QuickBooks® Online

Comprehensive

Fall 2018 Edition

By Patricia Hartley, MBA

Chaffey College

LABYRINTH

LEARNING™

QuickBooks Online: Comprehensive, Fall 2018 Edition
by Patricia Hartley, MBA

Copyright © 2018 by Labyrinth Learning

LABYRINTH
LEARNING™

Labyrinth Learning
PO Box 2669
Danville, CA 94526
800.522.9746
On the web at lablearning.com

President:
Brian Favro

Product Manager:
Jason Favro

Development Manager:
Laura Popelka

Production Manager:
Debra Grose

Senior Editor:
Alexandra Mummery

Junior Editor:
Alexandria Henderson

Indexing:
Valerie Haynes Perry

Cover Design:
Mick Koller, SuperLab Design

eBOOK ITEM: 1-64061-034-0
ISBN-13: 978-1-64061-034-7

PRINT ITEM: 1-64061-033-2
ISBN-13: 978-1-64061-033-0

Manufactured in the United States of America.

GPP 10 9 8 7 6 5 4 3 2 1

Contents in Brief

Contents

CHAPTER 13
Bringing It All Together! 247

Preface

This textbook is designed to help address the various challenges faced by learners and educators in computerized accounting courses, including the challenges inherent in teaching QuickBooks Online. We've kept the best elements of our proven instructional design and added powerful, interactive elements and assessments that offer enormous potential to engage learners in a new way.

Our goal is to simplify the entire learning experience and help every learner develop the practical, real-world skills needed to be successful at work and in school. Using a combination of text, videos, interactive elements, and assessments, we begin with fundamental concepts and take learners through a systematic progression of exercises to reach mastery. We're delighted with the results, and we hope that you are, too!

Key Themes

We had conversations with dozens of educators at community colleges, vocational schools, and other learning environments in preparation for this textbook. We listened and have adapted our learning solution to match the needs of a rapidly changing world, while keeping these common themes in mind:

Keep it about skills. Our content focus is on critical, job-ready topics and tasks, with a relentless focus on practical, real-world skills and common sense as well as step-by-step instruction to ensure that learners stay engaged from the first chapter forward. We've retained our method of exercise progression to ensure mastery—an approach that has been successfully developing skills for more than 20 years.

Keep it simple. Our integrated solutions create an engaging experience built on a dynamic instructional design that brings clarity to even the most challenging topics. We've focused our content on the things that matter most and have presented it in the easiest way for today's learners to absorb.

Keep it relevant. Fresh, original, and constantly evolving content helps educators keep pace with today's student and work environments.

How to Use This Book

Our comprehensive learning solution consists of a groundbreaking interactive ebook that delivers learning content in an engaging manner. Features include elements such as videos, self-assessments, slide shows, and more. The ebook also supports highlighting, note-taking, and searching. We understand that some students will still appreciate a print textbook, and that's available too. And every print purchase includes the ebook so all users have access to all content and features.

Every textbook purchase comes with the following:

- *eLab Course Management System:* This robust tool provides additional learning content for students, such as chapter overviews, and automatically graded reports and tests. And educators will enjoy the grading and tracking features. eLab can be fully integrated with a school's LMS, making course management even easier.

- *Instructor resources:* This course is also supported on the Labyrinth website with a comprehensive instructor support package that includes detailed lesson plans, PowerPoint presentations, a course syllabus, test banks, additional exercises, and more.

- *Learning Resource Center:* Files needed to complete exercises in this textbook can be found within eLab or on the Learning Resource Center at: **labyrinthelab.com/lrc**

 This textbook also carries the ProCert Certified logo, indicating that the content covers all course objectives included in the QuickBooks Certified User (QBCU) exam.

We're excited to provide this innovative approach with you, and we'd love you to share your experience with us at: lablearning.com/share

Visual Conventions

This book uses visual conventions and typographic cues to guide learners through the chapters. Some of the cues are indicated here.

Cue	What It Does
`Type this text`	Text to type at the keyboard is shown in this typeface.
Action words	Important action words in exercise steps are shown in a dark red font.
accounting cycle	Glossary terms are highlighted with a light yellow background.
Note! Tip! Warning!	Tips, notes, and warnings are called out with special icons.
☁	Videos and other multimedia content that are a required part of this course are indicated by this icon.
QG	Exercises that can be used with eLab's Quick Grader solution are indicated with this icon.
Command→Command→Command	Multistep menu commands are presented like this.
Vendors Center→New Vendor→ Import Vendors	Reference steps present shortcut steps for executing certain tasks.

Acknowledgements

Many individuals contribute to the development and completion of a textbook. We appreciate the careful attention and informed contributions of our Advisory Group members for their assistance in the development of this book. We would like to express our appreciation for the significant contributions of these educators in the development of this text.

Marie Campbell, *Idaho State University*

Paul Croitoru, *Wilbur Wright College*

Janine Fiorito, *Spartanburg Community College*

Helen Hall, *College of Southern Maryland*

Carol Jensen, *City College of San Francisco*

Patricia Johnson, *Canisius College*

Sandy Linn, *Northwest Arkansas Community College*

Michelle Masingill, *North Idaho College*

Kathy Moreno, *Abraham Baldwin Agricultural College*

Kathleen O'Neill, *West Contra Costa Adult Education*

Bill Pate, *Whatcom Community College*

Kevin Peck, *Eastern Arizona College*

Howard Randall, *Mission College*

Erik Richter, *Colorado Community College System*

Patrick Rogan, *Cosumnes River College*

Garrett Westbrook, *Southern Regional Technical College*

We are also grateful to the instructors and professionals who provided feedback and suggested improvements. This book has benefited from the feedback and suggestions of the following reviewers.

Kim Anderson, *Elgin Community College*

Renee Hall, *College of the Canyons*

Shmuel Fink, *Touru College*

Julie Hurtt, *East Central Community College*

Buz Jacobson, *Bryan University*

Steven Manske, *Mission Community College*

Ray McGrady, *Adult Learning Center, Virginia Beach*

Gregory B. Swango, *CPA, NorthWest Arkansas Community College*

Garrett Tedeman, *St. Augustine College*

Jill Wright, *Colusa County Office of Education Adult Career Tech Education/ROP*

About the Author

Patricia Hartley (MBA) is an Advanced Certified Pro Advisor for QuickBooks and part of the Intuit Trainer/Writer Network. Pat is an independent accounting and business consultant for small businesses as well as an Associate Instructor at Chaffey College in Rancho Cucamonga, CA, among others. Pat's "QuickBooks in a Day" workshops, targeted at small-business owners, managers, and accountants, offer hands-on training in basic to advanced QuickBooks skills.

1 | Getting Started with QuickBooks Online

QuickBooks Online is the web-based accounting software of choice for many small businesses. It's popular because it enables access anywhere, anytime, on any device (with an Internet connection) and provides many robust features and functions. In this chapter, you will review the QuickBooks Online editions to determine the right choice for you. You will also navigate the QuickBooks Online Dashboard and review some accounting basics that are vital to your success as a QuickBooks Online user. Finally, you will find out how to access the training tools for this course.

LEARNING OBJECTIVES

▸ Decide which QuickBooks Online level is best for your business

▸ Access the test drive data file

▸ Navigate the Gear menu

▸ Define and use features in the top-right navigation tools

▸ Identify features that appear on the Dashboard

▸ Use the Navigation bar to access the Sales and Expenses centers

▸ Discuss some accounting basics

Introducing QuickBooks Online

QuickBooks Online is a cloud-based accounting system that allows companies to:

- Access and update data from multiple platforms

- Access and update data from various mobile devices

- Track logins and activity via the Activity log

- Track inventory using the first-in, first-out (FIFO) accounting method

- Track customer, vendor, and employee transactions

- Process sales and cash receipts

- Process purchase orders and payments to vendors

- Synchronize bank and credit card transactions

- Easily collaborate with their accountants

An important benefit of having your accounting online and accessible anytime, anywhere, from any device is that the software is automatically updated and backed up. You do not need to back up your data files to your computer or servers, and you will not have to reinstall the software due to a system crash or when you get a new computer.

QuickBooks Online Subscriptions

QuickBooks Online is subscription-based accounting software that is suitable for most business types in a variety of industries. As a business grows and needs more robust features, it can take advantage of dozens of add-on applications, or apps, available in the QuickBooks Online Apps store.

QuickBooks Online has three subscription levels: Simple Start, Essentials, and Plus. This course covers the features and practices used for QuickBooks Online Plus. To determine which subscription level is appropriate for a company, consider which features the business needs now or in the near future. As a business needs more features, a subscriber can easily upgrade to a more robust version without losing data.

> **Tip!** Use Simple Start for a simple service business that is primarily cash-based. Use Essentials if the business needs recurring invoices or accounts payable. Use Plus if the business has inventory with FIFO valuation, employees, budgets, and multiple users.

Feature	Simple Start	Essentials	Plus
Track your income and expenses	✓	✓	✓
Send unlimited estimated and invoices	✓	✓	✓
Download transactions from your bank and credit card accounts	✓	✓	✓
Print checks and record transactions	✓	✓	✓
Import data from Excel® or QuickBooks Desktop	✓	✓	✓
Back up your data online automatically	✓	✓	✓
Same security and encryption as banks	✓	✓	✓
Access your data from a tablet or smartphone	✓	✓	✓
Invite up to two accountants to access your data	✓	✓	✓
Integrate with available applications	✓	✓	✓
Set up invoices to automatically bill on a recurring schedule		✓	✓
Manage and pay bills from vendors		✓	✓
Enter bills and schedule payments for later		✓	✓
Compare your sales with profitability with industry trends		✓	✓
Control what your users can access		✓	✓
Create and send purchase orders			✓
Track inventory			✓
Prepare and print 1099s			✓
Give employees and subcontractors limited access to enter time worked			✓
Track billable hours by customer			✓
Create budgets to estimate future income and expenses			✓
Categorize your income and expenses using class tracking			✓
Track sales and profitability for each of your locations or divisions			✓
Number of people who can access QuickBooks Online			✓
Number of built-in business reports			✓
Pay W-2 employees and file payroll taxes	Free trial, then continue using for an additional monthly fee.		
Accept online and mobile payments	QuickBooks Payments: pay per use		

Subscription Level Feature Comparison

Mobile Devices

You can use a mobile device (smartphones and tablets using iOS or Android) to perform many important QuickBooks activities, including:

- Creating, viewing, and emailing estimates, invoices, and sales receipts

- Accessing customer information

- Converting estimates to invoices

- Receiving payments, tracking expenses, and downloading and reconciling bank transactions

- Using your custom QuickBooks Online forms

You can even use your mobile device's camera, phone, and GPS with QuickBooks Online! The QuickBooks Online application for mobile devices is available through resources such as the App Store or Google Play.

Updates and the Ever-Evolving User Interface

Intuit introduces new features and images frequently to improve QuickBooks Online. As you work through this course, you may notice images and functionality in QuickBooks Online that differ from the text. The names of menus, tools, and other features may also change.

Updates are not pushed out at the same time to all users, so you may have a slightly different interface than other users. In addition, your test drive and one-year trial subscription may differ during update periods. Each time you log in to your QuickBooks Online account, you will see messages about any available updates. You can also keep up-to-date on what's new by visiting the following blog: quickbooks.intuit.com/blog/

Before You Begin

Throughout this course, you will use various tools during exercises and reviews. The following sections describe these tools and how to access them. You'll also find tips and other important details about using the tools.

Course Organization

The first part of this course (Chapters 1–6) focuses on setting up a service business. You will use Craig's Design and Landscaping Services in the QuickBooks Online Plus test drive for most of the discussions, examples, and Develop Your Skills (DYS) exercises. You will use your free QuickBooks Online Plus trial subscription and create the Puppy Luv Pampered Pooch business to complete end-of-chapter exercises. In Chapter 6, "All in a Day's Work," you will complete a project that draws on your newfound skills.

The second part of this course (Chapters 7–12) focuses on setting up a merchandising business. You will continue using the test drive for this discussion and demonstration. You will also continue with the company setup for Puppy Luv Pampered Pooch by adding merchandising features.

The course ends with a cumulative project in Chapter 13, "Bringing It All Together," in which you will use all of the features you have explored throughout the course. You will use a free, 30-day trial subscription to QuickBooks Online for this project.

Using the Browser

QuickBooks Online is web-based, so you must use a browser to access it. QuickBooks Online operates with most current browsers, but Google Chrome is recommended because all the screen captures in this course were captured in Chrome; if you use a different browser, the same window may look different. In addition, you may have trouble accessing some tools if you do not use Chrome.

Here are some tips and best practices for using QuickBooks Online in Chrome:

- **Create a QuickBooks Online user.** Chrome allows you to create multiple users that can be customized with different bookmarks and preferences. You can also create a Desktop shortcut for users that can be used exclusively for QuickBooks Online. To create a new user in Chrome, go to Customize→Settings→People. Click Add Person, choose an icon, and give the new user a name (e.g., QBO user).

- **Customize the bookmark bar.** Customizing the bookmark bar streamlines using QuickBooks Online. You can add bookmarks for the windows you use most and organize them in folders. To enable the bookmark bar, choose Customize→Bookmarks→Show Bookmark Bar. Add bookmarks by clicking the star at the top-right of the address bar.

- **Duplicate your window.** Duplicate your window by right-clicking the open tab and then clicking Duplicate. Doing so will open a new window.

- **Clear the browsing history.** If you receive errors or get unexpected results while working in QuickBooks Online, you may need to clear your cache and cookies. To clear your cache and cookies, choose Customize→History→Clear Browsing Data.

Intuit's YouTube channel offers many other best practices and tips related to browsing and other tasks. New suggestions are added all the time.

Security

QuickBooks Online uses the same encryption technology used by top financial institutions. Privacy is protected by the creation of a unique password for each user and an always-on Activity log that displays a complete record of each user's activities.

For more information, go to quickbooks.intuit.com/accountants/resources/advanced-security and click the buttons for Download Whitepaper and Read Our Security One-Pager.

The Test Drive

Intuit provides the QuickBooks Online test drive free of charge so interested users can try out the software without a subscription and learners can practice their skills. Users simply complete a security verification to access the test drive.

The test drive comes preloaded with a complete company (in this case, Craig's Design and Land-scaping Services) so you can try new features and functions without worrying about mistakes. Remember, you'll use the test drive for most of the Develop Your Skills exercises in this course.

The test drive is updated daily, so the dates displayed change daily to the current date. You will work in the year 2021 throughout the course so you can more easily see the results of your own entries in the test drive.

Access the QuickBooks Online test drive with this link, which you may want to bookmark in your browser: qbo.intuit.com/redir/testdrive

Warning! The test drive DOES NOT store data. Once you close or log out of the test drive, all of the data you entered is lost! Because of this, make sure to allow enough time in one sitting to complete all Develop Your Skills exercises in a chapter.

Your Trial Subscription and the Company File

You will use the QuickBooks Online Plus trial subscription, included with this course, to set up a company file called Puppy Luv Pampered Pooch. You will use this file for the end-of-chapter exercises, the Develop Your Skills exercises in Chapter 2, and the Chapter 6 project. The data in this company file is cumulative, and QuickBooks Online does not include a backup or restore feature, so be sure your work in each chapter is correct before moving to the next chapter.

Note that QuickBooks Online allows only one company file per license. This means you cannot change certain settings once you have completed the initial account creation steps. This is important because the settings you choose dictate the types of functionality available to you.

> **Note!** If you already have a QuickBooks Online account, use a different email address for your trial subscription for this course. The user ID (your email address) and password must be unique. At the second layer of security, be sure to include a phone number that can receive text messages. Also, don't forget to write down your password.

Other Tools You'll Need

Throughout this course you will be instructed to print a hard copy, print to PDF file, or export to Excel to upload coursework. Therefore, it is important that you have access to Microsoft® Excel, a printer, and PDF software (e.g., Adobe Acrobat or Cute PDF).

> **Note!** Different classrooms have different needs. Your instructor may direct you to save/ submit deliverables in formats that differ from what is indicated in an exercise step.

DEVELOP YOUR SKILLS 1-1

In this exercise, you will access the test drive for Craig's Design and Landscaping Services.

Before You Begin: *Visit the Learning Resource center at labyrinthelab.com/lrc to retrieve the student files for this course before beginning the exercises in this course. Also, make sure you are using the most current version of your Internet browser (ideally Google Chrome).*

1. In your Internet browser, type: `qbo.intuit.com/redir/testdrive`
2. Enter the security verification that appears and click **Continue**.
3. Keep the Dashboard open.

Navigating the User Interface

The QuickBooks Online user interface comprises all the software design features that allow you to interact with QuickBooks Online. The user interface includes shortcut icons that allow access to the Settings and the Help menus, as well as tools such as the Navigation bar that allows access to various centers. In QuickBooks Online, a center refers to a location that consolidates relevant transaction and contact information.

 View the video "User Interface Highlights" at: labyrinthelab.com/2017/video/QBO-V0101

The Gear Menu

The Gear ⚙ menu provides quick access to the Your Company, Lists, Tools, and Profile menus.

Your Company

When you first create your company, you will use tools in Company to customize your account, create transaction forms, and perform other tasks related to your business. For example, Account and Settings displays information about your company settings and more.

The Edit 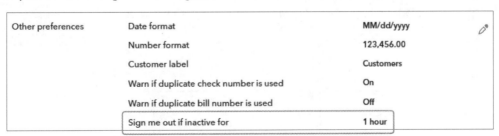 icon allows you to edit your address, tax ID, and contact information, as well as add your company logo.

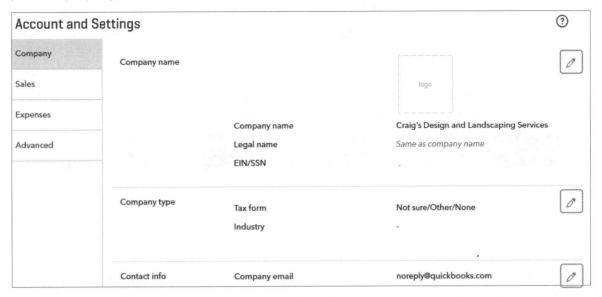

You can also set and edit default settings for sales and expenses. You can set many other defaults on the Advanced tab. If you plan to use account numbers for your Chart of Accounts, you can turn on that feature here.

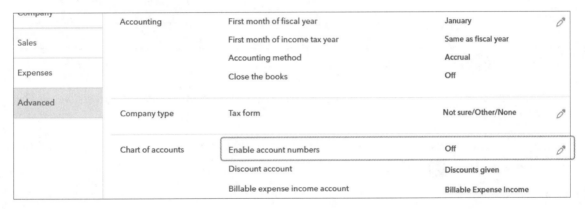

Pay attention to the last Advanced option under Other Preferences: Sign Me Out If Inactive For. If you do not change this setting, QuickBooks Online will close if it has been inactive for one hour.

Other preferences	Date format	MM/dd/yyyy	
	Number format	123,456.00	
	Customer label	Customers	
	Warn if duplicate check number is used	On	
	Warn if duplicate bill number is used	Off	
	Sign me out if inactive for	1 hour	

Lists

The foundation of QuickBooks Online is the lists that the program uses to store information about your accounts and the products and services used by your business. When these lists are set up and coded properly, the program is easy to use and provides accurate financial information.

The Lists menu includes links to the three most frequently used lists, which are usually Products and Services, Recurring Transactions, and Attachments. If you choose All Lists, you can view the lists and a narrative of what each list contains.

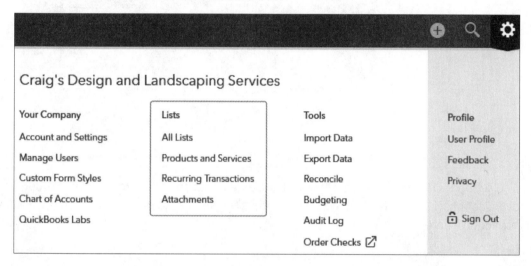

DEVELOP YOUR SKILLS 1-2

In this exercise, you will access the test drive and then explore some of the features accessible within the Gear menu.

1. Return to the Dashboard by clicking **Dashboard** on the Navigation bar.
2. Click the **Gear** ⚙ icon.
3. Choose **All Lists** from the Lists menu to see all of your accounting lists.
4. Click **Chart of Accounts** and then click the **See Your Chart of Accounts** button.

   The Chart of Accounts for Craig's Design and Landscaping Services is displayed along with the account type and balance and a shortcut to view the register for each account.

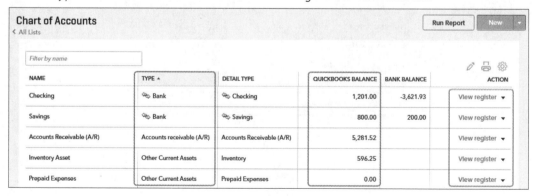

5. Click the **Gear** ⚙ icon and choose **Account and Settings** to see the types of information you can set up or change.

   If this were an account for your own company, you would use these settings to set up your company information. Because the account information related to Craig's Design and Landscaping Services is okay as is, you will change only the preference related to account inactivity.

6. Click the **Advanced** tab on the left and then scroll to the bottom.

7. In the Other Preferences section, click **Edit** ✎ and change the Sign Me Out If Inactive For setting to **3 hours**.

8. Click **Save** and then **Done**.

9. Return to the Dashboard by clicking **Dashboard** on the Navigation bar.

The Top-Right Navigation Tools

The top-right navigation tools make it easy to search for and create transactions as well as view recent transactions.

Clicking Create ⊕ displays a menu of transactions, which are grouped by Customers, Vendors, or Employees. The transactions under Other are not specific to a group. They provide a shortcut to making a bank deposit, transfer, journal entry, statement, or inventory adjustment.

Create			
Customers	**Vendors**	**Employees**	**Other**
Invoice	Expense	Payroll 🎁	Bank Deposit
Receive Payment	Check	Single Time Activity	Transfer
Estimate	Bill	Weekly Timesheet	Journal Entry
Credit Memo	Pay Bills		Statement
Sales Receipt	Purchase Order		Inventory Qty Adjustment
Refund Receipt	Vendor Credit		
Delayed Credit	Credit Card Credit		
Delayed Charge	Print Checks		

DEVELOP YOUR SKILLS 1-3

In this exercise, you will explore the top-right navigation tools.

1. Click the **Create** ⊕ button.

2. Choose **Expense** in the **Vendors** menu.

   This form lets you quickly create an expense transaction.

3. Click **Recent Transactions**  to view recent expenses and then **close** ✕ the window.

4. Click the **Create** ⊕ button and choose **Invoice** from the **Customers** menu.

   This feature allows you to quickly create a customer invoice for a service or product.

↻ Invoice			⚙ ⑦ ✕
Choose a customer ▾	Email (Separate emails with a comma)	Payment Options	BALANCE DUE
	☐ Send later	Cc/Bcc	**$0.00**

5. Close the window.

6. Click the **Search Transactions** 🔍 button to display a list of all recent transactions.

7. Choose the Cash Expense for $5.66 paid to Bob's Burger Joint.

   QuickBooks Online takes you to the Expense transaction window.

8. Close the Expense window.

9. Click **Search Transactions** 🔍 and then click **Advanced Search**.

   Here, you can search by various transactions and filters.

10. Click **Dashboard** on the Navigation bar.

The Help Menu

The Help menu provides a robust directory of topics and tasks as well as access to dozens of videos and phone and text support.

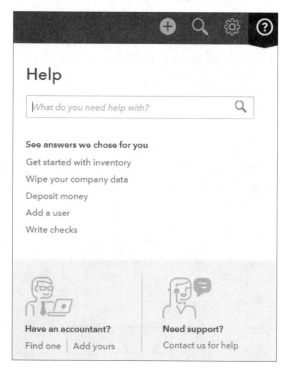

In this exercise, you will explore the Help menu.

1. Click **Help** 🔘, type **videos** in the search box, click **Search** 🔍, and select **Videos: Explore the power of QuickBooks Online**.

   Here you will find links to short videos that explore the power of QuickBooks Online.

2. Close the window.

3. Click **Help** 🔘, type **chart of accounts** in the search box, and click **Search** 🔍.

   Here you should find answers to the topic, as well as a link for contacting the Small Business Community at Intuit.

4. Close the Help window.

The Navigation Bar

The Navigation bar allows you to easily access the Banking, Sales, Expenses, and Workers centers, as well as other important information.

- **Banking center:** Allows you access to all banking and credit card accounts

- **Sales center:** Shows details and transactions related to sales and accounts receivable

- **Expenses center:** Shows details and transactions related to purchases and accounts payable

- **Workers center:** Allows you to sign up for a payroll subscription and keep track of your employee and contractor information

For each of these centers, you can add, edit, or make inactive list items such as contact names, addresses, terms, and telephone numbers. You can also view a summary of transactions or similar information in these and other centers. The Sales center, for example, has four folders that allow access to All Sales, Invoices, Customers, and Products and Services.

Selecting the Customers folder in the Sales center will provide you with a list of all customers.

Clicking a money bar section displays details for that section. In the following figure, the Overdue section is chosen, displaying details of overdue invoices.

Notice the Action menu, which allows you to quickly take action on items in the list. The Action menu provides similar tools in the Expenses and Employees centers, too. Also, notice the icons above the Action menu. Clicking on these icons allows you to quickly print, export to Excel, or change the appearance of the listed details.

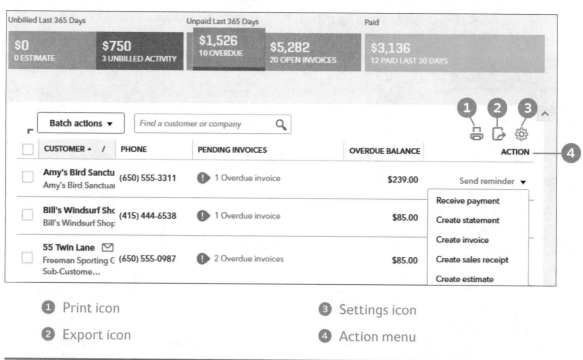

1. Print icon   3. Settings icon
2. Export icon   4. Action menu

DEVELOP YOUR SKILLS 1-5

In this exercise, you will use the Navigation bar.

1. Click **Sales** on the Navigation bar and then choose **Customers**.

2. Click **Cool Cars**.

   Notice the two folders: Transaction List and Customer Details

3. Click the **Customer Details** tab.

   Here, you can edit customer information if necessary.

4. Click the **Transaction List** tab.

5. Hover the mouse pointer over each icon above the Action menu and then click the **Settings** icon and notice you can add more fields to the list.

6. Click **Expenses** on the Navigation bar, click **Vendors**, and examine the money bar.

   Notice that four bills are overdue.

7. Click the **Overdue** section of the bar.

   Notice that only the four overdue items appear.

Unbilled Last 365 Days	Unpaid Last 365 Days		Paid
$125 1 PURCHASE ORDER	**$848** 4 OVERDUE	**$1,603** 5 OPEN BILLS	**$3,892** 21 PAID LAST 30 DAYS

8. Return to the Vendors list by selecting **Clear Filter / View All** in the upper-left part of the window.

Vendors [Clear Filter / View All]

   You will add a phone number for Bob's Burger Joint.

9. Click **Bob's Burger Joint**, switch to the **Vendor Details** tab, and click **Edit**.

10. Add this phone number: **800-555-1112**

11. Click **Save**.

    Doing so returns you to the Vendor Details list, where the new phone number is now displayed.

Vendor	Bob's Burger Joint
Email	
Phone	(800) 555-1112

12. Return to the **Dashboard**.

Accounting—Behind the Scenes

The primary focus of accounting is the accurate recording and categorizing of a firm's transactions so that reports can be accurately prepared to define the health of the organization.

The basic accounting equation that governs all accounting is:

Assets = Liabilities + Equity

Many business owners use some type of accounting software to keep their books. Although most online accounting forms, including QuickBooks Online, are intuitive, business owners may not understand the accounting concepts that govern what QuickBooks Online is actually doing behind the scenes.

In QuickBooks Online, each form used is completing a transaction. Having a basic understanding of accounting and the functions of the software reduces mistakes and provides good financial information for the business owner.

BEHIND THE SCENES

Throughout this course you will find a section called "Behind the Scenes." This section reviews the behind-the-scenes accounting that QuickBooks Online performs when you record a transaction. It is not meant to teach these principles; it is only to remind you of the concept or principle as you proceed.

Generally Accepted Accounting Principles (GAAP)

The term Generally Accepted Accounting Principles (GAAP) refers to a collection of commonly followed accounting rules and standards for financial reporting. Specifications include definitions of concepts and principles. The purpose of GAAP is to ensure that financial reporting is transparent and consistent from one organization to another. You will find notes throughout this course to remind you of the GAAP principles behind the transactions presented.

Accrual Basis vs. Cash Basis Accounting

The two main types of accounting methods are:

- **Accrual basis:** Income is recorded when the sales transaction is made and expenses are recorded when the obligation is incurred.

- **Cash basis:** Income is recorded when it is received and expenses are recorded when paid.

The method you choose depends on the nature of your business. QuickBooks Online makes it easy to look at reports in either basis. Speak with your accountant or tax professional to determine which method is best for your business.

Account Types and Financial Reports

Each business transaction is recorded in several types of ledgers, or accounts. Each account summarizes the transactions that increase and decrease the equity in an organization. Each account is listed in the company Chart of Accounts, and each account has a type. The five main types of accounts are assets, liabilities, equity, income, and expense.

The following account types are associated with the balance sheet used to analyze the net worth of a business:

- **Assets:** Assets are everything a company owns. Examples could be money in all bank accounts, accounts receivable, equipment, and property.

- **Liabilities:** Liabilities are everything a company owes. Examples could be a vehicle loan, mortgage, credit card balance, and accounts payable.

- **Equity:** Equity is the investment into the company and any profit or loss the company has retained over the life of the business.

The following account types are associated with the profit and loss report used to analyze the operating profit or loss of a business over a specific time period:

- **Income:** Income reflects all the sales/fees earned during a period. An accounting period could be a month, quarter, or year.

- **Expenses:** Expenses are any expenditure the company incurs while conducting business during a period. An accounting period could be a month, quarter, or year.

DEVELOP YOUR SKILLS 1-6

In this exercise, you will use the Chart of Accounts to practice determining which report each account is associated with. You will also change an account name and add an account to the Chart of Accounts.

1. Click the **Gear** ⚙ icon and choose **Chart of Accounts** from the **Your Company** menu.

   Tip! You can also access your Chart of Accounts from the left Navigation bar by clicking Accounting.

2. Scroll though the list to view the account names and types.

3. Refer to the preceding discussion to determine whether these accounts are associated with a balance sheet or a profit and loss statement.

Checking	Balance sheet or profit and loss statement
Truck Original Cost	Balance sheet or profit and loss statement
Accounts Payable	Balance sheet or profit and loss statement
Loan Payable	Balance sheet or profit and loss statement
Design Income	Balance sheet or profit and loss statement
Legal and Professional Fees	Balance sheet or profit and loss statement

Edit an Account Name and Add a New Account

Craig would like the checking account name to be the name of his bank.

4. Click **Edit** 🖉.

5. In the Name field type **Center City Bank Checking** to rename the account.

6. Click **Save and Close**.

   Craig would also like to add a second checking account.

7. Click **New** and choose the following account settings:

   - Account Type: **Bank**
   - Detail Type: **Checking**
   - Name: **Chase Checking**

8. Click **Save and Close** to return to Chart of Accounts listing.

   Now you will print the Chart of Accounts for handy reference.

9. Click the **Print** 🖨 icon above the **Action** column.

10. Choose **Portable Document Format (PDF)** from your list of printers and save the list to your **Chapter 01** folder as: **CH01 Chart of Accounts**

Tackle the Tasks

This is your opportunity to apply some of the skills learned in this chapter to accomplish additional tasks for Craig's Design and Landscaping Services. Close the test drive and then reopen it to accomplish these tasks.

1. Craig would like you to make the following changes to the Chart of Accounts:

   • Add the **AMEX** credit card account.

   • Change the name of the *Services* income account to: **Services Income**

   • Add an **Interest Paid** Expense account.

2. Print the list in PDF, saving the file in your **Chapter 01** folder as: **CH01 TTT Chart of Accounts**

Self-Assessment

Check your knowledge of this chapter's key concepts and skills using the Self-Assessment quiz here or in your eLab course.

1. Budgets can be created in QuickBooks Online Simple Start. *True   False*

2. FIFO is the inventory tracking method used in QuickBooks Online. *True   False*

3. The Your Company menu is located in the Gear menu. *True   False*

4. By default, QuickBooks Online automatically logs off if there is no activity for one hour. *True   False*

5. Accrual-based accounting means you record income when you receive the payment. *True   False*

6. You can view recent transactions on the Dashboard by clicking Search 🔍. *True   False*

7. QuickBooks Online is constantly being updated and improved. *True   False*

8. One purpose of the Navigation bar is to provide access to the Sales, Expenses, and Workers centers. *True   False*

9. In accrual-based accounting, you record expenses when you pay them. *True   False*

10. A balance sheet is used to analyze the operating profit or loss of a business. *True   False*

11. You CANNOT access your QuickBooks Online subscription from any device except your PC. *True   False*

12. Payroll CANNOT be done in QuickBooks Online Plus. *True   False*

13. The basic equation that governs accounting is:
    A. Assets = Liabilities + Equity
    B. Equity – Expenses = Assets
    C. Assets + Banking = Equity
    D. Liabilities + Assets = Expenses

14. Which subscription level allows for the creation of budgets?
    A. Simple Start
    B. Essentials
    C. Plus
    D. You cannot create budgets in QuickBooks Online.

15. Which inventory tracking method is used in QuickBooks Online Plus?
    A. General Counting
    B. FIFO
    C. Physical
    D. You cannot track inventory in QuickBooks Online Plus.

(cont'd.)

16. The Help menu offers you:
    A. Topic search
    B. Videos
    C. Links to contact Intuit
    D. All of these options

17. From the Dashboard you can easily access:
    A. Sales and Expenses centers
    B. Company settings
    C. Create transaction menu
    D. All of these options

18. The Checking account is an:
    A. asset account associated with the profit and loss report
    B. expense account associated with the profit and loss report
    C. asset account associated with the asset report
    D. asset account associated with the balance sheet

19. The recommended Internet browser for QuickBooks Online is:
    A. Internet Explorer
    B. Edge
    C. Chrome
    D. Firefox

20. Which of these is NOT a list in QuickBooks Online?
    A. Employees
    B. Other
    C. Customers
    D. Chart of Accounts

21. What are the three areas on the Dashboard that let you find and perform every feature and function you need in QuickBooks Online.
    A. List, Activities, Reports
    B. Activity bar, Activity feed, New icon
    C. Navigation bar, top Navigation bar, Gear menu
    D. Select, Action, Tools

2 | Setting Up a New Company File

A company file in QuickBooks Online is where the financial records for a company are stored. It's a critical element for a business. In this chapter, you will prepare for and create a company file in QuickBooks Online. You will build on the company file throughout this course to learn the skills you need to set up an account for your own company.

LEARNING OBJECTIVES

▸ Create a new company file

▸ Customize the company settings

▸ Edit the Chart of Accounts

▸ Add users

▸ Add and categorize services

▸ Enter the opening balances

🗂 Project: Puppy Luv Pampered Pooch

Sadie Garrison is a professional dog groomer. She worked with another groomer for many years and has just opened her own dog grooming salon. Sadie has decided to provide only dog grooming services. She knows owning a small business is going to keep her busy taking care of the dogs and doing marketing. She also realizes that the accounting must be done on a regular basis to ensure that all sales and deposits are recorded and all monies spent are tracked. Sadie has asked you to set up and maintain her QuickBooks Online accounting software. In this chapter, you will create the Puppy Luv Pampered Pooch company file. You will use this file to add customers and vendors and to process the daily, weekly, and monthly transactions.

Planning and Creating Your Company File

Before you set up a company file, it is critical that you have all the data you need. This data includes general information about the company, its address, its banking account names, and knowledge of the types of services that the company will provide. Within your Chapter 02 folder is the "Example QuickBooks Setup Checklist" file. It shows information typically needed when setting up a business. Imagine that you interviewed Sadie using this checklist as part of her business setup.

Start Date

Deciding on the start date is critical. It can affect the amount of work you need to do to set up your QuickBooks Online company file. Sadie will open her Puppy Luv Pampered Pooch salon on August 1, 2021, but she incurred expenses prior to that date. In this case, the start date can still be August 1, 2021. You just need to record all initial business setup expenses as part of Sadie's investment. Always choose the first day of a period, month, quarter, or year. Doing so allows for meaningful, accurate data comparison reports with future periods.

Setup Checklist—Elements of the Plan

Sadie has already invested $75,000 of her own savings. She has spent $16,000 in new equipment, $2,500 in supplies, and $800 in some marketing and social media material. The landlord in the strip mall included the signage in the monthly rent of $550 per month, and Sadie has paid $450 for the business license. Sadie paid six months' rent in advance on July 30. Sadie has given you her menu of services, a list of customers that will be coming from the other salon, and a list of vendors she plans to purchase from.

Company Name	Puppy Luv Pampered Pooch by Your Name
Street Address	104 Main Street Suite #100
City, State, Zip	Los Angeles, CA 90051
Phone	310-555-4567
Website	www.puppyluvpamperedpooch.net
Industry Type	Pet Care (except Veterinary) Services
Business Type	Sole proprietor
Fiscal Year	January
EIN number	10-1111100
Logo	See email from Sadie
Chart of Accounts	Use default and customize
Bank Account	Los Angeles City Bank
Credit Card Account	City Credit Union MC
Services Sold	See menu
List of Customers	See list
List of Vendors	See list
Accounting Basis	Accrual
Start Date	August 1, 2021
Currently Using	Excel
	Online Banking

DEVELOP YOUR SKILLS 2-1

In this exercise, you will access your trial subscription to QuickBooks Online and use Sadie's information for Puppy Luv Pampered Pooch. **If you have already accessed your trial subscription, skip this exercise and continue on to the next topic.**

You will go to a web page for the access instructions. The steps are not included in your textbook because Intuit may change the process at any time.

1. In your web browser, go to: **lablearning.com/QBO-install**
2. Follow the steps to access your trial subscription to QuickBooks Online.

   As you provide information on your business, be sure to complete the fields as indicated on the web page, setting the business name to Puppy Luv Pampered Pooch - Your Name *and the time in business to* Less Than 1 Year. *Also, choose the the options to have QuickBooks:* Send and Track Invoices, Organize Your Expenses, *and* Track Your Bills.

Customizing Your Company File

QuickBooks Online is now ready for you to start working, but it is a good practice to select all the settings for your specific business right from the beginning. QuickBooks Online allows you to easily customize settings to your own preferences; for example, you can refer to customers as clients, patients, members, and more.

In this exercise, you will use information collected from your interview with Sadie to customize your settings for Puppy Luv Pampered Pooch. You will also add a logo to your account.

Before You Begin: *Your Puppy Luv Pampered Pooch Dashboard will display similarly to the Dashboard for Craig's Design and Landscaping Services. Some helpful links in the Setup Guide will get you started.*

1. Click the **Gear** ⚙ icon and choose **Account and Settings** under **Your Company**.

    As you move forward, instructions like this will appear as: "Choose Gear ⚙ → Your Company→Accounts and Settings."

2. Click the **Edit** ✎ icon in the Company Name portion of the window.

3. Click the **plus sign** ➕.

    Notice that you can also edit your business name in this window and add the legal name of the business if you're operating as a DBA.

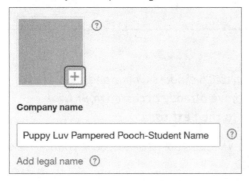

4. Navigate to your **Chapter 02** folder and double-click the **Puppy Luv Logo.jpg** file.

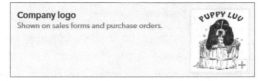

5. Type **10-1111100** in the EIN field and click **Save**.

6. Click the **Edit** ✎ icon in the Company Type section.

7. Select **Sole Proprietor (Form 1040)** in the Tax Form field.

8. Type **Pet Care (except Veterinary) Services** in the Industry field.

9. Click **Save**.

10. Click the **Edit** ✎ icon in the Contact Info section.

11. Fill in the fields as indicated and click **Save** when finished:

Company Phone	**310-555-4567**
Website	**www.puppyluvpamperedpooch.net**

12. Click the Address section **Edit** icon and enter the following address in the appropriate fields, clicking **Save** when finished:
    ```
    104 Main Street #100
    Los Angeles CA 90051
    ```
    Confirm that Customer-Facing Address and Legal Address are checked.

13. Click the **Advanced** tab.

14. Verify that the accounting method is set to Accrual; edit the setting if necessary.

15. Verify that the tax form type is set to Sole Proprietor (Form 1040); edit the setting if necessary.

16. In the Categories section, make sure that both options are set to **Off**.
    Sadie would like to call her customers, Clients.

17. Click the Other Preferences section **Edit** icon.

18. Click the drop-down menu arrow for **Customer Label** and choose **Clients** from the list.

19. Click **Save** and then **close** ☒ the Settings window.
    Any text in the QuickBooks interface that previously referred to customers *now says* clients *instead.*

The Chart of Accounts

The Chart of Accounts is located in the Gear menu and is a list of accounts for each transaction in your accounting system or general ledger. An important purpose of the Chart of Accounts is to categorize expenditures, revenues, assets, and liabilities so you can quickly assess the company's financial health. The Chart of Accounts can also be accessed via the left Navigation bar; choose Accounting.

↗ Gear ⚙ →Your Company→Chart of Accounts

BEHIND THE SCENES

Every transaction requires at least two accounts. An example of a transaction is a check written for a business license. One account would be your checking account, where assets are tracked; the other account would be business license expenses, where expenses are tracked.

QuickBooks Online is a double-entry accounting system, meaning every time one account is affected, there is an equal and opposite effect on a corresponding account. Take a look behind the scenes.

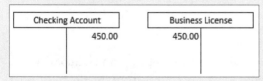

Checking Account		Business License	
	450.00	450.00	

When an item (for example, a business license) is purchased, the checking account—an asset—will decrease by the amount of the check, and the business license account—an expense—will increase by the same amount. Assets decrease on the balance sheet, and expenses increase on the profit and loss report.

Assigning Account Types

QuickBooks Online creates a Chart of Accounts for each company, based on the industry chosen at setup. The Chart of Accounts has the following account types: Assets, Liabilities, Equity, Income, and Expenses.

The Assets and Liabilities account types are broken down even further.

- **Assets** include Bank, Accounts Receivable, Other Current Assets, Fixed Assets, and Other Assets.

- **Liabilities** include Accounts Payable, Credit Card, Other Current Liabilities, and Long Term Liabilities.

As you create a new account, you choose the account type. QuickBooks Online then displays detail types for that account. Each detail type has a brief narrative on what type of transaction may be recorded in that account type.

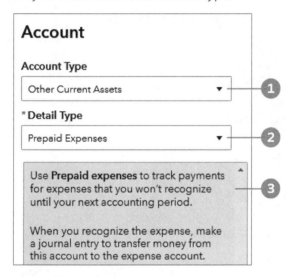

1. Account type

2. Detail type choices

3. Brief narrative of the detail type chosen

These account and detail types define placement order on the Financial Reports and Income Tax Report forms.

Accounts can be added from within the Chart of Accounts. In addition, if you need to create a new account while creating an expense or deposit transaction, you can quickly add it from within the form. It is not necessary to go back to the Chart of Accounts.

Editing the Default Chart of Accounts

Intuit provides the default Chart of Accounts to give you suggested settings and help you get started on your QuickBooks Online account. You can add new accounts from the default Chart of Accounts. You can also edit, delete, or merge existing accounts to fit your desired account list. Note that you can merge only accounts of the same type. For example, an income account cannot be merged with an expense account because they are different types.

Warning! You cannot un-merge.

Some accounts cannot be deleted. These accounts are preset by Intuit as defaults, or they have been linked to another feature. Examples of preset (default) accounts are Undeposited Funds, Uncategorized Asset, Uncategorized Income, Uncategorized Expense, and Opening Balance Equity. You will get an error message with a brief explanation if you try to delete them.

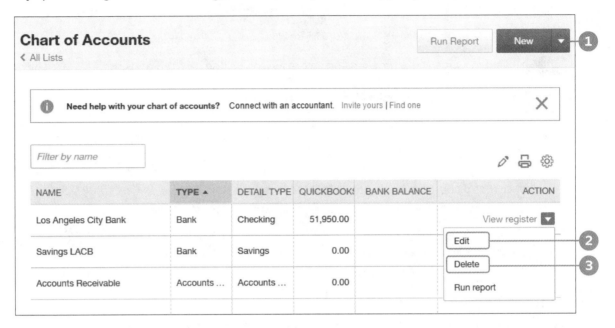

1 Add a new account

2 Edit an account

3 Delete an account

DEVELOP YOUR SKILLS 2-3

In this exercise, you will use information from your interview with Sadie to add, delete, and change some accounts in the Chart of Accounts for Puppy Luv Pampered Pooch.

1. To add an account, choose **Gear** ⚙ →**Your Company**→**Chart of Accounts**.

2. Click the **New** button and make these settings:
   - Account Type: **Bank**
   - Detail Type: **Checking**
   - Name: `Los Angeles City Bank`

3. Click the **Save and Close menu** ▼ button and then choose **Save and New**.

4. Make these settings to add an income account:
   - Account Type: **Income**
   - Detail Type: **Service/Fee Income**
   - Name: `Services`

5. Click the **Save and New menu** ▼ button and then choose **Save and Close**.

Delete an Account

As you reviewed the default Chart of Accounts, you identified at least one account that Sadie does not need. You will now delete an account.

6. Scroll to the Ask My Accountant account and click the **downward-facing arrow** icon.

    You must click the arrow—not the words—to see the menu of available actions.

Tip! Moving forward, the downward-facing arrow icon will be referred to as the Action menu.

7. Choose **Delete** and then click **Yes** to confirm the deletion.

Ask My Accountant	Expenses	Utilities			Run report ▼
					Edit
Automobile Expense	Expenses	Auto			
					Delete

Notice that a pop-up message states that the account is now inactive. In QuickBooks Online you can never really delete anything. QuickBooks will only make it inactive.

QuickBooks Online allows you to delete an account, customer, or vendor even if there is a balance. QuickBooks Online creates a transaction to offset the balance. The transaction memo will contain the text Created by QB Online.

Edit an Account

Now you will change the name of the Services account, an Income account, to something more appropriate for Puppy Luv Pampered Pooch.

8. Choose **Services→Action menu→Edit**.

Services	Income	Service...		Run report ▼
				Edit
Uncategorized Income	Income	Sales o...		Delete

9. In the Name field, change Services to: **Pooch Services**

10. Click **Save and Close**.

11. Click **Dashboard** on the Navigation bar.

    On a Chart of Accounts, you might notice more than one account of the same type. You can merge accounts, as long as they are the same type. For example, the Pooch Services account and the Sales account could be one account. The Pooch Services account cannot be merged with Job Supplies because they are different types.

Products and Services

The Products and Services features are the magic in QuickBooks Online. When you set up these features correctly, each time you use a product or service to create a Sales form or Purchase form, the accounting is done automatically and linked to the correct detail and summary reports. Each Product and Services item is linked to at least one account in the Chart of Accounts. At this time, Sadie has decided not to sell any products, so you will work only with services. Services items are necessary to capture sales information on sales forms, such as invoices and sales receipts.

QuickBooks Online provides a default list of products and services based on the information provided at setup. All of these features can be edited (changed) as well as inactivated if you do not wish to use them; however, you cannot delete them. Besides providing a default list of products and services, QuickBooks Online also lets you add your own unique list of products and services.

NAME		SKU	TYPE	SALE	INCOME ACCOUNT
	Grooming		Service		Pooch Services

In the Products and Services list, you can create categories of products and services to quickly organize what you sell. This feature can save you time when you create sales transactions. For example, you can use categories for types of services or products. You will categorize Puppy Luv by Service: Bath and Brush, Mini Pet Groom, Full Pet Groom, and Add-Ons.

> ✔ **Best Practice**
>
> To take full advantage of categories, set up all of your categories before you set up your individual products and services. (If you decide not to do this, you can still assign the products and services to a category later.)

Sadie gave you her menu of services and prices for Puppy Luv Pampered Pooch. In this exercise, you will use this menu to create a new list of services. You will use the Categories feature to group the services.

Puppy Luv Pampered Pooch
List of Services

Bath and Brush: Nails, ears, paw pads, sanitary, and bath and brush
Mini Pet Groom: All of the above plus light trim around head, face, and eyes
Full Pet Groom: All of the above and complete haircut, anal gland extraction, and bow or bandana plus cologne

Bath and Brush		Mini Pet Groom	
Small	$20	Small	$25
Medium	$30	Medium	$35
Large	$40	Large	$45
X Large	$55	X Large	$65

Full Pet Groom	
Small	$40
Medium	$45
Large	$55
X Large	$75

ADD ONS

Nails Painted	$8.00	Ears Cleaned	$15.00
Teeth Brushed	$5.00	Bow/Bandana	$1.00
Flea Bath	$10.00	Extra for Matted Pets	$5.00

Hours: Thursday – Friday 9:00 am to 6:00pm; Saturday 8:00 am to 1:00 pm

1. Choose **Gear** ⚙ →**Lists**→**All Lists** and then click **Product Categories** on the Lists screen.

2. If a window pops up asking you if you want to add a product or service, click the **Add a Product or Service** button provided.

> **Note!** Pop-ups should always be closed unless otherwise directed.

3. Click the **New Category** button, type **Full Pet Groom** in the Name field, and click **Save**.

4. Add the following new categories: **Mini Pet Groom** and **Bath and Brush**

5. Click the **Products and Services** link in the top-left portion of the window.

> Name *
>
> Full Pet Groom
>
> ☐ Is a sub-category

Product categories
‹ Products and services

Add a New Service Item

Now that you have a category, you can add the services for that category.

6. Click **Add a Product or Service** and choose **Service**.

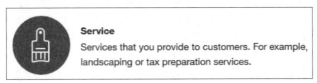

7. Fill in the fields as shown:

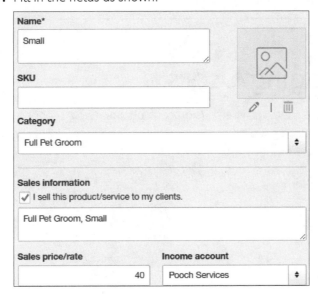

8. Click **Save and Close**.

Your Products and Services list now has the category you added. Next you will use Sadie's menu to add the remaining services for the Full Pet Groom category.

9. Add these services and prices to the Products and Services list for the Full Pet Groom category.

Service	Price
Medium	$45
Large	$55
X Large	$75

Click Save and New after entering the data for the Medium and Large service; click Save and Close after the X Large entry.

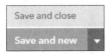

Create a Products/Services List Report

Now you will create a report so Sadie can view the result of your categorizing the services.

10. Click the **Run Report** button from the More menu at the top-right corner.

At the top of the report, notice the icons that allow you to email the report, print it, and export to Excel or PDF. Also notice the Save Customization button at the top-right corner.

11. To return to the Products and Services list, click the **Back to Report List** link at the top-left corner.

12. Return to the **Dashboard**.

Adding and Managing Users

QuickBooks Online Plus allows up to five users with permission controls and two Accountant users. The Manage User feature lets you control user access and monitor activity. Users can be managed from the Gear icon under Your Company list.

Puppy Luv Pampered Pooch - Your Name

Your Company	Lists
Account and Settings	All Lists
Manage Users	Products and Services
Custom Form Styles	Recurring Transactions
Chart of Accounts	Attachments
QuickBooks Labs	

The Manage Users feature allows the Master Administrator (you, in this case) to add new users and edit what features each user can access. The permissions can also be edited or modified. Users that are no longer employed or active users can be deleted. An important management feature is Activity, which allows you to view the activity of each user. If you highlight a user name and choose Activity, all of the Activity will be listed, including login and logout times.

 **Best Practice**

To help protect confidential information (for example, payroll information), when you set up users, allow users to access only the activities they need to perform their jobs.

DEVELOP YOUR SKILLS 2-5

In this exercise, you will add Sadie Garrison as a user and define her permissions.

1. Choose **Gear** ⚙ →**Your Company**→**Manage Users**.
2. Click **New**. (You may need to enable popups within your browser.)

   A Mini Interview window appears with various permissions attached to each user type.

3. Because Sadie is the owner and needs to have all access rights, choose **Company Administrator** and then click **Next**.

   You must enter an email address for each new user. The new user will be sent an email invitation that includes a link to your company account.

4. Enter your own email address so you can respond to the invitation.

5. Click **Next** and then click **Finish**.

   Your new user is listed as pending until that person responds to the email invitation.

6. Return to the **Dashboard**.

Opening Balances and Historical Transactions

You are almost ready to get started with current business transactions. Sadie spent some of her investment on equipment and supplies, and she prepaid rent prior to opening on August 1. You need to record those transactions to ensure you capture the investment, asset purchases, and correct bank balance. You can enter all of these opening balances in a journal entry or directly into the account register.

If Puppy Luv Pampered Pooch were an ongoing business with many historical transactions, you would need to carefully evaluate whether to enter those transactions by summary total or individual transaction. You could use a journal entry to record beginning balances from the closing Trial Balance report. Or, you could create a new transaction form for each opening balance.

To record Puppy Luv's opening balances, you will enter Sadie's transactions directly into the bank account register. This will allow you to practice adding vendor names and the Chart of Accounts name from within the register.

> ✔ **Best Practice**
>
> If you have an ongoing business with historical transactions, use a hybrid of summary totals and individual transactions. Enter the open transactions for accounts receivable and accounts payable and a journal entry for the remaining accounts. This can be tricky. The other side of the entry must be an equity account. It would be in your best interest to check with your accounting professional for advice on historical transactions.

DEVELOP YOUR SKILLS 2-6

Sadie has given you a list of her investments and purchases. In this exercise, you will use this list to enter Sadie's initial opening deposit and other transactions into her checking account register.

Sadie's Transactions	
Invested	$75,000
Purchases	$16,000 Equipment
	$ 2,500 Supplies
	$ 800 Marketing/Social Media
	$ 450 Business license
Prepaid Rent	$ 3,300 $550 per month (6 months)

1. From the right side of the Dashboard, at the bottom of the Bank Accounts section, choose **Go to Registers→Los Angeles City Bank**.

2. Close the pop-up message if you get one.

3. To enter Sadie's initial deposit, choose **Add Check menu button** ▾→**Deposit** on the left side of the Bank Register window.

4. Add this information to complete the deposit:

5. Click **Save** on the Bank Register.

Enter the Remaining Banking Transactions

Now you will enter the remaining transactions into the Los Angeles City Bank register.

6. Click the **Add Deposit menu** ▾ button and choose **Check**.

7. Type **07/05/2021** in the Date field and **10001** in the Ref No. field.

8. Type **Ace Groomer and Supply Company** in the Payee field, tap ⌷Tab⌷ to add the new name as a vendor, and click **Save**.

9. Type **16,000** in the Payment field.

10. Type **Equipment** in the Account field and tap ⌷Tab⌷.

11. In the Account window, complete the fields as indicated:

Account Type	Fixed Assets
Detail Type	Machinery & Equipment
Name	Equipment

12. Click **Save and Close** to close the Account window and then click **Save**.

13. Return to the **Dashboard**.

Self-Assessment

Check your knowledge of this chapter's key concepts and skills using the Self-Assessment quiz here or in your eLab course.

1. Categories can be added to the QuickBooks Online Products and Services list. *True   False*

2. QuickBooks Online allows you to delete items from the default list of products and services. *True   False*

3. QuickBooks Online Plus allows you to add only two users and two Accountant users. *True   False*

4. QuickBooks Online Plus allows you to restrict users' access to some features. *True   False*

5. When you record a check written in QuickBooks Online, you must select the account in the register. *True   False*

6. If you record a check written to a new vendor, you must add a new vendor in the Expenses center and then record the check. *True   False*

7. Some accounts on the Chart of Accounts cannot be deleted. *True   False*

8. The Chart of Accounts lists accounts for each transaction in your accounting system. *True   False*

9. If you merge two accounts and discover you made a mistake, you can choose Un-Merge. *True   False*

10. To change your company address in the Company Settings, the first step is to click Search 🔍. *True   False*

11. When setting up a new company file, which start date is best to choose?
    A. July 25, 20xx
    B. December 31, 20xx
    C. April 1, 20xx
    D. January 10, 20xx

12. You can upload your company logo into QuickBooks Online from the:
    A. Navigation bar
    B. Company setting
    C. Create icon
    D. None of these options

13. You can choose to label your customers:
    A. Clients
    B. Members
    C. Tenants
    D. All of these options

(cont'd.)

14. Asset accounts include:
    A. bank accounts
    B. credit card accounts
    C. Accounts Payable
    D. advertising expenses

15. QuickBooks Online creates a default Chart of Accounts based on:
    A. what state you are in
    B. the business type selected during setup
    C. how long you have been in business
    D. None of these options

16. Within the Chart of Accounts list, you can:
    A. edit or change the account name
    B. add a new account
    C. merge accounts
    D. All of these options

Reinforce Your Skills

Set Up the Chart of Accounts for Puppy Luv Pampered Pooch

Now that you have discovered the features you need to customize in Quickbooks Online for Puppy Luv Pampered Pooch, you will continue to edit the Chart of Accounts. You have reviewed the Chart of Accounts and made some notes on what you want to delete, change, and add. In this exercise, you will continue to customize the Chart of Accounts by deleting the accounts you don't think will be used.

1. Choose **Gear** ⚙ →**Your Company**→**Chart of Accounts.**

2. In the Inventory Asset line, click the **Action** menu and choose **Delete**.

3. Delete these accounts:

   - Sales of Product Income
   - Cost of Goods Sold
   - Contractors
   - Purchases

Edit an Account and Add an Account

Now that you have reduced the size of the Chart of Accounts, you are going to rename an account.

4. In the Advertising & Marketing line, choose **Action menu**→**Edit**.

5. Type **Marketing** in the Name field and then click **Save and Close**.

   Sadie wants to open a savings account at the same bank so that she can save for taxes and new equipment. You will now add that account.

6. Scroll to the top of the screen and click the **New** button at the top-right corner.

7. Complete the fields as indicated:

   - Account Type: **Bank**
   - Detail Type: **Savings**
   - Name: **Savings LACB**

8. Click **Save and Close** and then return to the **Dashboard**.

Set Up Products and Services for Puppy Luv Pampered Pooch

To make Sadie's first day go smoothly, you need to correct the Products and Services list. You have the Puppy Luv Pampered Pooch lists of services as well as the Products and Services default list. After a review, you decide to make some changes. In this exercise, you will edit all the services linked to Sales so that they link to Pooch Services.

1. Choose **Gear** ⚙ →**Lists**→**Products and Services**.
2. Change the Income Account for the **Hours** and **Sales** accounts from *Sales* to **Pooch Services**.

Add Products and Services

Previously you added the categories for the services. Now you will add the service to the appropriate category.

3. Click the **New** button at the top right of the Products and Services window and choose **Service** as the type.
4. Complete the Product/Service Information fields as indicated:
   - Name: **Small**
   - Category: **Bath and Brush**
   - Sales Information: **Bath and Brush, Small**
   - Sales Price/Rate: **20**
5. Choose **Save and Close**→**Save and New**.
6. Add the following services for **Bath and Brush**:

Service	Price
Medium	$30
Large	$40
X Large	$55

7. Return to the **Dashboard**.

Add a User

Sadie mentioned that it would be great if her tax accountant could log in to QuickBooks Online and review her records on a quarterly basis to be sure everything is categorized correctly and the appropriate tax amount has been paid. In this exercise, you will add an Accountant user.

1. Choose **Gear** ⚙ →**Your Company**→**Manage Users**.

2. Click **Invite Accountant**.

3. In the Mini Interview window, type **Accountant@accountant.net** in the Accountant's Email Address field.

Note! Your instructor may want to be your Accountant user.

4. Click **Next** and then click **Finish**.

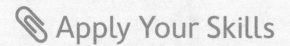

Apply Your Skills

Complete the Chart of Accounts Setup

Sadie has reviewed the Chart of Accounts and would like you to make some additional changes. In this exercise, you will complete the Chart of Accounts setup for Puppy Luv Pampered Pooch.

1. Delete these accounts from the Chart of Accounts, if they are displayed:
   - Inventory Asset
   - Sales
   - Sales of Product Income
   - Cost of Goods Sold
   - Purchases

2. Rename the *Job Supplies* account to: **Pooch Supplies**

3. Add an expense account: *Postage* (Office/General Administrative Expenses)

4. Add Sadie's **City Credit Union** credit card.

5. Click **Run Report** to run an Account List.

6. Click the **Export** button and save as an Excel file in your **Chapter 02** folder as:
   CH02 Chart of Accounts

   Depending on the browser being used, the file may automatically appear in your download bar or tray at the bottom of the web browser window. Retrieve the downloaded file and save it in your Chapter 02 folder.

7. Return to the **Dashboard**.

Complete the Products and Services Setup

In this exercise, you will complete the Product and Services setup for Puppy Luv Pampered Pooch.

1. Add the services for the Mini Pet Groom category (shown on the next page).

2. Add a new category called **Add Ons** and then use the Add Ons information in the Puppy Luv Pampered Pooch List of Services brochure shown here to add the remaining services:

3. Run a **Product/Service List** report.

4. Click the **Export** button, choose **Export to Excel**, and then save the file in your **Chapter 02** folder as: CH02 Products and Services List

5. Return to the **Dashboard**.

APPLY YOUR SKILLS 2-3 QG

Enter Opening Balances

In this exercise, you will enter the opening balances from information provided by Sadie.

1. From the Dashboard, choose **Go to Registers→Los Angeles City Bank**.

2. Use this information to add a check:
   - Date: **07/10/2021**
   - Check: **10002** (confirm or type)
   - Payee: **City of Los Angeles Clerk**
   - Memo: **Business License**
   - Payment: **450**
   - Account: **Taxes & Licenses**

3. Click **Save**.

4. Enter the three remaining transactions into the Los Angeles City Bank checking account register:

Check Number	Date	Amount	Payee	Account
10003	07/15/2021	$2,500	Doggies Plus	Pooch Supplies
10004	07/17/2021	$800	George's Pet Media	Marketing
10005	07/30/2021	$3,300	Capital Properties	Prepaid Expenses

Hint: Prepaid Expenses is an Other Current Asset account type.

5. Return to the **Dashboard**.

The ending balance in the Los Angeles City Bank checking account is $51,950.

6. Run a Chart of Accounts report.

 CHECK FIGURE *Your figures should match those shown here.*

Account	Balance
Los Angeles City Bank	$51,950
Prepaid Expenses	$3,300
Equipment	$16,000
Owner's Equity	$-75,000

Warning! At the end of each chapter, make sure your ending report figures match those in the Check Figure sections before moving to the next chapter. Each chapter builds on the previous one. If your figures are incorrect, any errors will carry over into the work you do in the next chapter.

7. Click the **Export** button, choose **Export to Excel**, and then save the file in your **Chapter 02** folder as: `CH02 Ending Chart of Accounts`

8. Return to the **Dashboard**.

Congratulations! You have set up the new company file for Puppy Luv Pampered Pooch. You will use this file in the following chapters to create day-to-day business transactions as well as reports and bank reconciliations for Puppy Luv Pampered Pooch.

Your Chart of Accounts should look like the one shown here.

Puppy Luv Pampered Pooch - Student Name ✎

ACCOUNT LIST

ACCOUNT	TYPE	DETAIL TYPE	DESCRIPTION	BALANCE
Los Angeles City Bank	Bank	Checking		51,950.00
Savings LACB	Bank	Savings		0.00
Prepaid Expenses	Other Current Assets	Prepaid Expenses		3,300.00
Uncategorized Asset	Other Current Assets	Other Current Assets		0.00
Equipment	Fixed Assets	Machinery & Equipment		16,000.00
City Credit Union	Credit Card	Credit Card		0.00
Opening Balance Equity	Equity	Opening Balance Equity		0.00
Owner's Investment	Equity	Owner's Equity	Money you invested in your bu...	-75,000.00
Owner's Pay & Personal Expenses	Equity	Owner's Equity	Money you took out of your bu...	0.00
Retained Earnings	Equity	Retained Earnings		0.00
Pooch Services	Income	Service/Fee Income		
Uncategorized Income	Income	Sales of Product Income		
Bank Charges & Fees	Expenses	Bank Charges	Fees or charges from your ban...	
Car & Truck	Expenses	Auto	Gas, repairs, insurance, and ot...	
Insurance	Expenses	Insurance	Liability, fire, theft, and other in...	
Interest Paid	Expenses	Interest Paid	Interest paid on loans, credit ca...	
Legal & Professional Services	Expenses	Legal & Professional Fees	Professional services including ...	
Marketing	Expenses	Advertising/Promotional	Ads, business cards, and other ...	
Meals & Entertainment	Expenses	Entertainment Meals	Client meals and entertainment...	
Office Supplies & Software	Expenses	Office/General Administrative ...	Office, kitchen, and bathroom s...	
Other Business Expenses	Expenses	Office/General Administrative ...	Other expenses for your busin...	
Pooch Supplies	Expenses	Supplies & Materials	Supplies you bought to compl...	
Postage	Expenses	Office/General Administrative ...		
Reimbursable Expenses	Expenses	Supplies & Materials	Purchases you made for a cust...	
Rent & Lease	Expenses	Rent or Lease of Buildings	Office space, storage, vehicle, ...	
Repairs & Maintenance	Expenses	Repair & Maintenance	Repairs, maintenance, and clea...	
Taxes & Licenses	Expenses	Taxes Paid	Property and business taxes, lic...	
Travel	Expenses	Travel	Business travel including trans...	
Uncategorized Expense	Expenses	Other Miscellaneous Service Cost		
Utilities	Expenses	Utilities	Phone, gas, electric, water, inte...	

3 | Working with Customers

Your customers are the people and businesses that you sell products and services to. In this chapter, you will learn the features of the Sales center that will assist you in the creation of sales documents, invoices, and sales receipts. You will also manage your business's Accounts Receivable, track customer-related transactions, and create customer and sales-related reports that help you determine what customers are buying and how often, as well as the volume of sales made to each customer.

LEARNING OBJECTIVES

▸ Set up customers and sub-customers

▸ Import customers

▸ Edit sales settings and preferences

▸ Create sales receipts and invoices

▸ Receive payments from customers

▸ Record bank deposits

▸ Create sales reports

📁 Project: Craig's Design and Landscaping Services

Craig Carlson learned from an associate that the next step in completing the setup for the QuickBooks Online company file is to track customers and sales transactions. Craig has decided to keep the Customer label for his Customers list and to use a sub-customer feature for each project. Finally, it is important that Craig have some customer and sales reports that can help him keep track of things such as how much customers owe and how much they spend.

The Sales Center

The Sales center (as it is known in the test drive; in your Puppy Luv Pampered Pooch data file in QuickBooks Online, this area is referred to as the Invoicing center) provides information about all of your customers and their transactions in a single place. It also allows you to perform customer-related tasks such as searching for customers, adding customers, importing lists of customers, editing and merging customer information, and making customers inactive.

The Sales center contains four tabs: All Sales, Invoices, Customers, and Products and Services. These allow the user easy access to these features and functions in one place. The Customers list within the Sales center contains a multi-colored money bar that gives you a quick snapshot of Accounts Receivable. You can click money bar sections to access more detailed information about unbilled, unpaid, and paid invoices.

The Customers list displays customer names, contact information, and open balances at a glance, as well as detailed information when you select a specific name. The Action menu lets you quickly create a statement, receipt, invoice, or other transaction for an individual customer.

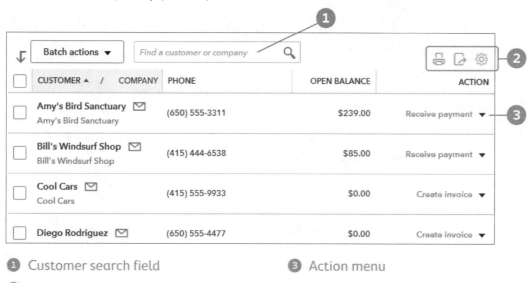

1. Customer search field
2. Print, Export, and Settings icons
3. Action menu

Adding Customers and Sub-Customers

The Display Name As field is the only required field when setting up a new customer, but by completing more fields, you will be able to create more useful management reports. For example, you could organize your Customers list by zip code, phone number, or email address.

QuickBooks Online does not allow you to add two customers with the same name. You must include a middle initial or other distinguishing identifier in the Display Name As field to make the names different.

To keep track of multiple projects, locations, or members of a single customer, you can create sub-customers. For example, if Jane Kim has two properties for which Craig's Design and Landscaping Services is maintaining the landscaping, you can make each property a sub-customer of Jane Kim.

> ✔ **Best Practice**
>
> As you create new customers, enter as much information as possible so you can fully utilize the power of QuickBooks Online data when creating management reports.

Tip! Using the Sales center is not the only way to add customers. You can also add new customers and sub-customers from within a sales form.

DEVELOP YOUR SKILLS 3-1

In this exercise, you will create a new customer and a sub-customer for Craig's Design and Landscaping Services. Remember, the user interface for QuickBooks Online is updated frequently, so some of the names and features in course exercises may differ from what you see on your interface.

Before You Begin: *Access the QuickBooks Online test drive at qbo.intuit.com/redir/testdrive. Leave the test drive open for the entire chapter. If you close it, you will lose your work needed for subsequent Develop Your Skills exercises in this chapter.*

1. Open the **Sales** center from the Navigation bar and click the **Customers** tab.
2. Click the **New Customer** button at the top-right corner of the browser window.
3. Complete the Customer Information form as follows:
   - First Name: **Edward**
   - Last Name: **Bruce**
   - Display Name As: This should auto-fill, but, if not, type **Edward Bruce**
   - Email: **eBruce@hotmail.net**
   - Phone: **619-555-1118**
   - Billing Address: **1452 Santiago Road, Bayshore, CA, 94326**
4. Click **Save** and then choose **Sales** on the Navigation bar and click **Customers** to return to the Customers list.

Add a Sub-Customer

Edward Bruce has accepted the proposal to landscape his front yard. He mentioned that he may want to landscape his backyard, too, so you will create a sub-customer to more easily track this specific project.

5. Click the **New Customer** button.

6. Follow these steps to create a sub-customer:

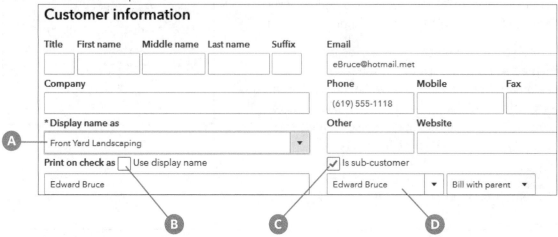

Ⓐ Type **Front Yard Landscaping** in the Display Name As field.

Ⓑ Uncheck **Use Display Name**.

Ⓒ Check the **Is Sub-Customer** checkbox.

Ⓓ Choose **Edward Bruce** from the Enter Parent Customer menu.

7. Click **Save** and then click **Sales** on the Navigation bar.

Importing Customers from an Excel or CSV File

QuickBooks Online allows you to import customer lists from an Excel or comma-separated values (CSV) worksheet. One way you can import customer lists is by accessing the Import Data tool from the Gear menu.

The Import Data tool allows you to import information about customers, vendors, Charts of Accounts, and products and services. The tool includes forms and prompts to help you upload and map your lists to QuickBooks Online format. This feature is a great time-saver for existing businesses that have large lists.

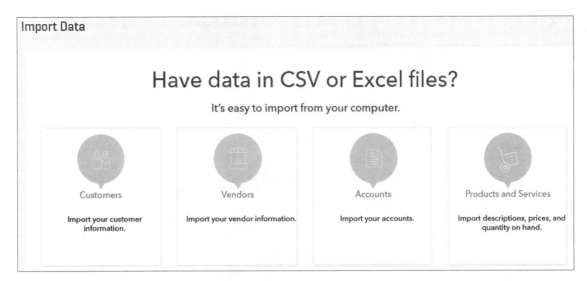

QuickBooks Online often provides multiple ways to do something, depending on where you are working within the application. Besides using the Import Data tool, you can also import data from within the Sales center.

Gear ⚙ →Tools→Import Data

Sales center→New Customer→Import Customers

DEVELOP YOUR SKILLS 3-2

In this exercise, you will work within the Customers list to import customers from an Excel file.

1. Click the **New Customer menu** ▼ and choose **Import Customers**.

2. Click **Browse**, navigate to your **Chapter 03** folder, and select **CH03 Import Customers.xlsx**.

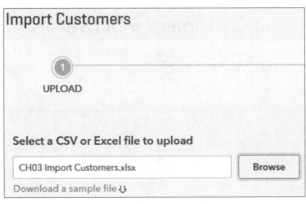

3. Click **Next** at the bottom-right corner of the browser window.

4. Review the mapping to verify that the fields selected for import match the figure.

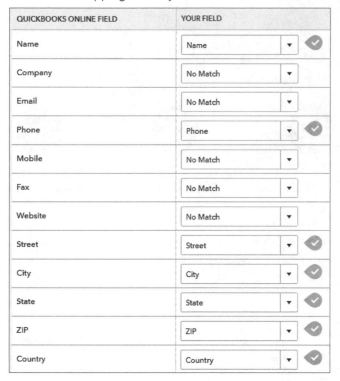

5. Click **Next** and then review the records ready for import.

6. Click **Import**.

A message appears informing you that the records were successfully imported.

Editing, Merging, and Making Customers Inactive

Your Customers list is customizable. After you add a customer, you can go back and edit the record. You can also merge two lists if you find that the same customer is listed twice. Doing so will combine all the customer's transactions into a single record. Finally, to keep your Customers list current and less cluttered, you can inactivate customer records that you are no longer dealing with.

> *Note!* In QuickBooks Online, customer, vendor, account, and other information can be made inactive but can never be deleted.

In this exercise, you will edit a customer address, merge two customers together, and make a customer inactive. You will start by editing the address for Cool Cars, which just notified you that they have moved.

1. Choose **Cool Cars** from the Customers list.

   Click the company name, not the checkbox to the left of the name.

2. Click the ⏐ Edit ⏐ button at the top-right corner.

3. Change the street address in the Billing Address field to **15851 N Ocean Dr** and then click **Save**.

4. Open the **Sales** center. Click the **Customers** tab if the center doesn't open to the Customers list.

Merge Two Customers

You have discovered that Rago Travel Agency is actually owned by John Melton. You need to merge these two records.

5. Choose **Rago Travel Agency** from the Customers list and then click the **Edit** button at the top-right corner.

6. Edit the Display Name As field to show **John Melton** and then click **Save**.

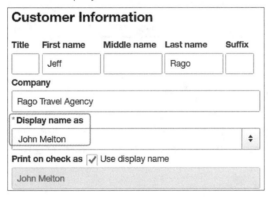

7. Choose **Yes** in the dialog box to confirm the change.

8. Click **Sales** on the Navigation bar and then click the **Customers** tab.

Make a Customer Inactive

Craig reviewed the Customers list and has asked you to remove old or inactive customers. Wedding Planning by Whitney is no longer an active customer.

9. Choose **Wedding Planning by Whitney** from the Customers list and then click the **Edit** button.

10. Click the ⏐ Make inactive ⏐ button at the bottom of the window.

11. Choose **Yes** when the prompt appears and then return to the Customers list.

> *Tip!* Use the keyboard shortcut ⏐Ctrl⏐+⏐Alt⏐+⏐C⏐ to go to the Customers list.

12. To see a complete listing of customers, including inactive customers, click the **Settings** icon above the Action menu and then click the checkbox for **Include Inactive**.

13. Scroll down the list to the customer Wedding Planning by Whitney.

The inactive customer is included in the list and is tagged as deleted.

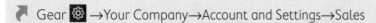

14. Return to the **Dashboard**.

Recording Sales Transactions

Sales transactions can be recorded in one of two ways: either with a sales receipt when a customer pays for a product or service at the time of sale or with an invoice when a customer pays after the sale of a product or service.

Customizing Sales Forms Settings: Content

Before you begin recording sales transactions, it's important to decide what information should appear on sales forms and then check that the sales form settings are appropriate for your business.

 View the video "Sales Form Settings: Content" at: labyrinthelab.com/2017/video/QBO-V0301.html

> 🔻 Gear 🔅 →Your Company→Account and Settings→Sales

Customizing Sales Forms Settings: Appearance

It's also important that sales forms reflect your company's image. You can use the Custom Form Styles settings to customize the appearance of your Invoice, Sales Receipt, and Estimate forms. You have five styles to choose from. After you choose a style, you can further customize the form's appearance, header, and footer. There is no limit to the number of forms you can create.

✔ *Best Practice*

To help brand your business and to help people easily find your contact information, include your logo, contact information, and website address on all forms that customers, vendors, and other members of the public will see.

DEVELOP YOUR SKILLS 3-4

Craig has asked you to create a sales receipt that reflects his business. He has told you what color, font, and other information he wants. In this exercise, you will create a customized sales receipt form for Craig's Design and Landscaping Services.

1. Choose **Gear** ⚙ →**Your Company**→**Custom Form Styles**.

2. Click the **New Style** button in the top-right corner of the browser window and choose **Sales Receipt** from the menu.

3. Set the name of the receipt to: **My Sales Receipt**

   The Give Your Template a Name field may be prepopulated. You can edit the existing text or type new text.

4. Click **Change Up the Template** and choose the **Airy** style.

5. Click **Splash on Some Color** and choose the green color with value **#79BD58** from the color palette.

6. Click **Get Choosy with Your Font** and choose **Courier** as the font type.

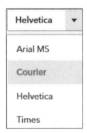

7. In the top creation bar, click the **Content** tab.

8. Click the top portion of the form on the right side of the browser window.

9. On the left side of the window, click the **+ Address** link to expand the list and then confirm that the Street Address field has a checkmark next to it.

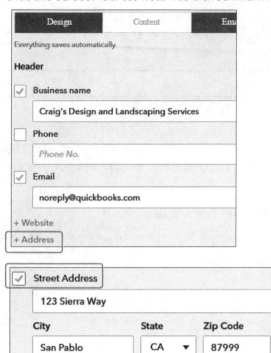

10. Click the middle portion of the form on the right side of the window.

11. On the left side of the window, click in the **Date** checkbox to add a Date column to the receipt.

12. Click the bottom portion of the form on the right side of the window.

13. On the left, edit the Message to Customer field to: `It has been a pleasure to have your business. Enjoy your day.`

14. Click **Done** and then return to the **Dashboard**.

Creating Sales Receipts and Invoices

QuickBooks Online forms are designed to work dynamically with one another. If you link your Chart of Accounts and your Products and Services lists correctly as you prepare your sales forms, the appropriate accounting transactions will be created when you make a transaction. For example, when you make a sale on account (to be paid later) and select the Invoice form, the Accounts Receivable account and the Sales account increase by the amount of the sale. When you receive payment at the time of sale and select the Sales Receipt form, the Sales account and an account called Undeposited Funds increase by the amount of the sale.

The Undeposited Funds account is unique to QuickBooks. It is where QuickBooks Online holds transactions until you deposit the corresponding checks and cash. It is important that your deposit in QuickBooks matches exactly what was deposited in the bank.

Warning! It's not a good practice to record sales on a journal entry or directly on a bank deposit form. The profit and loss report would be correct, but the sales would not appear on sales reports.

Edward Bruce just dropped off his signed contract and paid for the design of his front yard. This type of transaction requires a sales receipt. In this exercise, you will create a sales receipt and a sales invoice. You will also see how these transactions impact various accounts in QuickBooks Online.

1. Choose **Create**  →**Customers**→**Sales Receipt**.
2. Complete the fields for the sales receipt as indicated:
   - Choose a Customer: **Edward Bruce: Front Yard Landscaping**
   - Sales Receipt Date: **09/01/2021**
   - Payment Method: **Check**
   - Reference No.: **4511**
   - Deposit To: **Undeposited Funds**
   - Product/Service: **Design**
   - Description: **Custom Design – Front Yard Landscaping**
   - Rate: **500**
3. Click **Save**.

View the Transaction Journal

Now you will view the behind-the-scenes accounting for this transaction.

4. Click **More** in the bottom tray and then choose **Transaction Journal**.

> Copy
> Void
> Delete
> Transaction journal
> Audit history

A debit has been made to Undeposited Funds, and a credit has been made to Design Income.

Craig's Design and Landscaping Services

JOURNAL
All Dates

DATE	TRANSACTION TYPE	NUM	NAME	MEMO/DESCRIPTION	ACCOUNT	DEBIT	CREDIT
09/01/2021	Sales Receipt	1038	Edward Bruce:Front Yard Land...		Undeposited Funds	$500.00	
				Custom Design	Design income		$500.00
						$500.00	$500.00
TOTAL						$500.00	$500.00

Create a Sales Invoice

Craig provided pest control services to Bill's Windsurf Shop. Now you will create an invoice for services rendered.

5. Choose **Create**  →**Customers**→**Invoice**.

6. Follow these steps to create an invoice form:

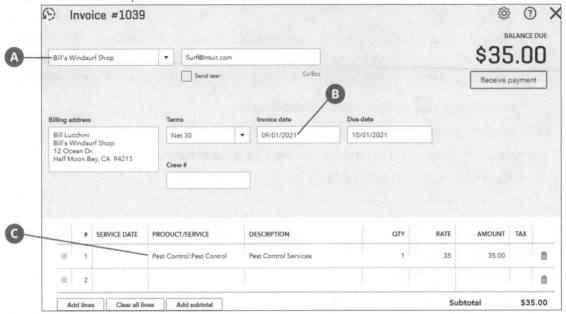

Ⓐ Choose **Bill's Windsurf Shop** as the customer.

Ⓑ Type **09/01/2021** for the invoice date.

Ⓒ Choose **Pest Control** as the product/service.

7. Click **Save**.

Notice that you can also change the payment terms for this specific invoice.

8. In the bottom tray, choose **More→Transaction Journal**.

QuickBooks Online displays the behind-the-scenes accounting. In this transaction, Accounts Receivable is the debit and Pest Control Services is the credit.

Receiving Customer Payments

Customer payments on open invoices are entered into QuickBooks Online and applied to the appropriate invoice through the Create menu. By default, all customer payments are deposited to Undeposited Funds, to be batched for deposit to your banking institution later.

In this exercise, you will record the receipt of payment from Amy's Bird Sanctuary.

1. Choose **Create** ⊕ →**Customers**→**Receive Payment**.
2. Complete the fields as indicated:
   - Choose a Customer: **Amy's Bird Sanctuary**
   - Payment Date: **09/01/2021**
   - Payment Method: **Check**
   - Reference No.: **55841**
3. In the Outstanding Transactions section, click in the **Invoice # 1021** checkbox to add a checkmark.

   Once you enter the customer, all the customer's open invoices appear in the bottom portion of the window.

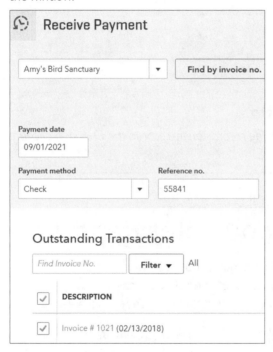

4. Choose **Save and New**→**Save and Close**.

   The Accounts Receivable account decreases by $239, and the Undeposited Funds account increases by $239.

Recording a Bank Deposit

In QuickBooks Online, you must record your bank deposits for the exact amount that went into the bank. By recording all the monies collected into the Undeposited Funds account, you can more easily choose the specific checks, cash, or credit card transactions that make up a single batch for deposit.

In this exercise, you will record the deposit of two customer payments.

1. Choose **Create** →**Other**→**Bank Deposit**.

   A list of all undeposited funds appears. You will select the payments to include in this one deposit.

2. If not already selected, choose **Checking** from the Choose an Account menu at the top of the browser window.

3. Type **09/01/2021** in the Date field.

4. In the Select Existing Payments section, click in the checkboxes for **Edward Bruce:Front Yard Landscaping** and **Amy's Bird Sanctuary** to choose these payments for deposit.

Select the payments included in this deposit

	RECEIVED FROM ▲	DATE	TYPE	PAYMENT METHOD	MEMO	REF NO.	AMOUNT
☑	Amy's Bird Sanctuary	09/01/2021	Payment	Check ▼		55841	239.00
☐	Cool Cars	03/07/2018	Payment	Enter Text ▼			1,675.52
☑	Edward Bruce:Front Yard Landscaping	09/01/2021	Sales Receipt	Check ▼		4511	500.00
☐	Freeman Sporting Goods:0969 Ocean View Road	03/07/2018	Payment	Enter Text ▼			387.00

5. Choose **Save and New**→**Save and Close**.

   After you save the record, QuickBooks Online records an increase in the Checking account and a decrease in the Undeposited Funds account.

Creating Customer and Sales Reports

The Reports center on the Navigation bar contains numerous customer- and sales-related reports. These reports help you analyze which products and services customers are buying, how much they are spending, how much money they owe, and how long they have owed it.

View the video "The Reports Center" at: labyrinthelab.com/2017/video/QBO-V0302

In this exercise, you will create a number of reports that will help you analyze Craig's customers and sales. You will start with a Customer Balance Summary report.

1. Click **Reports** in the Navigation bar.

2. Click the **All** tab, choose the **Who Owes You** category, and then choose **Customer Balance Summary**.

   The summary displays all balances due for each customer; each sub-customer's balance is also listed as a subtotal for the customer.

CHECK FIGURE *Verify that your total is $5,077.52 and that your figures match those shown here.*

Craig's Design and Landscaping Services	
CUSTOMER BALANCE SUMMARY	
All Dates	
	TOTAL
Bill's Windsurf Shop	120.00
▾ Freeman Sporting Goods	
0969 Ocean View Road	477.50
55 Twin Lane	85.00
Total Freeman Sporting Goods	562.50
Geeta Kalapatapu	629.10
Jeff's Jalopies	81.00
John Melton	450.00
Kookies by Kathy	75.00
Mark Cho	314.28
Paulsen Medical Supplies	954.75
Red Rock Diner	226.00
Rondonuwu Fruit and Vegi	78.60
▾ Shara Barnett	
Barnett Design	274.50
Total Shara Barnett	274.50
Sonnenschein Family Store	362.07
Sushi by Katsuyuki	160.00
Travis Waldron	414.72
Weiskopf Consulting	375.00
TOTAL	$5,077.52

3. Click the **Back to Report List** link in the top-left corner of the window.

4. Click the **All** tab to return to the menu of report categories.

Create a Customer Balance Detail Report

Now you will create a report that allows you to see more detail, such as invoice dates and amounts for each customer.

5. Choose **Who Owes You→Customer Balance Detail**.

Craig's Design and Landscaping Services ✎

CUSTOMER BALANCE DETAIL

All Dates

DATE	TRANSACTION TYPE	NUM	DUE DATE	AMOUNT	OPEN BALANCE	BALANCE
▾ Bill's Windsurf Shop						
01/18/2018	Invoice	1027	02/17/2018	85.00	85.00	85.00
09/01/2021	Invoice	1040	10/01/2021	35.00	35.00	120.00
Total for Bill's Windsurf Shop				**$120.00**	**$120.00**	
▾ Freeman Sporting Goods						
▾ 0969 Ocean View Road						
03/07/2018	Invoice	1036	04/06/2018	477.50	477.50	477.50
Total for 0969 Ocean View Road				**$477.50**	**$477.50**	
▾ 55 Twin Lane						
01/18/2018	Invoice	1028	02/17/2018	81.00	81.00	81.00
02/26/2018	Invoice	1005	03/28/2018	54.00	4.00	85.00
Total for 55 Twin Lane				**$135.00**	**$85.00**	
Total for Freeman Sporting Goods				**$612.50**	**$562.50**	

Here and throughout this course, remember that your dates will differ from those in the provided images.

6. Click the **Back to Report List** link and then click the **All** tab.

Create a Sales by Customer Summary

7. Choose **Sales and Customers→Sales by Customer Summary**.

8. Choose **All Dates** from the Report Period menu.

9. Click **Run Report**.

The summary displays the total sales to each customer.

Craig's Design and Landscaping Services

SALES BY CUSTOMER SUMMARY

All Dates

	TOTAL
Amy's Bird Sanctuary	630.00
Bill's Windsurf Shop	295.00
Cool Cars	2,194.00
Diego Rodriguez	140.00
Dukes Basketball Camp	422.00
Dylan Sollfrank	337.50
▾ Edward Bruce	
Front Yard Landscaping	500.00
Total Edward Bruce	**500.00**
▾ Freeman Sporting Goods	
0969 Ocean View Road	1,058.75
55 Twin Lane	205.00
Total Freeman Sporting Goods	**1,263.75**
Geeta Kalapatapu	582.50

10. Click the **Back to Report List** link.

Create a Sales by Product/Service Detail Report

Now you will create a report that details each product and service, who it was sold to, and the sales amount.

11. Choose **Sales and Customers→Sales by Product/Service Detail**.

12. Choose **All Dates** in the Report Period field and then click **Run Report**.

Craig's Design and Landscaping Services

SALES BY PRODUCT/SERVICE DETAIL
All Dates

DATE	TRANSACTION TYPE	NUM	CUSTOMER	MEMO/DESCRIPTION	QTY	SALES PRICE	AMOUNT	BALANCE
▼ Design								
▼ Design								
02/10/2018	Invoice	1007	John Melton	Custom Design	10.00	75.00	750.00	750.00
02/10/2018	Sales Receipt	1008	Kate Whelan	Custom Design	3.00	75.00	225.00	975.00
03/02/2018	Sales Receipt	1003	Dylan Sollfrank	Custom Design	4.50	75.00	337.50	1,312.50
03/05/2018	Invoice	1010	Weiskopf Consulting	Custom Design	5.00	75.00	375.00	1,687.50
03/05/2018	Invoice	1015	Paulsen Medical Supplies	Custom Design	4.00	75.00	300.00	1,987.50
03/06/2018	Invoice	1033	Geeta Kalapatapu	Custom Design	3.50	75.00	262.50	2,250.00
09/01/2021	Sales Receipt	1039	Edward Bruce:Front Yard Lan...	Custom Design +Front Yard L...	1.00	500.00	500.00	2,750.00
Total for Design					31.00		$2,750.00	
▼ Fountains								
▼ Concrete								
01/18/2018	Invoice	1029	Dukes Basketball Camp	Concrete for fountain installat...	5.00	15.00	75.00	75.00
03/07/2018	Invoice	1037	Sonnenschein Family Store	Concrete for fountain installat...	5.00	9.50	47.50	122.50
Total for Concrete					10.00		$122.50	

Correcting Errors

There may be times when you need correct, void, or delete a transaction in QuickBooks Online. Errors are easy to fix, but you must be watchful of the dates and transaction numbers.

To correct a transaction, you only need to locate it, make the correction, and click Save.

To void or delete a transaction you need to locate it, click the More icon at the bottom of the window, and select the action you wish. Choosing Void will void the transaction but maintain the integrity of the accounting. Delete completely removes the transaction.

QuickBooks Online assigns sequential document numbers on sales documents, and you will need to keep the sales receipts and invoices in the exact order in which they are presented throughout the textbook. You can customize your document numbers to suit your needs, after enabling the setting that allows this.

> ↱ Gear ⚙ →Accounts and Settings→Sales tab→Sales Form Content→Custom Transaction Numbers→On

Account and Settings

	Sales form content		
Company		Preferred invoice terms	**Net 30**
		Preferred delivery method	**Print later**
Sales		Shipping	**Off**
		Custom fields	**On**
Expenses		Custom transaction numbers	**On**
		Service date	**Off**
Advanced		Discount	**On**
		Deposit	**Off**

Tackle the Tasks

This is your opportunity to apply some of the skills learned in this chapter to accomplish additional tasks for Craig's Design and Landscaping Services. To refresh your memory, refer to the concepts and Develop Your Skills exercises as needed.

Before You Begin: Close the current test drive window and then open a new test drive window.

Task	Use This Information
Add New Customers	• James Steen, 123 College Ave., Bayshore, CA 94211 • Cook's House of Design, 458 Holly Ave., Bayshore, CA 94215 • David Seth, 4881 National Blvd., Bayshore, CA 94214
Create Sales Receipts	James Steen paid cash for pest control services at the College Avenue address on 09/02/2021. Kate Whelan paid with check number 5584 for six bags of soil and four sprinkler heads on 09/02/2021. David Seth paid with check number 8871 for repairs for $225 on 09/02/2021.
Create Deposit Records	On 9/03/2021, deposit the receipt for James Steen's 09/02/21 payment.
Create Reports	Craig would like to see a summary of sales by customer for all dates. Craig would like to see a summary of customer balances for all dates.

Self-Assessment

Check your knowledge of this chapter's key concepts and skills using the Self-Assessment quiz here or in your eLab course.

1. You can import customer and vendor lists only from Excel. *True   False*

2. You can merge customers in QuickBooks Online. *True   False*

3. A long-time customer has gone out of business; you can delete the customer. *True   False*

4. A sales receipt is used when you are collecting payment at the time of sale. *True   False*

5. Undeposited Funds is an account to use for unpaid invoices. *True   False*

6. You should use the Bank Deposit form to record sales because it is faster. *True   False*

7. You CANNOT complete a sales form until you have set up all of the customer's information. *True   False*

8. To customize sales forms, you click the Customize button on the Dashboard. *True   False*

9. You can customize several different sales forms. *True   False*

10. To receive a customer payment on an open invoice, you click Make Deposit on the Navigation bar. *True   False*

11. Which lists can be imported from Excel into QuickBooks Online?
    A. Transactions
    B. Customers, Vendors, Products and Services, and Chart of Accounts
    C. Bank statements and open invoices
    D. You cannot import anything into QuickBooks Online.

12. How should you handle two customers with the same name?
    A. If the addresses are different, do nothing.
    B. Give them different customer numbers.
    C. Add an initial to one of the names to make it different.
    D. It does not matter; you can have identical customer names.

13. What is the difference between an invoice and a sales receipt?
    A. An invoice is for future sales; a sales receipt is for current sales.
    B. An invoice is for sales that will be paid in the future; a sales receipt is for sales that are paid at the time of sale.
    C. An invoice records the sale; a sales receipt records the payment.
    D. They can be used interchangeably; there is no difference.

(cont'd.)

14. You made a sale for which the customer paid the whole amount. To record the sale, click
    Create ⊕ and then choose:
    A. Invoice
    B. Record Sale
    C. Sales Receipt
    D. Receive Payment

15. Which statement is true regarding Undeposited Funds?
    A. The account is used for unpaid invoices.
    B. The account is used for unknown deposits.
    C. Undeposited Funds is not an account in QuickBooks Online.
    D. The account is used to record payments prior to making a deposit.

16. What would be a reason to NOT use deposits or journal entries to record sales?
    A. You don't know how to make a journal entry.
    B. The profit and loss report will be incorrect.
    C. The sales reports will not include these sales.
    D. It is okay to record sales using deposits or journal entries.

17. Where can you find reports related to customers' Accounts Receivable?
    A. Reports→Recommended→Customers
    B. Reports→All tab→Who Owes You
    C. Reports→All tab→Review Sales
    D. Reports→Recommended→Sales

18. Where can you find reports related to sales?
    A. Reports→Recommended→Sales
    B. Reports→All tab→Sales and Customers
    C. Reports→All tab→Business Overview
    D. There are no sales reports in QuickBooks Online.

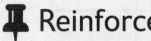

Reinforce Your Skills

For these exercises, you will work with Puppy Luv Pampered Pooch, the company account created in your trial subscription to QuickBooks Online. Remember that the area known as the Sales center in the test drive is called the Invoicing center when working with your Puppy Luv Pampered Pooch company file in the full version of QuickBooks Online.

REINFORCE YOUR SKILLS 3-1

Add New Clients

In this exercise, you will add new clients (customers) and their pets in the Puppy Luv Pampered Pooch Clients list. Besides giving you the name of her new clients, Sadie has given you an Excel file with a list of existing clients that will be moving to her new pooch salon. To save time and reduce the possibility of input errors, you will import the client list into QuickBooks Online. The Clients list is found within the Invoicing tab on the Navigation bar.

Before You Begin: *Access your trial subscription to QuickBooks Online. Read any alerts or reminders that appear and close any unnecessary windows.*

1. From the **Clients list**, add and save this client:
   - Name: **Mary Beth Dunham**
   - Phone number: **702-555-4489**
   - Click **Add Client**

2. Add Mary Beth's small mixed-breed dog as a sub-client (i.e., sub-customer) by creating these settings:
   - Click **New Client**
   - Display Name As: **Elvis**
   - Print on Check As: Click in the checkbox to uncheck
   - Is Sub-Client: Click in the checkbox
   - Parent customer: **Mary Beth Dunham**

3. Click **Import Clients** from the **New Client** drop-down menu, navigate to your **Chapter 03** folder, and choose **CH03 Import Clients.xlsx**.

4. Click **Next**.

5. Review the mapping to verify the correct fields are selected and then click **Next**.

6. Review the records ready for import and then click **Import**.

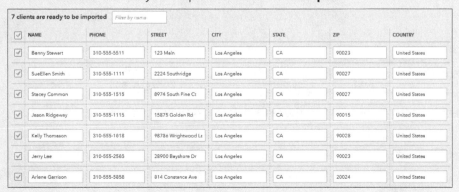

	NAME	PHONE	STREET	CITY	STATE	ZIP	COUNTRY
✓	Benny Stewart	310-555-5511	123 Main	Los Angeles	CA	90023	United States
✓	SueEllen Smith	310-555-1111	2224 Southridge	Los Angeles	CA	90027	United States
✓	Stacey Common	310-555-1515	8974 South Pine Ct	Los Angeles	CA	90027	United States
✓	Jason Ridgeway	310-555-1115	15875 Golden Rd	Los Angeles	CA	90015	United States
✓	Kelly Thomason	310-555-1818	98786 Wrightwood Lr	Los Angeles	CA	90028	United States
✓	Jerry Lee	310-555-2585	28900 Bayshore Dr	Los Angeles	CA	90023	United States
✓	Arlene Garrison	310-555-5858	814 Constance Ave	Los Angeles	CA	20024	United States

7 clients are ready to be imported

The Clients list now includes the names of the imported clients.

Set Default Sales Settings

In this exercise, you will review and set default settings for Puppy Luv Pampered Pooch. You and Sadie have discussed the sales terms for her business and the design of sales forms. Sadie wants to change some of the sales terms and has decided on a pink color scheme for sales receipts and invoices.

1. Choose **Gear** ⚙ →**Your Company**→**Account and Settings**.

2. Click **Sales** on the left, click the **Sales Form Content** section **Edit** 🖉 button, and make these changes:

   • Preferred invoice terms: **Net 15**

   • Service Date: **On**

3. Click **Save** and then click **Done**.

4. Choose **Gear** ⚙ →**Your Company**→**Custom Form Styles**.

5. To create a new style of sales receipt:

   • Choose **Sales Receipt** from the **New Style** button.

   • Type the name as: **Pink Sales Receipt**

   • Choose the **Modern** template.

   • Choose the pink color **#f4749b**.

   • Change the font to **Courier, 10pt** and adjust all margins to **0.50**.

   • On the **Content** tab, choose to include the company address and click **Hide Country** if the country is displayed.

   • On the **Content** tab, add this message to the footer: **Thank you for choosing Puppy Luv Pampered Pooch!**

6. Preview the form and click **Done**.

7. Use the **Edit** drop-down menu to make **Pink Sales Receipt** the default.

Create Sales Forms, a Deposit, and a Report

Opening day was a pooch party! Many owners and their pooches came over to meet Sadie and tour the salon. Sadie also managed to get in a few groomings and flea baths. In this exercise, you will create sales receipts for Puppy Luv Pampered Pooch's first day of business. You will also add clients and clients' pooches as sub-clients, make a bank deposit, and create a Sales by Client Summary report.

1. Choose **Create** ⊕ →**Clients**→**Sales Receipt**.

2. Prepare sales receipts for the following services provided on August 5, 2021.

   Hint: Choose Undeposited Funds in the Deposit To field. Where needed, add clients and pooches as sub-clients. You may need to add Undeposited Funds as a Current Asset account.

   - Jason Ridgeway brought in his medium-sized terrier mix, Butch, for a Full Pet Groom. He paid with check number 4844.

     - To add Butch as a sub-client of Jason Ridgeway from with the Sales Receipt form, type `Jason Ridgeway:Butch` in the pop up, choose **+Details**, and select **Is a Sub-Client of Jason Ridgway**. The Sales Receipt number should be #1001.

   - Jerry Lee brought in his large Lab, King, for a Flea Bath after a walk in the woods. He paid with check number 9887.

   - Bonnie Zoe brought in her tiny Chihuahua, Missy, for a Bath and Brush and paid cash.

3. To prepare the bank deposit for August 5, 2021, choose **Create**→**Other**→**Bank Deposit**.

4. Return to the **Dashboard**.

5. To run a report for August 5, 2021, click **Reports** on the Navigation bar and then choose **All tab**→**Sales and Customers**→**Sales by Client Summary**.

6. Enter the appropriate data and then click **Run Report**.

   Your report amounts should match those shown in this figure.

Puppy Luv Pampered Pooch - Your Name	
SALES BY CLIENT SUMMARY	
August 5, 2021	
	TOTAL
Bonnie Zoe	
Missy	20.00
Total Bonnie Zoe	20.00
Jason Ridgeway	
Butch	45.00
Total Jason Ridgeway	45.00
Jerry Lee	
King	10.00
Total Jerry Lee	10.00
TOTAL	$75.00

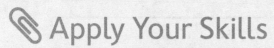

Apply Your Skills

The Apply Your Skills exercises give you a chance to figure out things on your own. You will apply critical thinking skills to prepare the remaining sales receipts and the bank deposit for the grand opening of Puppy Luv Pampered Pooch.

APPLY YOUR SKILLS 3-1

Create Sales Receipts, a Bank Deposit, and a Report

Sadie did not get in many groomings, but she did meet some wonderful pooch owners and their pooches. After closing for the day, Sadie received a call from Esther Green, a dog breeder who is very interested in contracting services for her kennel. A meeting was scheduled for the afternoon of August 6. In this exercise, you will create the remaining sales receipts for August 5, 2021, record a bank deposit, and create a sales report for Sadie.

1. Create sales receipts for these services:

   - Benny Stewart decided it would be a treat for his small Terrier, Maggie, to get a nice Bath and Brush along with a teeth brushing. Benny paid with check number 12678.

   - Arlene Garrison's small Terrier, Joe, got a Mini Pet Groom and his ears cleaned. Arlene paid with check number 9981.

   - Stacey Common was curious about the new boutique and decided Agnes, her medium-sized Terrier mix, could use a Bath and Brush. Stacey paid in cash.

2. Create the bank deposit for August 5, 2021, to Los Angeles City Bank.

3. Create a Sales by Client Summary report for August 5, 2021.

 CHECK FIGURE *Your figures should match those shown here.*

Account	Amount
Bank deposit	$95
Bank balance	$52,120
Sales by Client Summary	$170

APPLY YOUR SKILLS 3-2

Create Transactions, a Deposit, and a Report

In this exercise, you will create all the transactions for August 6, 2021, and then create a bank deposit and report.

1. Use the following information to create the appropriate transaction:

   - Julie Walton brought in both of her large Boxers, Alice and Suzy, for Full Groom, Teeth Brushed, and Ears Cleaned. She paid with check number 1515. Set up two sub-clients, create two sales receipts, and apply half of the payment to each.

   - Doug Sherrill brought in his extra-large Husky, Skeeter, for a Bath and Brush. He paid with check number 8987.

   - Brett Johnson brought in his large Bassett, Romeo, for a Bath and Brush and Teeth Brushed. He paid with cash.

- Amanda Brown found a terribly matted, small terrier mix in a field. She brought him in for a Flea Bath and Full Groom. Don't forget the extra charge for matted pets. Amanda has not named him yet. She paid cash. (Do not create a sub-client.)

- Jamee Thompson brought in her tiny teacup poodle, Peaches, for a Full Groom and had her nails painted. Jamee paid with check number 58581.

2. Sadie closed the salon a bit early to meet with the kennel owner. You will take the checks and cash from today's sales to the bank and deposit them, so you need to record a bank deposit. Then, leave a Sales by Client Summary report for August 6, 2021 for Sadie to review.

 CHECK FIGURE *Your figures should match those shown here.*

Account	Amount
Bank deposit	$353
Bank balance	$52,473
Sales by Client Summary	$353

APPLY YOUR SKILLS 3-3

Set Up a New Account, Create Transactions, and Create a Report

Sadie met with Esther Green about setting up weekly appointments for the twenty-nine dogs in Esther's kennel. She will bring in seven medium-sized dogs for Bath and Brush each week on a rotating basis. She would also like the dogs' ears cleaned and their teeth brushed as needed. Sadie jumped at this opportunity and signed a contract with Esther. You will bill her weekly, and she will pay in fifteen days.

Esther brought in seven medium-sized dogs Saturday morning, August 7, 2021, to get their teeth brushed, and all were given a Bath and Brush. That was all Sadie had time to service on Saturday. In this exercise, you will prepare the invoice.

1. Create a custom invoice for GreenWay Kennels using these criteria:

- Style: **Modern**

- Color: **pink (value #f4749b)**

- Font: **Courier, 10pt**

- All margins: **0.50**

- Include the company address

- Add the message: **Thank you for choosing Puppy Luv Pampered Pooch!**

2. Prepare the invoice for GreenWay Kennels. (The Invoice number should be 1013.)

3. Sadie would like an overview of how sales by client were for August 5 through August 7, 2021. Create a report for her.

Your report should have the values shown here.

Puppy Luv Pampered Pooch
SALES BY CLIENT SUMMARY
August 5-7, 2021

	TOTAL
Amanda Brown	55.00
▾ Arlene Garrison	
Joe	40.00
Total Arlene Garrison	**40.00**
▾ Benny Stewart	
Maggie	25.00
Total Benny Stewart	**25.00**
▾ Bonnie Zoe	
Missy	20.00
Total Bonnie Zoe	**20.00**
▾ Brett Johnson	
Romeo	45.00
Total Brett Johnson	**45.00**
▾ Doug Sherrill	
Skeeter	55.00
Total Doug Sherrill	**55.00**
GreenWay Kennels	245.00
▾ Jamee Thompson	
Peaches	48.00
Total Jamee Thompson	**48.00**
▾ Jason Ridgeway	
Butch	45.00
Total Jason Ridgeway	**45.00**
▾ Jerry Lee	
King	10.00
Total Jerry Lee	**10.00**
▾ Julie Walton	
Alice	75.00
Suzy	75.00
Total Julie Walton	**150.00**
▾ Stacey Common	
Agnes	30.00
Total Stacey Common	**30.00**
TOTAL	**$768.00**

4. Export your report to Excel, saving the file in your **Chapter 03** folder as: `CH03 Sales By Client Summary`

 CHECK FIGURE *Your figures should match those shown here.*

Account	Amount
Los Angeles City Bank	$52,473
Accounts Receivable	$245
Pooch Services (Sales by Client)	$768

Now you will review some of the decisions you made to set up the GreenWay Kennels account and create an invoice.

5. Consider these questions:

- What were the necessary actions?
- Will there be a bank deposit today? Why?
- What is the invoice amount?

4 | Working with Vendors

Vendors are the people and businesses you buy products and services from. In this chapter, you will build a Vendors list. You will prepare vendor-related purchase and expense transactions, such as creating an Accounts Payable bill and recording a credit card and debit card purchase. You will also create vendor Accounts Payable and purchase-related management reports to assist with purchase history and unpaid bills.

LEARNING OBJECTIVES

▶ Set up vendors

▶ Edit settings and preferences

▶ Create expense transactions

▶ Make payments to vendors

▶ Create vendor reports

📂 Project: Craig's Design and Landscaping Services

Craig Carlson purchases supplies from a number of businesses. He would like to set up all these businesses as vendors in QuickBooks Online. Craig pays for his purchases in several different ways. He has an account with some of his vendors, so that he can make purchases and then receive a bill to be paid later. Craig also uses his credit and debit cards for many purchases.

The Expenses Center

The Vendors list is located in the Expenses center on the Navigation bar. It provides information about your vendors and your transactions with them in a single place. It allows you to perform vendor-related tasks such as searching for vendors, adding vendors, importing vendor lists, editing and merging vendor information, and making vendors inactive. The Expenses center also includes tools that allow you to quickly perform tasks such as printing and exporting Vendors lists, and adjusting list settings.

1. ● Money bar

2. ● New Vendor icon

3. ● Print, Export, and Settings icons

4. ● Individual vendor actions menu

5. ● Vendor search field

Tip! Use the keyboard shortcut Ctrl + Alt + V to go to the Vendors list.

The Money Bar

The Vendors list contains a multi-colored money bar that gives you a quick snapshot of Accounts Payable, including open, past-due, and paid bills. You can click the money bar sections to access more detailed information about these bills.

The Vendors List

The Vendors list displays vendor names, contact information, and open balances at a glance, as well as detailed transaction information when you select a specific name. The Action menu lets you quickly create transactions for the selected vendor.

You can add vendors individually or you can import them from an Excel or CSV worksheet.

Adding Vendors

QuickBooks Online does not allow you to add two vendors with the same exact name. You must include a middle initial or other distinguishing identifier in the Display Name As field to make the names different.

> **Tip!** Using the Expenses center is not the only way to add vendors. You can also add new vendors from within a purchase/expense form by typing the vendor name and adding details as directed.

> ✔ **Best Practice**
>
> As you create new vendors, enter as much information as possible so you can fully utilize the power of QuickBooks Online data when creating management reports. For example, be sure to include address and contact information in the Vendors list.

DEVELOP YOUR SKILLS 4-1

In this exercise, you will add a new vendor in Craig's Design and Landscaping Services.

Before You Begin: *Access the QuickBooks Online test drive at qbo.intuit.com/redir/testdrive and leave the test drive open for the entire chapter.*

> **Note!** Remember, the QuickBooks Online user interface is updated frequently, so some of the names and features in course exercises may differ from what you see on your interface.

1. Click **Expenses** on the Navigation bar and then click the **Vendors** tab.
2. Click the **New Vendor** button at the top-right corner of the browser window.
3. Type **Morning Supplies** as the company name and then tap Tab.
4. The display name should fill automatically; if not, type **Morning Supplies** here and then tap Tab twice.
5. For the address, type **1458 Magnolia** and tap Tab, type **Bayshore** and tap Tab, type **CA** and tap Tab, and then type **94305** and tap Tab five times.
6. Type **650-555-8814** in the Phone field.

7. Choose **Net 10** in the Terms field.

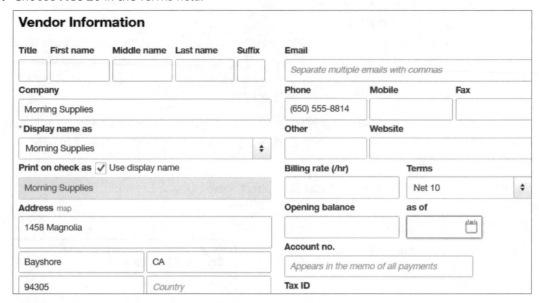

Vendor Information

Title	First name	Middle name	Last name	Suffix

Email

Separate multiple emails with commas

Company

Morning Supplies

* Display name as

Morning Supplies

Print on check as ✓ Use display name

Morning Supplies

Address map

1458 Magnolia

Bayshore	CA
94305	*Country*

Phone

(650) 555-8814

Mobile	Fax

Other   Website

Billing rate (/hr)   Terms

Net 10

Opening balance   as of

Account no.

Appears in the memo of all payments

Tax ID

8. Click **Save**.

The Display Name As field is the only required field to set up a new vendor. By completing more fields, you will be able to create more vendor management reports.

Importing Vendor Data from an Excel or CSV File

QuickBooks Online allows you to import vendor lists from an Excel or comma-separated values (CSV) worksheet. One way you can import vendor lists is by accessing the Import Data tool from the Gear menu.

The Import Data tool allows you to import information not only about vendors, but also about customers, Charts of Accounts, and products and services. The tool includes forms and prompts to help you upload and map your lists to QuickBooks Online format. This feature is a great time-saver for existing businesses that have large lists.

Tools

Import Data

Export Data

Reconcile

Budgeting

Audit Log

Order Checks ⤢

QuickBooks Online often provides multiple ways to do something, depending on where you are working within the application. Besides using the Import Data tool, you can also import data from within the Expenses center.

🖱 Gear ⚙ →Tools→Import Data

🖱 Expenses center→New Vendor menu ▾ →Import Vendors

Editing, Merging, and Making Vendors Inactive

Your Vendors list is customizable. After you add a vendor, you can go back and edit the record. You can also merge two vendors if you find that the same one is listed twice. Doing so will combine all the vendor's transactions into a single record. Finally, to keep your Vendors list current and less cluttered, you can inactivate vendor records that you are no longer dealing with. As with customers, you can inactivate vendors but never truly delete them.

DEVELOP YOUR SKILLS 4-2

In this exercise, you will edit vendor data, merge two vendor records, and make one vendor inactive. Books by Bessie notified you that they have moved. You will start by editing the address.

1. Choose **Books by Bessie** from the Vendors list.

2. Click the **Edit** button and then type the new address as shown:

3. Click **Save**.

4. Return to the **Vendors** list.

Merge Two Vendors

You have discovered that Lee Advertising is actually owned by Tony Rondonuwu. You will now merge these two records.

5. Choose **Tony Rondonuwu** from the Vendors list.

6. Click the **Edit** button and then change the display name to: **Lee Advertising**

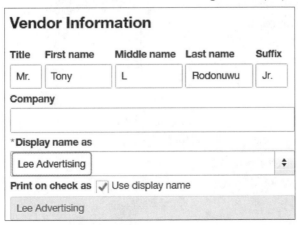

7. Click **Save** and confirm the change, and then return to the **Vendors** list.

Make a Vendor Inactive

Craig reviewed the Vendors list and wants to remove old or inactive vendors. Squeaky Kleen Car Wash closed last month, so you will make this vendor inactive.

8. Select **Squeaky Kleen Car Wash** from the Vendors list.

9. Click the **Edit** button and then click **Make Inactive** at the bottom of the window; confirm the change when prompted.

10. Return to the **Vendors** list.

11. To see a complete list of vendors, including inactive vendors, click the **Settings** icon above the Action menu and then click in the checkbox for **Include Inactive**.

The inactive vendor is now included in the list, but it has been deleted.

> ☐ **Squeaky Kleen Car Wash (deleted)**

Creating Vendor Transactions: Purchases and Expenses

Vendor transactions in QuickBooks Online are recorded either as an expense when you pay at the time of purchase, or as a bill if you make a purchase and pay later. Expense forms are used for all payments made with a debit card, credit card, automatic withdrawal, or wire transfer. If you have an account with your vendors, you will enter the bill on the date you made the purchase and pay the bill at a later time.

Remember that all QuickBooks Online forms are intuitive. An expense form will always credit the bank or credit card account chosen. A check form will always credit the bank account chosen. A bill form will always credit Accounts Payable; this default setting cannot be changed.

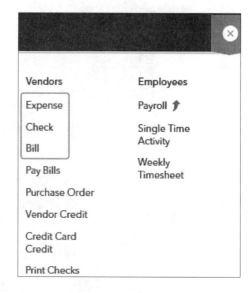

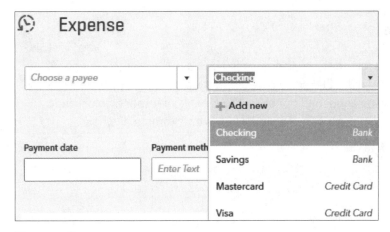

Expense form

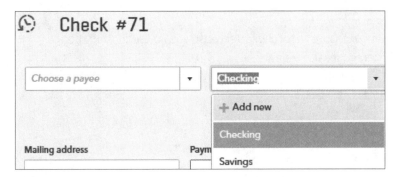

Check form

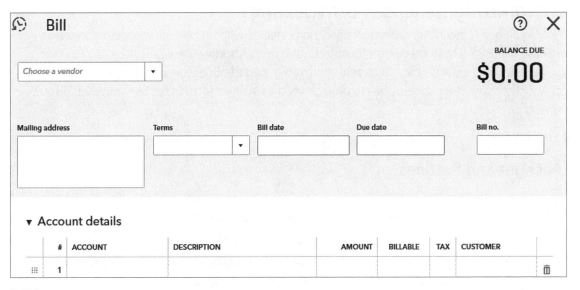

Bill form

BEHIND THE SCENES

In accrual basis accounting, you record the expense when you have the obligation to pay. Remember, QuickBooks Online is a double-entry accounting system, meaning every time one account is affected, there is an equal and opposite effect on a corresponding account. QuickBooks Online handles all the accounting for you. Here is an example of what's happening behind the scenes.

When entering a bill for General Supplies for $230, the Supplies Expense record increases with a debit and the Accounts Payable (liability) record increases with a credit.

Supplies Expense	Accounts Payable
230	230

When the bill is paid, the Checking Account record will decrease with a credit, and the Accounts Payable account will decrease with a debit.

Checking Account	Accounts Payable
230	230

Customizing Expense Form Settings

Before you begin recording expense transactions, decide what information should appear on expense forms and then check that form settings are appropriate for your business. Although you can customize the content of expense forms by using the Edit icon in the Expenses folder, you cannot customize their appearance (as you can with customer forms such as invoices and sales receipts).

In the following figure, all of the defaults are "On" for Craig's Design and Landscaping.

Account and Settings

Company			
	Bills and expenses	Show Items table on expense and purchase forms	On
Sales		Track expenses and items by customer	On
		Make expenses and items billable	On
Expenses		Default bill payment terms	
Advanced	Purchase orders	Use purchase orders	On

When you click the Edit ✏ icon in the Bills and Expenses section, you can change the terms, markup, sales tax, and more.

Company	Bills and expenses	☑ Show Items table on expense and purchase forms ⑦	**On**
		☑ Track expenses and items by customer ⑦	**On**
Sales		☑ Make expenses and items billable ⑦	**On**
Expenses		☐ Markup with a default rate of 0.00 % ⑦	
		☑ Track billable expenses and items as income ⑦	
Advanced		● In a single account	
		○ In multiple accounts ⑦	
		☐ Charge sales tax ⑦	
		Default bill payment terms	[▾]
		Cancel **Save**	

> ↗ Gear ⚙ →Account and Settings→Expenses

Creating Check, Expense, and Bill Records

QuickBooks Online forms are designed to work dynamically with one another. If you link your Chart of Accounts and your Products and Services lists correctly as you prepare your expense or purchase forms, the appropriate accounting transactions will be created when you make a transaction.

If you write a check at the time of a purchase, you will use a check form to record your transaction. If you use a credit card or debit card to pay for items at the time of purchase, you will use an expense form. If you purchase goods and services and pay for them later, then you will enter the transaction in a bill form and pay the bill at a later date.

> **Warning!** It's not a good practice to record expenses on a journal entry or directly on a bank withdrawal form. The profit and loss report would be correct, but the purchases/expenses would not appear on vendor reports.

DEVELOP YOUR SKILLS 4-3

In this exercise, you will record a check, a credit card purchase, and a debit card purchase for purchases made on September 1, 2021. You will start by recording a purchase made by check at Morning Supplies.

Craig stopped by Morning Supplies to purchase some materials he needed. It was a small purchase, so he used a check that he happened to have in his wallet.

1. Choose **Create** ⊕ →**Vendors**→**Check**.
2. Choose **Morning Supplies** as the payee field and tap [Tab].
3. Choose **Checking** as the account type, if necessary, and tap [Tab] twice.
4. Type **09/01/2021** for the payment date and tap [Tab].
5. If necessary, enter **71** as the check number (it will likely AutoF ill for you).
6. Choose **Job Materials:Plants and Soil** in the Account field and tap [Tab].

7. Type **Misc. Plants and Plant Feed** in the Description field and tap Tab.

8. Type **42.75** in the Amount field.

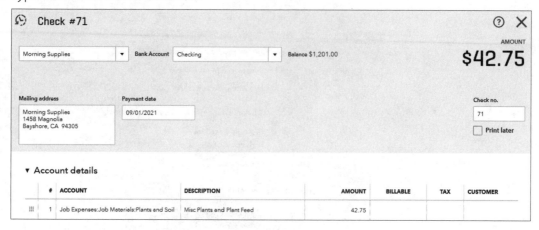

9. Choose to **Save and Close** the check form.

Create an Expense Form

Craig met Bill for a quick lunch at Bob's Burger Joint on 09/01/2021. Craig paid with his debit card. You will now use an expense form to record the transaction.

Tip! When entering an expense transaction, it's important to indicate from which account it was paid.

10. Choose **Create** ⊕ →**Vendors**→**Expense**.

11. Choose **Bob's Burger Joint** in the payee field and tap Tab.

12. Choose **Checking** as the account type, if necessary, and tap Tab.

13. Type **09/01/2021** for the payment date and tap Tab twice.

14. Type **Debit** in the Ref. No. field and tap Tab.

15. Choose **Meals and Entertainment** in the Account field and tap Tab.

16. Type **Lunch with Bill** in the Description field and tap Tab.

17. Type **24.97** in the Amount field.

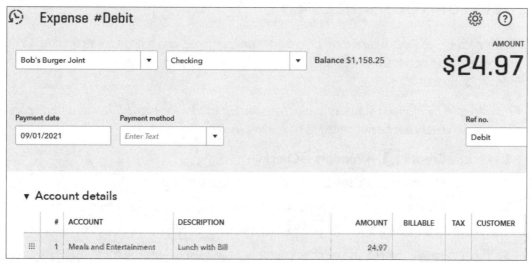

18. Choose **Save**.

   Now you will view the accounting behind the scenes for this transaction.

19. In the bottom tray, click the **More** button and then choose **Transaction Journal**.

Craig's Design and Landscaping Services
JOURNAL
All Dates

DATE	TRANSACTION TYPE	NUM	NAME	MEMO/DESCRIPTION	ACCOUNT	DEBIT	CREDIT
09/01/2021	Expense	Debit	Bob's Burger Joint		Checking		$24.97
				Lunch with Bill	Meals and Entertainment	$24.97	
						$24.97	$24.97
TOTAL						**$24.97**	**$24.97**

In this example, Meals and Entertainment is the debit and Checking is the credit.

Record a Credit Card Purchase

In this transaction, you will enter a credit card purchase for coffee mugs with a logo from Mahoney Mugs.

20. Choose **Create** ⊕ →**Vendors**→**Expense**.

21. Complete the Expense form as noted, tapping [Tab] to navigate the fields:

   • Payee: **Mahoney Mugs**

   • Account: **Mastercard**

   • Payment Date: **09/01/2021**

   • Ref No.: **MC**

   • Account: **Office Expenses**

   • Description: **Mugs with Logo**

   • Amount: **36.50**

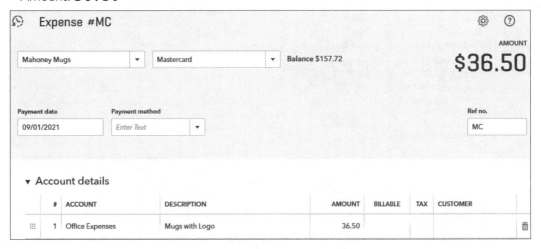

22. Choose **Save and Close**.

Managing Accounts Payable

You can use QuickBooks Online to manage your Accounts Payable—that is, purchases that will be paid later or on account. When vendors send you bills and you enter these bills in QuickBooks Online, you can keep track of the amount you owe for purchases in any given period. As you set up each vendor, you can specify the terms for that vendor. You can also enter the terms directly on the bill form.

DEVELOP YOUR SKILLS 4-4

Craig has ordered new computers and monitors for his office from Computers by Jenni. They will be delivered today, 9/1/2021, and the terms are net 15 days. In this exercise, you will enter a bill for purchases made today and payable in 15 days.

1. Choose **Create ⊕ →Vendors→Bill**.
2. Complete the Bill form as follows, using ⎡Tab⎤ to navigate the fields:
   - Vendor: **Computers by Jenni**
   - Terms: **Net 15**
   - Bill Date: **09/01/2021**
   - Bill No.: **2021-1515**
   - Account: **Office Expenses**
   - Description: **Computer and Monitor**
   - Amount: **1345.00**

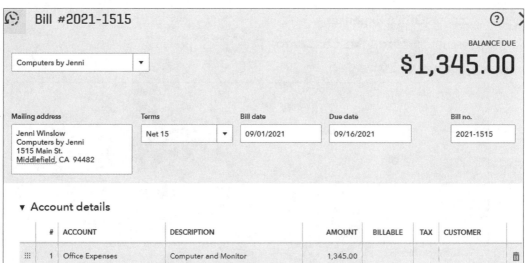

3. Choose **Save**.
4. In the bottom tray, choose **More→Transaction Journal**.

   Accounts Payable is the credit, which increases liabilities on the balance sheet. Office Supplies is the debit, which increases expenses on the profit and loss statement.

Accounts Payable Reports

The Reports center on the Navigation bar contains a number of vendor-related reports to help you manage your Accounts Payable. For example, the What You Owe section in the All folder lets you track what you owe and when payments are due so that you can manage your cash flow. The Accounts Payable Aging Summary report in the Recommended folder shows your unpaid bills and how long you have owed on them.

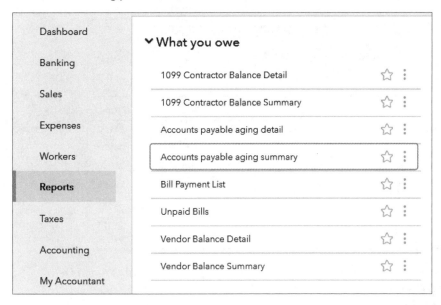

DEVELOP YOUR SKILLS 4-5

In this exercise, you will create reports to assist you in managing the Accounts Payable for Craig's Design and Landscaping Services.

1. Click **Reports** on the Navigation bar.
2. In the What You Owe section, click **Accounts Payable Aging Summary**.
3. Type **09/30/2021** in the As Of field.
4. Click **Run Report**.

   This report summarizes the vendors and the amounts due.

Craig's Design and Landscaping Services

A/P AGING SUMMARY
As of September 30, 2021

	CURRENT	1 - 30	31 - 60	61 - 90	91 AND OVER	TOTAL
Brosnahan Insurance Agency					241.23	$241.23
Computers by Jenni		1,345.00				$1,345.00
Diego's Road Warrior Bodyshop					755.00	$755.00
Norton Lumber and Building Mate...					205.00	$205.00
PG&E					86.44	$86.44
Robertson & Associates					315.00	$315.00
TOTAL	$0.00	$1,345.00	$0.00	$0.00	$1,602.67	$2,947.67

5. To see details about various totals, click any amount.

6. Review details as you like and then return to the **Reports** center.

7. Click the **All** tab, choose **What You Owe**, and then choose **Vendor Balance Summary**.

8. Ensure that *All Dates* appears in the Report Period field and then click **Run Report**.

   This report gives you similar information as the Accounts Payable Aging Summary but in a different format.

Craig's Design and Landscaping Services

VENDOR BALANCE SUMMARY

All Dates

	TOTAL
Brosnahan Insurance Agency	241.23
Computers by Jenni	1,345.00
Diego's Road Warrior Bodyshop	755.00
Norton Lumber and Building Materials	205.00
PG&E	86.44
Robertson & Associates	315.00
TOTAL	**$2,947.67**

Craig would like to know whether any bills are overdue. The Accounts Payable Aging Detail Report will provide this information.

9. Return to the **Reports** center.

10. Choose **Accounts Payable Aging Detail** and notice the report lists each bill, the number of days it is past due, and the amount.

Craig's Design and Landscaping Services ✎

A/P AGING DETAIL
As of April 7, 2018

DATE	TRANSACTION TYPE	NUM	VENDOR	DUE DATE	PAST DUE	AMOUNT	OPEN BALANCE
▼ 31 - 60 days past due							
01/26/2018	Bill		PG&E	02/25/2018	41	86.44	86.44
Total for 31 - 60 days past due						**$86.44**	**$86.44**
▼ 1 - 30 days past due							
03/12/2018	Bill		Robertson & Associates	03/12/2018	26	315.00	315.00
03/12/2018	Bill		Norton Lumber and Building ...	03/12/2018	26	205.00	205.00
03/05/2018	Bill		Brosnahan Insurance Agency	03/15/2018	23	241.23	241.23
Total for 1 - 30 days past due						**$761.23**	**$761.23**
▼ Current							
03/10/2018	Bill		Diego's Road Warrior Bodysh...	04/09/2018	-2	755.00	755.00
Total for Current						**$755.00**	**$755.00**
TOTAL						**$1,602.67**	**$1,602.67**

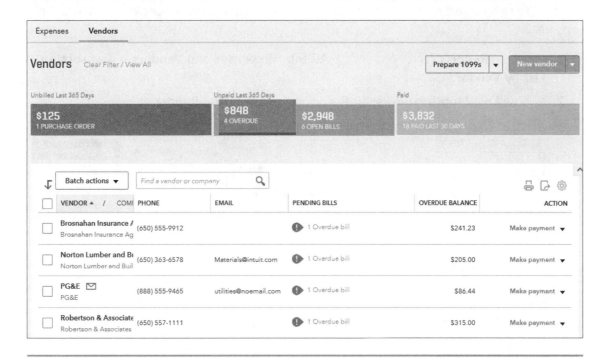

Other Vendor Reports

The All folder includes a category called Expenses and Vendors. These reports provide summaries and/or detailed information about purchases by vendor, as well as purchases by Product/Service.

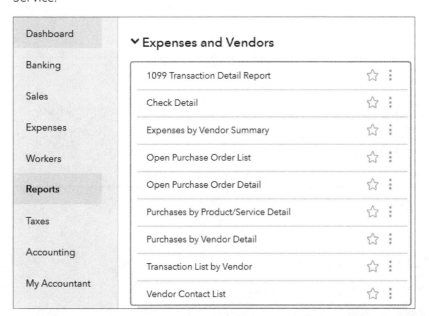

Reports center→All tab→Review Expenses and Purchases

In this exercise, you will prepare a vendor report to show Craig the transactions for each vendor last month.

1. Open the **Reports** center and choose **All tab→Expenses and Vendors→ Transaction List by Vendor**.

2. Choose **Last Month** in the Report Period field and click **Run Report**.

   A partial list of the report appears here. Your dates will vary.

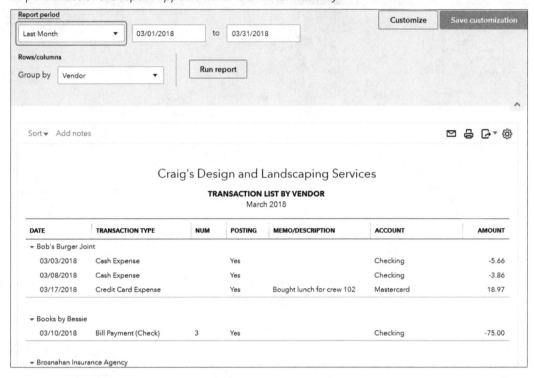

Paying Bills

When you pay bills in QuickBooks Online, you choose the account to make the payment from. When you pay with a check, the Accounts Payable (liability) decreases *and* the checking account balance (asset) decreases. You can also pay bills with a credit card.

In this exercise, you will pay all the bills that are past due and print checks.

1. Choose **Create** ⊕ **→Vendors→Pay Bills**.

2. Choose **Checking** as the payment account and tap [Tab].

3. Type **09/01/2021** as the payment date field and tap [Tab].

4. The Starting Check No. field should fill in with check number 72; if not, update it accordingly.

5. Click the checkboxes to the left of the first four vendors (payees).

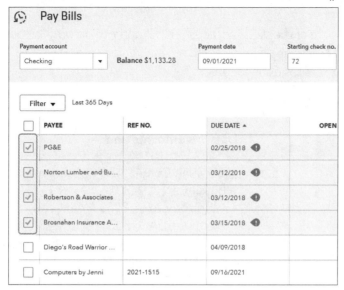

Print Checks

6. Click **Save and Print**.

7. Choose **Voucher** as the check type.

8. Click the **Yes, I'm Finished with Setup** button at the bottom-right corner of the browser window.

9. At the top of the Print Checks window, verify that **Checking** is selected as the account type.

10. Enter **72** in the Starting Check No. field and then click **Preview and Print**.

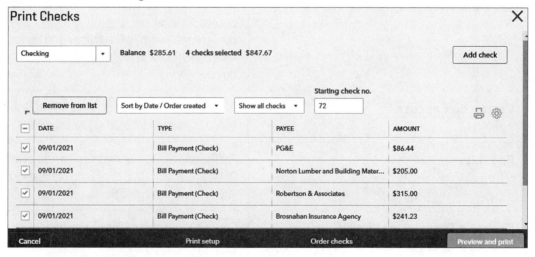

If this were a real work situation, you would now load your checks into your printer. For this example, you will print on plain paper or to a PDF file.

11. On the Print Preview screen, click **Print** and choose to print on blank paper or to a PDF file. (If printing to PDF, choose an appropriate name for the file.)

12. Close ☒ the Print Preview screen.

13. Click **Done** in the next window and then **Close** ☒ the Print Check window.

14. Return to the **Expenses** center.

No bills are overdue now.

Tackle the Tasks

This is your opportunity to apply some of the skills learned in this chapter to accomplish additional tasks for Craig's Design and Landscaping Services. To refresh your memory, refer to the concepts and Develop Your Skills exercises as needed.

Before You Begin: Close the current test drive window and then open a new test drive window.

Task	Use This Information
Set Up New Vendors	• Christina Gomez, 456 College Ave., Bayshore, CA 94301 • Gloria's Garden, 8585 Main Drive, Bayshore, CA 94302 • KGS Tax and Accounting, PO Box 145, Bayshore, CA 94302
Record a Check	Paid Gloria's Garden for purchase of Custom Garden Art; Job Expenses: Job Materials account; paid $255 with check number 77 on 9/01/2021
Create a Bill	Billed $100 by Books by Bessie for accounting services (Legal & Professional Fees account); bill number 2021-902; dated 9/2/2021; due in 15 days
Create a Bill	Dated 9/2/2021 from Cal Telephone for purchase of a new speaker gadget for conference room; bill number 15188 for $89.23; Office Expenses account; due in 15 days
Create an Expense	Paid Squeaky Kleen Car Wash $19.99 with MasterCard on 9/3/2021; Automobile
Pay Bills	For Books by Bessie and Cal Telephone on 9/17/2021 from the checking account; start with check number 78
Create a Transaction List by Vendor Report and Export It to Excel (XLSX); Save the File in Your Chapter 04 Folder As: CDLS Transaction List by Vendor	September 1 through September 30, 2021

Your report should look like this.

Craig's Design and Landscaping Services

TRANSACTION LIST BY VENDOR
September 2021

DATE	TRANSACTION TYPE	NUM	POSTING	MEMO/DESCRIPTION	ACCOUNT	AMOUNT
▾ Books by Bessie						
09/02/2021	Bill	2021-902	Yes		Accounts Payable (A...	100.00
09/17/2021	Bill Payment (Check)	78	Yes	1345	Checking	-100.00
▾ Cal Telephone						
09/02/2021	Bill	15188	Yes		Accounts Payable (A...	89.23
09/17/2021	Bill Payment (Check)	79	Yes		Checking	-89.23
▾ Gloria's Garden						
09/01/2021	Check	77	Yes		Checking	-255.00
▾ Squeaky Kleen Car Wash						
09/03/2021	Expense	MC	Yes		Mastercard	19.99

Self-Assessment

Check your knowledge of this chapter's key concepts and skills using the Self-Assessment quiz here or in your eLab course.

1. You can delete a vendor in QuickBooks Online. *True   False*

2. You can have two vendors with the same name. *True   False*

3. A vendor is a person or business you sell services or products to. *True   False*

4. You can set up a new vendor only from the Vendors list. *True   False*

5. You can record purchases with a credit card in QuickBooks Online. *True   False*

6. The Manage Accounts Payable report in the All folder categorizes unpaid bills based on how overdue they are. *True   False*

7. You can customize the appearance of a bill form in QuickBooks Online. *True   False*

8. You can import vendor information into QuickBooks Online. *True   False*

9. A Vendor Balance Summary report is useful for knowing the total amount purchased from each vendor. *True   False*

10. Hector is a supplier who sells you products. Which list should you add him to?
    A. Contacts
    B. Customers
    C. Vendors
    D. Chart of Accounts

11. To enter a transaction for a service paid for using a debit card, you would:
    A. choose Create→Vendors→Debit Card
    B. choose Create→Vendors→Payment
    C. choose Create→Vendors→Expense
    D. choose Create→Vendors→Bill

12. How can you track Accounts Payable in QuickBooks Online?
    A. Record an expense and then pay it.
    B. Enter a bill and then pay it.
    C. Write a check for the expense.
    D. You cannot track Accounts Payable in QuickBooks Online.

13. To take a quick look at all past-due bills, you should:
    A. create a Transaction List by Vendor report.
    B. click the orange Past Due section on the money bar in the Expenses center.
    C. create a Chart of Accounts and check the balance in Accounts Payable.
    D. choose Create→Vendors→Pay Bills.

Reinforce Your Skills

For these exercises, you will work with Puppy Luv Pampered Pooch, the company account created in your trial subscription to QuickBooks Online.

Sadie has given you some bills that have been paid with a check, debit, or credit card. She also has a few bills that need to be scheduled for payment later. Recording these expenses for Puppy Luv Pampered Pooch is an opportunity to reinforce some of the skills learned about vendors and expenses.

REINFORCE YOUR SKILLS 4-1

Add and Edit Vendors

In this exercise, you will add new vendors to the Puppy Luv Pampered Pooch company file.

Before You Begin: *Access your trial subscription to QuickBooks Online. Read any alerts or reminders that appear and close any unnecessary windows.*

1. Open the **Expenses** center and then click the **Vendors** tab.
2. Click the **New Vendor** button and set up the following new vendors:
   - Sundown District Water, PO Box 1455P, Los Angeles, CA 90051
   - Silva's Catering, 123 East Southside, Los Angeles, CA 90022; 310-555-1414
   - Steve Nguyen, 78441 Normandie Ct., Los Angeles, CA 90005; 310-555-8138
3. Edit the Ace Groomer and Supply Company vendor with this new information:

   1475 West Main St.

   Bullhead City, AZ 86426

   800-555-7491

   Hector@Ace.email.net

REINFORCE YOUR SKILLS 4-2

Review and Set Default Expense Settings

In this exercise, you will review and set the Expense form defaults for Puppy Luv Pampered Pooch.

1. Choose **Gear→Your Company→Account and Settings**.
2. Click **Expenses** in the Navigation bar.
3. Edit the default bill payment terms to **Net 15**.
4. Ensure that the option to use purchase orders is turned **Off**.

Create Purchase and Expense Forms

The Grand Opening party for Puppy Luv Pampered Pooch was a great success. Sadie has given you all the receipts for the party expenses, plus a few bills that need to be scheduled for payment. In this exercise, you will create the purchase/expense transactions for Puppy Luv Pampered Pooch. You will need to add a vendor.

1. Choose **Create→Vendors→Check** and record the following: Check number 10006 for $200 to Silva's Catering for all food and beverages for the Grand Opening; Meals and Entertainment account; dated 08/01/2021.

2. Choose **Create→Vendors→Expense** and record the following: $125 paid by debit card to Steve Nguyen for Window Display; Marketing account; paid on 07/28/2021.

3. Choose **Create→Vendors→Bill** and record the following: Bill number 2021-115 dated 7/28/2021 for $55.50; from Bonni's Dog Biskits, 144 Beach Rd., Ventura, CA 93003; for some treats for the pooches; Pooch Supplies account; due in 15 days.

Create a Vendor Report

Sadie would like a report to show all of the vendor transactions to date. In this exercise, you will create some vendor- and expense-related reports for Sadie.

1. Open the **Reports** center.

2. Click the **All** tab, choose **Expenses and Vendors**, and then choose **Transaction List by Vendor**.

3. Choose **All Dates** as the report period and then click **Run Report**.

   Your report should look like this.

Puppy Luv Pampered Pooch - Student Name

TRANSACTION LIST BY VENDOR
All Dates

DATE	TRANSACTION TYPE	NUM	POSTING	MEMO/DESCRIPTION	ACCOUNT	AMOUNT
▾ Ace Groomer and Supply Company						
07/05/2021	Check	10001	Yes		Los Angeles City Bank	-16,000.00
▾ Bonni's Dog Biskits						
07/28/2021	Bill	2021-115	Yes		Accounts Payable (A/P)	55.50
▾ Capital Properties						
07/30/2021	Check	10005	Yes		Los Angeles City Bank	-3,300.00
▾ City of Los Angeles Clerk						
07/10/2021	Check	10002	Yes	Business License	Los Angeles City Bank	-450.00
▾ Doggies Plus						
07/15/2021	Check	10003	Yes		Los Angeles City Bank	-2,500.00
▾ George's Pet Media						
07/17/2021	Check	10004	Yes		Los Angeles City Bank	-800.00
▾ Silva's Catering						
08/01/2021	Check	10006	Yes		Los Angeles City Bank	-200.00
▾ Steve Nguyen						
07/28/2021	Expense	Debit	Yes		Los Angeles City Bank	-125.00

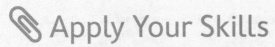

Apply Your Skills

Now it's time to use your new skills to prepare all the Puppy Luv Pampered Pooch purchase and expense transactions for the first few weeks of August. The first step in the accounting cycle is to analyze the transaction, determine what accounts will be affected, and then choose the appropriate action—in the right sequence and on the right form. The second step is to record the transaction.

In these exercises, you will perform these steps of the accounting cycle. To simulate a real-world accounting environment, some of the information to be entered is presented in a random fashion— imagine a pile of bills, receipts, and notes that you have to sort through and analyze. Take your time and think carefully about your choices.

APPLY YOUR SKILLS 4-1

Add and Edit Vendors

Sadie has been busy looking for new suppliers and networking with local dog breeder associations, shelters, and Chambers of Commerce. She has found a couple new vendors and received additional information from an existing vendor. In this exercise, you will add and edit vendors.

1. Add these vendors:
   - Sundown District Gas and Electric, PO Box 259RT, Los Angeles, CA 90051
   - District Party Décor, 1411 E Magnolia, Los Angeles, CA 90052
2. Edit the George's Pet Media vendor with this new information:

   310-555-7711

   GPM@email.net

APPLY YOUR SKILLS 4-2

Create Purchase and Expense Transactions

Sadie has left you some receipts for payment made and a few bills to enter. She has written notes so you know which account to record the transaction in. In this exercise, you will create the transactions for these receipts and bills. (Hint: You may need to add vendors and accounts.)

1. Review the list and then create the necessary transactions:
   - Debit card transaction for decorations for the Grand Opening; 7/30/2021 at District Party Décor; $37.88; Office Supplies & Software
   - Debit card transaction for raffle tickets, tissue paper, and ribbons; $25.66 at Office Plus; 7/28/2021; Office Supplies & Software
   - Credit card purchase; 7/25/2021; Sundown District Chamber of Commerce lunch meeting; $45; Meals and Entertainment
   - Credit card purchase; 7/28/2021 for $389.10 from District Party Décor for rental of tables and chairs, balloons, and music for the Grand Opening party; Equipment Rental Expense
   - Credit card purchase; 7/27/2021 to US Post Office for 100 stamps; $47.00; Postage
   - Bill dated 7/30/2021 from Sundown District Water for $16.84; for service from 7/20/2021 to 7/28/2021; due in 15 days; Utilities

- Bill dated 7/30/2021 from PetEdge, PO Box 100, Beverly, MA 01915; for pooch nail clippers; bill number 89774; $48.96; due in 15 days; Pooch Supplies

- Bill dated 7/28/2021 from Designs for You, 1004 Makers Road, Los Angeles, CA 90022; bill number 21-8944; due in 15 days; for 1000 business cards; $108; Marketing

- Bill dated 8/05/2021 from Sundown District Chamber of Commerce for one-year membership; $250.00; bill number PLPP 2021; due in 15 days; Dues and Subscriptions

---

APPLY YOUR SKILLS 4-3 QG

Prepare Report and Pay Bills

Sadie has asked you to provide a list of all unpaid bills. She will advise you about which bills to pay and any additional reports she would like to review. In this exercise, you will prepare a report of unpaid bills for Sadie.

1. Prepare an **Accounts Payable Aging Summary** report as of August 15, 2021.

2. Export the report to Excel, saving it in your **Chapter 04** folder as: **CH04 AP Aging 8.15.21**

3. Pay all the bills due by 8/12/2021 on **8/10/2021**. The beginning check number is **10007**.

4. Print the checks to a PDF file and then save checks **10007–10008**.

5. Print a **Vendor Balance Summary** report for all dates.

   The balance should be $315.80.

6. Export the report to Excel, saving it in your **Chapter 04** folder as: **CH04 Vendor Balance Summary**

Puppy Luv Pampered Pooch

VENDOR BALANCE SUMMARY

All Dates

	TOTAL
PetEdge	48.96
Sundown District Chamber of Commerce	250.00
Sundown District Water	16.84
TOTAL	**$315.80**

7. Prepare a **Transaction List by Vendor** report for all dates; export it to Excel, saving it in your **Chapter 04** folder as: **CH04 Transaction List By Vendor**

 CHECK FIGURE *Your figures should match those shown here.*

Account	Balance
Los Angeles City Bank	$51,920.96
Accounts Payable	$315.80
City Credit Union	$481.10

5 | Banking and Credit Card Transactions

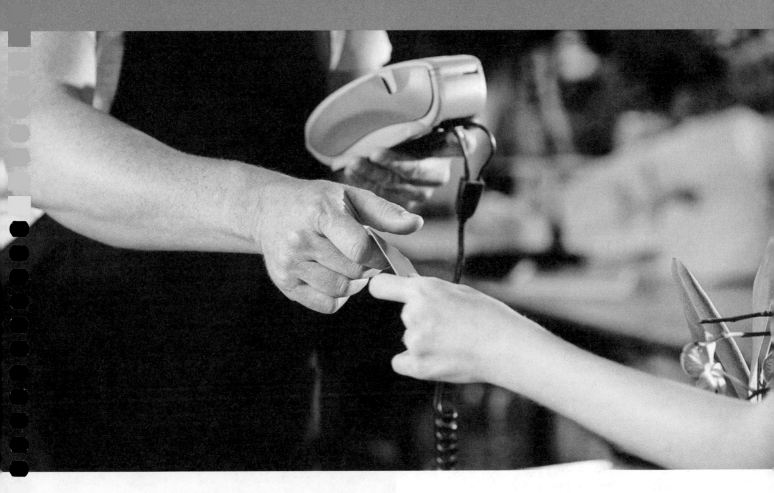

In this chapter, you will record other non-customer and vendor-related transactions. You will also import, set up, and use bank feeds to match recorded transactions or add your transactions. Doing so will make your bank and credit card accounts self-reconciling. You will also import bank feeds even if your financial institution is not linked to QuickBooks Online. Finally, you will reconcile the bank and credit card accounts and produce banking and financial reports.

LEARNING OBJECTIVES

▸ Identify Banking center features
▸ Set up bank feeds
▸ Set up bank rules
▸ Manage credit card transactions
▸ Match and add transactions
▸ Reconcile bank and credit card accounts
▸ Create reconciliation reports
▸ Create financial statement reports

📂 Project: Craig's Design and Landscaping Services

Craig Carlson knows that in any business it's important to manage the bank balances daily. If the business uses credit cards to pay expenses, managing those balances is equally important. QuickBooks Online has a unique bank feeds feature that links your online banking and credit card accounts directly to the QuickBooks Online Banking center. Craig has noticed that the accounts for his business are not current. He has asked you to check into and reconcile the bank and credit card accounts.

Managing the Banking Center

The Banking center is located on the Navigation bar. You can also access it from the Dashboard below Bank Accounts. The Banking center provides a list of all banking and credit card accounts, as well as the bank balance and the QuickBooks Online balance.

 View the video "Banking Center Tour" at: labyrinthelab.com/2017/video/QBO-V0501

Setting Up and Using Bank Feeds

Bank feeds are a unique feature of QuickBooks Online. Bank feeds allow your bank and credit card providers to share information with QuickBooks Online about money going in and out of your accounts. This is a read-only transfer of information into your business accounting software. You also have options to match, add, or exclude transactions. Your bank and credit card data is downloaded automatically, usually once a day, saving you hours of manual data entry time.

More than 15,000 financial institutions allow customers to link their accounts with QuickBooks Online. A few institutions do not participate, but you can still upload bank feeds to QuickBooks Online by importing the data provided by the bank via a CSV, QFX, QBO, or OFX format.

You can set up automatic bank feeds from the Dashboard by clicking the Connect Accounts link, providing the requested banking and user identification information, and following the onscreen instructions.

> Connect accounts

The first download could take a few minutes; subsequent downloads will be much quicker. Be aware that ninety days of transactions will download. If you need a shorter period of time or a specific range, be sure to select the appropriate option.

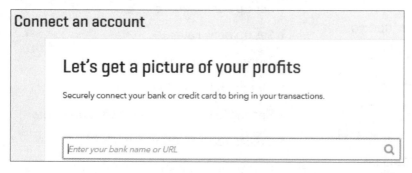

Connect an account

Let's get a picture of your profits

Securely connect your bank or credit card to bring in your transactions.

| Enter your bank name or URL | 🔍 |

DEVELOP YOUR SKILLS 5-1

In this exercise, you will add transactions to the register from the bank feeds, as well as match transactions in the banks feeds. Keep in mind your dates will differ.

Before You Begin: *Access the QuickBooks Online test drive at qbo.intuit.com/redir/testdrive and leave the test drive open for the entire chapter.*

Note! Remember, the user interface for QuickBooks Online is updated frequently, so some of the names and features in course exercises may differ from what you see on your interface.

1. From the Dashboard, click **Checking** (in the Bank Accounts section).

2. Notice that twenty-five transactions are waiting to be matched or added to the Checking account register.

3. In the Category or Match column in the table, notice the transactions marked as "uncategorized."

   Transactions listed as Uncategorized Income or Uncategorized Expense indicate that QuickBooks Online did not a find a match; this is because the transaction has not yet been recorded in QuickBooks Online or a match was not found.

CATEGORY OR MATCH	SPENT	RECEIVED
Uncategorized Income		$55.00
Uncategorized Income		$200.00
Uncategorized Expense	$1,200.00	

4. Click anywhere in the A Rental row where **$800.00** was spent.

5. Change the category from Uncategorized Expense to **Equipment Rental** and tap Tab.

From this window you can Add, Find Match, or Transfer, using the icons in the upper-left part of the window.

Notice that the other A Rental entry for money spent also changes from Uncategorized Expense to Equipment Rental. A Rental will now use Equipment Rental as the default account type. QuickBooks Online "learns" to categorize like transactions automatically. If you do not want to permanently categorize A Rental this way, click the Edit This Setting link. For this exercise, leave the setting as is.

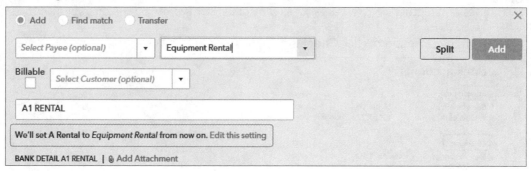

6. Click the **Add** button.

This adds the banking transaction into the QuickBooks Online Checking Account register as an Equipment Rental expense.

7. Click **Add** in the A Rental row where **$1,200** was spent.

The transaction is added into your register in QuickBooks Online. QuickBooks Online remembers the previous Spent transaction and suggests the Equipment Rental (in green) category for all of A Rental's Spent transactions.

Match Transactions

Now you will match transactions. The green 1 Record Found icon indicates a definite match in the QuickBooks Online checking account register, while the white Records Found icon indicates one or more transactions are a potential match.

8. Scroll to the Pg E transaction.

QuickBooks Online has found a matching transaction that was already recorded: a bill payment to PG&E for $114.09.

9. Click **Match** in the Action column.

Now you will review the register.

10. Click **Go to Register**.

11. Notice that the two transactions for A Rental are recorded on the register with this icon: [icon]. Hover your mouse pointer over the icon.

This icon indicates the transaction was manually added from the bank feeds. And the "C" above the icon indicates that the bank has cleared this transaction through the bank feed.

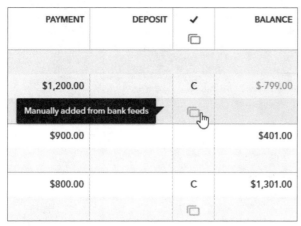

PAYMENT	DEPOSIT	✓	BALANCE
		[icon]	
$1,200.00		C	$-799.00
Manually added from bank feeds		[icon]	
$900.00			$401.00
$800.00		C	$1,301.00
		[icon]	

12. Click **Dashboard** on the Navigation bar.

Managing Bank Rules

The Bank Rules feature allows you to go beyond the automatic categorization of transactions to a finite level of control. Bank rules allow you to save time and minimize errors in the bank feeds. Rules for both money in and money out can be created. This feature may take a bit of time to set up in the beginning, but over time, bank rules will save you a lot of work.

DEVELOP YOUR SKILLS 5-2

Craig has started using Chin's Gas to fuel the company trucks. He set up an account with Chin's to allow drivers to fill up their tanks as needed. Chin's automatically deducts the charges from Craig's company checking account on a monthly basis. You want to be sure the account is coded correctly when the transaction is downloaded in the bank feeds. In this exercise, you will set up a bank rule for Chin's Gas.

1. On the Navigation bar, choose **Banking→Bank Rules**.
2. Click the **New Rule** button in the upper-right corner of the window; read and close any pop-up windows that appear.
3. Type **Chins** in the Rule Name field and tap [Tab].
4. Choose **Money Out** in the For field and tap [Tab].
5. Click the menu button for the In field and make sure that only the Checking checkbox has a checkmark (uncheck other boxes as necessary).

6. Complete all of the remaining fields as shown:

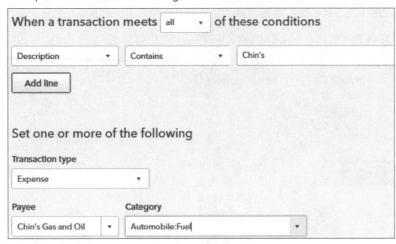

7. Click **Save** and then view your new rule.

8. Click the **Banking** tab at the top of the window.

9. Scroll to the Chin's Gas transaction and note that it is categorized with a rule.

10. Click **Add** for Chin's Gas and then return to the **Dashboard**.

Other Banking Transactions

You will perform many different types of banking transactions in your business. You may transfer funds from checking to savings accounts. You may deposit funds that are not customer related; for example, loan proceeds, refunds on insurance overpayments, or rebates on purchases. You will spend money that is not associated with a specific vendor or deposit money that is not from a specific customer. QuickBooks Online provides a way to carry out all these types of transactions.

Businesses may use electronic funds transfers (EFTs), online payments, and wire transfers to move funds into or out of accounts. You can easily record these in QuickBooks Online. If these transactions are "money out," create an expense and use the transaction type in the Ref No. field. If the transactions are "money in," create a deposit and use the transaction type in the Memo field.

DEVELOP YOUR SKILLS 5-3

In this exercise, you will transfer funds from the Craig's Design and Landscaping Services' savings account to the checking account. You will then make a couple of deposits.

1. Choose **Create** ⊕ →**Other**→**Transfer**.

2. Complete the form as shown, using [Tab] to navigate the fields:

Transfer Funds From	Balance
Savings ▼	**$800.00**
Transfer Funds To	Balance
Checking ▼	**$ -984.00**
Transfer Amount	Date
50.00	09/05/2021

3. Choose to **Save and Close** the transfer.

Make Deposits

Now you will make a bank deposit for a loan from Craig's bank and then deposit the proceeds from a Cash and Carry Parking Lot Sale.

4. Choose **Create→Other→Bank Deposit**.

5. Use **Checking** as the account type and **09/06/2021** as the date.

6. In the Add New Deposits section, click in the **Account** field for the first row, choose **Loan Payable**, and then tap [Tab].

7. Now, add funds to this deposit. Enter **Loan Proceeds** as the description and tap [Tab].

8. Choose **Check** as the payment method field and tap [Tab].

9. Enter **124599** as the reference number (Ref. No. field) and tap [Tab].

10. Enter **10000** as the amount and tap [Tab] twice.

11. Complete the fields for Row 2 as shown:

▼ Add funds to this deposit

	#	RECEIVED FROM	ACCOUNT	DESCRIPTION	PAYMENT METHOD	REF NO.	AMOUNT	
⠿	1		Loan Payable	Loan Proceeds	Check	124599	10,000.00	🗑
⠿	2		Other Income	Parking Lot Sale			426.00	🗑

12. Choose to **Save and Close** the deposit.

> **Tip!** You may need to refresh your page to view the change in your checking account balance.

Entering Debit and Credit Card Transactions

Many businesses use credit cards to purchase products and services. In QuickBooks Online, entering credit card transactions is similar to entering banking transactions. Instead of decreasing the checking account balance, QuickBooks Online increases the amount due to the credit card institution. You can pay bills with the debit or credit card as well.

BEHIND THE SCENES

Bank accounts are assets in the Chart of Accounts. As you spend money—by writing a check or using a debit card—your bank account balance decreases and your expenses account increases. Credit cards are liabilities on the Chart of Accounts. As you make purchases, your credit card liability increases and your expenses account increases.

Checking		Office Supplies	
	45.00	45.00	

Assets decrease and the expenses account increases when a debit card or check is used to purchase office supplies for $45.00.

Credit Card Payable		Office Supplies	
	45.00	45.00	

Liability increases and the expenses account increases when the same purchase is made with a credit card.

Checking		Credit Card Payable	
	45.00	45.00	

When you pay the credit card balance with monies from your checking account, both assets and liabilities decrease.

To enter credit card charges, you must first create a Credit Card account in your Chart of Accounts. As you make charges on the credit card, you enter them as expense transactions. If you have returns or credits on the credit card, you can create a Credit Card Credit transaction.

 Create→Vendors→Credit Card Credit

DEVELOP YOUR SKILLS 5-4

Craig has notified you of a new credit card he is using, Capital Two. He gave you a few receipts and a return. In this exercise, you will set up the new credit card account and enter the transactions for the receipts.

1. Use the **Chart of Accounts** to create a new credit card account for Capital Two.

   Hint: From the Navigation bar, choose Accounting→Chart of Accounts.

2. Choose **Create→Vendors→Expense** and create the following expenses for the Capital Two credit card, adding vendors if necessary.

Date	Payee	Amount	Account
09/01/2021	Bob's Burger Joint	$23.15	Meals and Entertainment
09/05/2021	Squeaky Kleen Car Wash	$19.99	Automobile
09/05/2021	Office Mart	$47.99	Office Expenses

3. Choose to **Save and Close** the final expense.

Enter a Return

Now you will enter a return that Craig made to Office Mart.

4. Choose **Create→Vendors→Credit Card Credit** and enter this information; be sure to choose the Capital Two credit card.
   - Payee: **Office Mart**
   - Credit Card Account: **Capital Two**
   - Date: **09/07/2021**
   - Account: **Office Expenses**
   - Amount: **15.99**

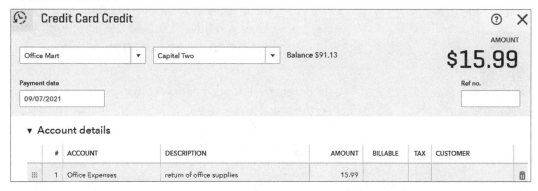

5. Choose to **Save and Close** the transaction and then return to the **Dashboard**.

Pay a Bill with a Debit or Credit Card

Now you will learn the steps to follow in order to record a bill payment for a credit card. You would use the same steps for a debit card.

6. Choose **Create→Vendors→Pay Bills**.

7. In the Payment Account field, choose **Mastercard** as the method used to pay the bills.

8. Enter the date as **09/07/2021**.

9. Select **PG&E** as the bill that was paid with the card.

10. Click **Save and Close**.

    Once saved, the bill will be recorded as paid, reducing the Accounts Payable account and increasing the Mastercard account balance.

11. Return to the **Dashboard**.

Reconciling Accounts

At the end of each accounting period—usually a month—it is a recommended best practice to compare the transactions you have entered into QuickBooks Online with your bank and credit card statements. This process is called reconciling. Although the focus in this chapter is on reconciling bank and credit card accounts, you can also reconcile almost all of your balance sheet accounts.

Consult this table if you encounter problems when reconciling an account in QuickBooks Online.

TIPS FOR RECONCILING ACCOUNTS IN QUICKBOOKS ONLINE	
Problem	**Solution**
Transactions on the bank statement are not in QuickBooks Online.	Add the transactions and then return to the Reconcile screen.
An error was made when entering a transaction.	Click the transaction inside the reconciliation, edit it, and continue.
The bank made an error.	Record the transaction to adjust your balance. After you have resolved the error with your institution, reverse the transaction.

At times you will need to void or delete a check that has been written, perhaps because a mistake was made when preparing the check, the check was lost, etc. QuickBooks Online makes this simple to accomplish. Using the Search feature, find the check that needs to be voided or deleted and click More at the bottom of the screen. Choosing Void keeps the transaction in place with zeros for all values and stamps the transaction as "VOID." Choosing Delete removes the check from QuickBooks Online completely.

Bank Feeds

If you use the Bank Feeds feature in QuickBooks Online, your reconciliation is pretty much done for you. However, it remains a good practice to manually complete the reconciliation to ensure accuracy. This process will assist you in finding errors, omissions, or other discrepancies between the bank and QuickBooks. It also marks the transactions as reconciled.

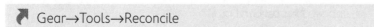 Gear→Tools→Reconcile

Undeposited Funds

It's important to have a good understanding of the Undeposited Funds default account in Quick-Books. It holds funds received from customer payments until you deposit them into your bank account. Each deposit recorded in the Undeposited Funds account must match exactly what the bank receives.

For example, on a specific day a customer paid $50.00 in cash, which you recorded on a sales receipt. On the same day, another customer paid with a check for $50.00, which you also recorded on a sales receipt. When you prepared both sales receipts, the deposit-to account was Undeposited Funds. You take both payments to the bank and make one deposit for $100.00. For the deposit to be properly recorded, you must choose to include both payments in the one deposit.

DEVELOP YOUR SKILLS 5-5

Craig has received the credit card statement from Mastercard and passed it along to you to reconcile with QuickBooks transactions. In this exercise, you will match or add the Mastercard transactions and then reconcile the account.

1. In the Navigation bar, choose **Banking** and, if necessary, click the **Mastercard** block.

2. Click to add a checkmark to the left of all of the transactions that are identified as **1 Record Found**.

   This action matches the banking and QuickBooks Online transactions.

	DATE ▼	DESCRIPTION	PAYEE	CATEGORY OR MATCH	SPENT	RECEIVED
☐	04/14/2018	Amazon		Uncategorized Expense		$89.99
☐	04/13/2018	Lara's Lamination		Uncategorized Expense	$150.00	
☐	03/31/2018	Squeaky Kleen Car	Squeaky Kleen Car ...	2 records found	$19.99	
☐	03/24/2018	Bob's Burger	Bob's Burger Joint	1 record found CC Expense 03/24/2018 $18.97 Bob's Burger Joint	$18.97	
☐	03/24/2018	Squeaky Kleen Car	Squeaky Kleen Car ...	2 records found	$19.99	
☐	03/19/2018	Norton Lumber And	Norton Lumber and...	1 record found Bill Payment 1 03/19/2018 $103.55 Norton Lumber and Building Materials	$103.55	
☐	03/13/2018	Tania's Nursery	Tania's Nursery	1 record found Expense 50 03/13/2018 $82.45 Tania's Nursery	$82.45	

3. Click the **Batch Actions menu** ▾ button and choose **Accept Selected**.

4. Click the **2 Records Found** transactions, select the appropriate transaction, and click **Match**.

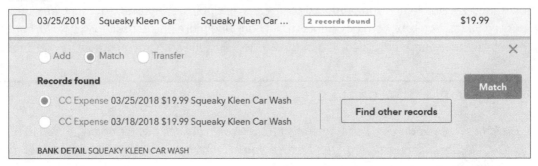

5. Assign the remaining two items to **Advertising Expense** and then click **Add** to add each transaction to QuickBooks Online.

Reconcile an Account

Craig has given you his Mastercard statement so you can reconcile the Mastercard account in QuickBooks. As you reconcile the account, note your dates will be different, depending on what month and year you are currently in.

6. Navigate to your **Chapter 05** folder and open **CH05 Mastercard Stmt.pdf**.

7. Choose **Gear→Tools→Reconcile**.

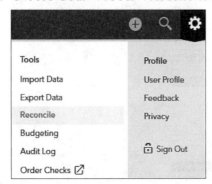

> *Tip!* You can also access Reconcile from the account register.

8. Click **Reconcile an Account** and then click **Let's Do It**, if prompted.

9. Choose **Mastercard** in the Account field.

10. Enter your current month end date in the Ending Date field and **123.72** in the Ending Balance field.

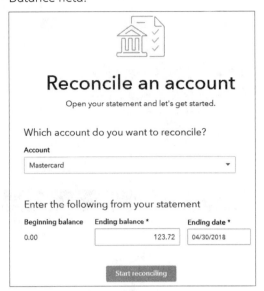

> ✔ *Best Practice*
>
> Be sure your Difference on the reconciliation screen is always 0.00 before clicking Finish Now. QuickBooks Online will create a new account on your chart of accounts named "Reconciliation Discrepancies" to record any differences that could cause unwanted consequences.

11. Click **Start Reconciling** and then place checkmarks to the right of all transaction rows on the statement that match up with those shown on your statement.

    You are finished and reconciled when the Difference equals 0.00.

12. Click **Finish Now**.

13. Choose **View Report**.

14. Return to the **Dashboard**.

    When an account is reconciled, the reconciliation reports remain in the reconciliation feature for review or to be printed. The transactions are all marked with an R in the register, indicating they have been reconciled.

Preparing Financial Reports

Once you have analyzed and recorded all the transactions for a period and reconciled all the bank and credit card accounts, it's usually a good time to prepare the balance sheet and profit and loss financial statements for a preliminary review.

DEVELOP YOUR SKILLS 5-6

Craig has requested the balance sheet and profit and loss statements for September 2021. In this exercise, you will prepare these financial reports for him.

1. Open the **Reports** center and then click the **Balance Sheet** report link.
2. Edit the transaction date range as shown and then click **Run Report**.

The following balance sheet appears.

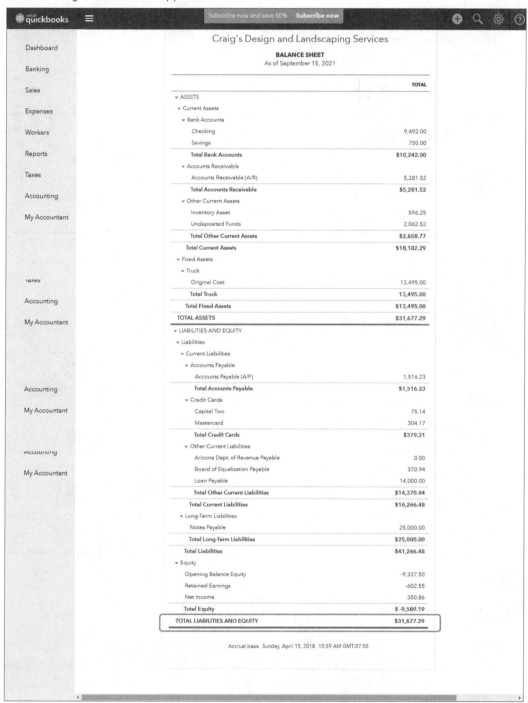

3. Return to the **Reports** center and then click the **Profit and Loss** report link.

4. Edit the transaction date range to show from **09/01/2021** to **09/15/2021** and then click **Run Report**.

Craig's Design and Landscaping Services
PROFIT AND LOSS
September 1-15, 2021

	TOTAL
Income	
Other Income	426.00
Total Income	$426.00
Gross Profit	$426.00
Expenses	
Automobile	19.99
Meals and Entertainment	23.15
Office Expenses	32.00
Total Expenses	$75.14
Net Operating Income	$350.86
Net Income	$350.86

Your Net Income on the Profit and Loss report should be the same as the Net Income on your balance sheet.

Tackle the Tasks

This is your opportunity to apply some of the skills learned in this chapter to accomplish additional tasks for Craig's Design and Landscaping Services. To refresh your memory, refer to the concepts and Develop Your Skills exercises as needed.

Before You Begin: Close the current test drive window and then open a new test drive window.

Complete these tasks in the Checking account. Keep in mind you need a unique name for each rule, and you may need to add a payee or vendor name.

Task	Use This Information
Set Up Bank Rules	• A Rental; money out; Category: Equipment Rental Expense • A Rental; money in; Category Equipment Rental Expense • Use all bank accounts
Match Transactions in the Checking Account	All the green transactions; 1 Record Found or Rule as indicated on the icon; there should be 17 transactions to match
Match More Transactions	The one green 1 Record Found and the one white 2 Records Found
Edit the Category and Add the Transaction	• Mahoney Mugs; Office Expense • Tim Philip Masonry; Job Expenses: Job Materials • Hicks Hardware; Supplies • Books by Bessie; Bookkeeper (there are two transactions)
Find a Match	Chin's Gas (should find check #70)
Reconcile the Checking Account	Use the **CH05 Bank Statement.pdf** file in your **Chapter 05** folder; use the current month end date
Prepare Profit and Loss Report	All dates; net income -$866.00
Prepare Balance Sheet Report	All dates; total assets $20,927.83.

Your checking account balance in QuickBooks should be -$1,307.46. The bank balance should be -$3,621.93.

Checking		Reviewed
Bank balance	$-3,621.93	Updated
In QuickBooks	$-1,307.46	moments ago

Self-Assessment

Check your knowledge of this chapter's key concepts and skills using the Self-Assessment quiz here or in your eLab course.

1. Only bank accounts are available in the Banking center in QuickBooks Online. *True   False*

2. The For Review folder in the Banking center is for all the transactions that need to be reviewed and matched. *True   False*

3. Undeposited Funds is a unique asset account to hold funds that have been received but have not yet been deposited into a bank account. *True   False*

4. Bank feeds can be set up only for the business's bank accounts. *True   False*

5. Bank feed transactions can be imported from CSV and OFX formats. *True   False*

6. You can set up bank rules only for money out transactions. *True   False*

7. You can reconcile only your banking accounts. *True   False*

8. To transfer funds from a checking account to a savings account, you would make a journal entry. *True   False*

9. When reconciling bank and credit card accounts, the difference must always be zero. *True   False*

10. When matching transactions in the Banking center, which of these indicates that a definite match has been located?
    A. A white Records Found icon
    B. A green 1 Record Found icon
    C. Uncategorized Expenses
    D. Uncategorized Income

11. What are the steps to create a new bank rule for money out?
    A. Choose Gear→Your Company→Chart of Accounts→New→Manage Rules.
    B. Choose Banking→Bank Rules→New Rule.
    C. Choose Reports→All tab→Setup Rules.
    D. Choose Gear→Tools→Reconcile→Setup New Rule.

12. What are the steps to deposit proceeds from a bank loan?
    A. Choose Create→Customers→Receive Payment and then enter the information and amount in Add New Deposits.
    B. Choose Create→Other→Journal Entry.
    C. Choose Create→Other→Bank Deposit and then enter the information and amount in Add New Deposits.
    D. Choose Gear→Bank Deposit.

13. What are the steps to reconcile bank and credit card accounts?
    A. Choose Gear→Tools→Reconcile and then choose the account.
    B. Choose Transactions→Banking and then choose Register→Reconcile.
    C. Choose Gear→Chart of Accounts→View Register→Reconcile.
    D. All of these options

(cont'd.)

14. What are the steps to create the balance sheet and profit and loss reports?
    A. Choose Gear→Account and Settings→Advanced→Reports.
    B. Choose Create→Reports and then select Balance Sheet *or* Profit and Loss.
    C. In the Reports center, choose Balance Sheet *or* Profit and Loss.
    D. Choose Transactions→Reports→Chart of Accounts.

15. What two pieces of information do you need to reconcile your bank and credit card accounts?
    A. Bank name and account number
    B. Total amount of checks written and total amount of deposits made
    C. Statement date and ending balance
    D. None of these

16. When reconciling bank or credit card accounts, when is it okay to click the Finish Now button?
    A. When the Cleared Balance is 0.00
    B. When the Difference is 0.00
    C. When Checks and Payments equals Deposits and Other Credits
    D. When every transaction has a checkmark

17. Creating bank rules can simplify accounting in QuickBooks Online by:
    A. suggesting the correct accounting categories prior to adding downloaded bank and credit card transactions
    B. automatically suggesting the account when creating an expense transaction
    C. adding the income account on deposits from Undeposited Funds
    D. None of these options

18. How does the QuickBooks Online bank feeds feature assist with daily cash flow?
    A. By displaying the balance in bank and credit card accounts each day
    B. By displaying the cleared transactions each day
    C. By matching transactions to what is recorded in QuickBooks Online
    D. All of these options

19. At the end of an accounting period, which financial reports should be prepared?
    A. Sales Summary report and Customer Sales report
    B. Unpaid Bills report and Accounts Payable Aging report
    C. Balance sheet and profit and loss statement
    D. Cash in the bank report and credit card report

20. If you discover that you made an error recording an amount on a transaction during the reconciliation process, how would you fix it?
    A. Add another transaction for the difference.
    B. Click on the transaction and then click Edit to correct it.
    C. You cannot fix an error during reconciliation.
    D. Exit the bank reconciliation, find/edit the transaction, and then return to reconciliation.

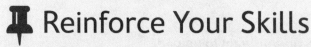

Reinforce Your Skills

For these exercises, you will work with Puppy Luv Pampered Pooch, the company account created in your trial subscription to QuickBooks Online.

Sadie has just returned from the bank, where she transferred money to the savings account and deposited proceeds of a bank loan into the checking account. Recording these transactions will reinforce some of the skills learned in this chapter.

REINFORCE YOUR SKILLS 5-1

Perform Bank Transactions

In this exercise, you will record a bank transfer and a deposit. You may need to add accounts.

Before You Begin: *Access your trial subscription to QuickBooks Online. Read any alerts or reminders that appear and close any unnecessary windows.*

1. Choose **Create→Other→Transfer** and record this transfer: $10,000; from Los Angeles City Bank checking account to LACB savings account; 8/7/2021

2. Choose **Create→Other→Bank Deposit** and record this deposit: Los Angeles City Bank; $5,000; loan payable; 8/7/2021 (Account Type: Other Current Liability)

REINFORCE YOUR SKILLS 5-2

Upload CSV Credit Card Transactions

Sadie's bank does not have a bank feed with QuickBooks Online, but it does have a CSV data file that can be downloaded from the bank and uploaded to QuickBooks Online. In this exercise, you will upload the CSV file.

1. On the Navigation bar, choose **Banking**.

2. Click the **Upload Transactions Manually** link at the bottom of the window.

    You will get this window only the first time you upload.

3. Browse to your **Chapter 05** folder, select the **CH05 CC Transactions.csv** file, and click **Next**.

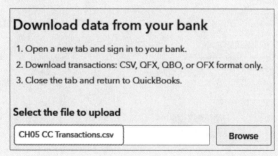

4. Select **City Credit Union** and click **Next**.

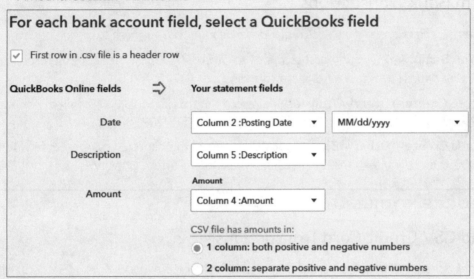

Select a QuickBooks account for the bank file you want to upload

Bank file	QuickBooks Account
CH05 CC transactions.csv	City Credit Union ▾

5. Verify QuickBooks Online fields map to the Your Statement Fields as follows:

   • Date: **Column 2 :Posting Date**

   • Description: **Column 5 :Description**

   • Amount: **Column 4 :Amount**

For each bank account field, select a QuickBooks field

☑ First row in .csv file is a header row

QuickBooks Online fields ⇒	Your statement fields	
Date	Column 2 :Posting Date ▾	MM/dd/yyyy ▾
Description	Column 5 :Description ▾	
Amount	**Amount** Column 4 :Amount ▾	

CSV file has amounts in:

● **1 column: both positive and negative numbers**

○ **2 column: separate positive and negative numbers**

6. Click **Next**, verify the four entries are selected, and click **Next**.

Select the transactions to import

☑	DATE	DESCRIPTION	AMOUNT
☑	07/29/2021	District Party	-389.10
☑	07/29/2021	USPS	-47.00
☑	07/27/2021	Sundown CC	-45.00
☑	07/06/2021	Sammy Gas	-18.35

7. Choose **Yes** to confirm that you want to import now.

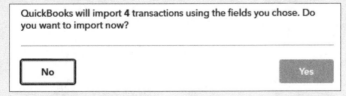

QuickBooks will import **4** transactions using the fields you chose. Do you want to import now?

No	Yes

8. Click **Let's Go!**

QuickBooks Online brings you back to the bank feeds window. Three transactions match transactions in QuickBooks Online, and one transaction did not get recorded. Sadie told you she may not have given you all the charges; it looks like the charge to Sammy Gas is one. With QuickBooks Online bank feeds, you can easily add the transaction here.

9. Match the three transactions.

10. Change the account for *Sammy Gas* to **Automobile Expense** (add the account) and then add the transaction.

11. Click **Go to Register**.

Your register should look like this. Leave this window open for the next exercise.

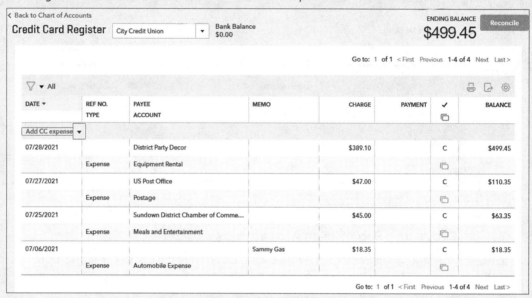

Reconcile the Credit Card Statement

Sadie has given you the recent credit card statement from City Credit Union. In this exercise, you will use the statement, shown here, to reconcile the credit card account with the QuickBooks account.

City Credit Union

	Statement Date	July 30, 2021
Make payments to:	Due Date	August 15, 2021
City Credit Union	Minimum Due	$25.00
PO Box 1485		
Bayshore, CA 94335	Balance	$ 110.35

Transaction Date	Posting Date	Description	Debits	Credits and Payments
7/6/2021	7/10/2021	Sammy Gas	18.35	
7/25/2021	7/27/2021	Sundown CC	45.00	
7/27/2021	7/30/2021	USPS	47.00	

Beginning Balance	Payments	New Charges	New Balance
$ -		$ 110.35	$ 110.35

1. Click **Reconcile→Reconcile an Account→Let's Do It**.

2. Enter the statement ending date and balance and then click **Start Reconciling**.

3. Verify that a checkmark is placed to the right of each transaction that appears on the statement and that the Difference is 0.00. You may need to uncheck a transaction that is not on your statement.

4. Click **Finish Now** and then click **Done**.

5. Return to the **Dashboard**.

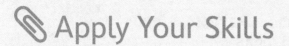 # Apply Your Skills

---

APPLY YOUR SKILLS 5-1

Create a Deposit

Sadie received a refund of $50 for overpayment of her business taxes. In this exercise, you will deposit the refund to the Los Angeles City Bank checking account.

1. Deposit $50; received from the City of Los Angeles Clerk on 7/29/2021; Taxes and Licenses account

---

APPLY YOUR SKILLS 5-2

Upload the Los Angeles City Bank Transactions

In this exercise, you will upload the CSV file that Sadie has downloaded from the bank.

1. Navigate to your **Chapter 05** folder and open the **CH05 Los Angeles City Bank Transactions.csv** file.
2. Choose **Banking→File Upload**.
3. Link to **Los Angeles City Bank**.
4. Map the **CSV** columns.
5. Select all transactions to import and then click **Yes** when prompted.
6. Click **Let's Go!**

APPLY YOUR SKILLS 5-3

Work with Bank Feeds and Bank Rules

In this exercise, you will match all the green Match transactions, add a transaction, and set up a bank rule.

1. The bank feeds indicate that nine matching transactions are already in QuickBooks Online. Match all of them.
2. Set up a money out bank rule for the Sammy Gas; Automobile Expense account.
3. Add the Sammy Gas transaction to QuickBooks Online.

APPLY YOUR SKILLS 5-4 `QG`

Bank Account Reconciliation and Financial Reports

In this exercise, you will reconcile the July 31, 2021, bank statement from Los Angeles City Bank in QuickBooks Online.

1. Navigate to your **Chapter 05** folder and open the **CH05 LA City Bank Statement.pdf** file.
2. Reconcile the Los Angeles City Bank account.
3. Prepare the balance sheet and profit and loss reports for July 31, 2021.

4. Export both reports to Excel, saving them in your **Chapter 05** folder as: **CH05 Balance Sheet** and **CH05 Profit and Loss**

5. Return to the Los Angeles City Bank Register by choosing **Banking** and then clicking **Go to Register**.

6. Export the register to Excel, saving it in your **Chapter 05** folder as: **CH05 Los Angeles City Bank Register**

7. Return to the **Dashboard**.

 CHECK FIGURE *Your figures should match those shown here.*

ACCOUNT BALANCES	
Account	**Balance**
Los Angeles City Bank	$46,955.73
City Credit Union	$499.45
Savings LACB	$10,000

STATEMENT BALANCES	
Statement	**Balance**
Total assets on balance sheet 7/31/2021	$71,096.23
Net loss on profit and loss statement 7/31/2021	–$4,632.52

6 | All in a Day's Work!

N ow it's your opportunity to see what it would be like to manage an
account from day to day. In this chapter, you will draw on all that
you have learned in the preceding chapters to manage the Puppy
Luv Pampered Pooch account. You will record the necessary transactions into
QuickBooks Online for August 2021.

📂 Project: Puppy Luv Pampered Pooch

Sadie Garrison has placed her trust in you to keep her QuickBooks Online data current and correct. She will give you a variety of transactions and tasks over the month. You will analyze each transaction to determine what the appropriate form is, and you will add vendors, clients, and accounts as you go. You will also reconcile statements and prepare financial reports as requested.

Use your problem-solving and analytical skills to complete this project. You are welcome to refer to previous chapters and to use QuickBooks Online Help. The Check Figures feature appears at the end of each week to keep you on track.

Before You Begin

Open Puppy Luv Pampered Pooch, the company account created in your trial subscription to QuickBooks Online. Create a profit and loss statement and a balance sheet report for 7/1/2021 through 8/10/2021, and then be sure they match the reports shown. It's very important to begin with the correct balances, as this helps ensure you end with the correct balances.

> **Tip!** If your balances are not correct, review each prior chapter to determine and correct the error.

Puppy Luv Pampered Pooch - Your Name
PROFIT AND LOSS
July 1 - August 10, 2021

	TOTAL
Income	
Pooch Services	768.00
Total Income	**$768.00**
Gross Profit	**$768.00**
Expenses	
Automobile Expense	33.58
Dues & Subscriptions	250.00
Equipment Rental	389.10
Marketing	1,033.00
Meals and Entertainment	245.00
Office Expenses	63.54
Pooch Supplies	2,604.46
Postage	47.00
Taxes & Licenses	400.00
Utilities	16.84
Total Expenses	**$5,082.52**
Net Operating Income	**$ -4,314.52**
Net Income	**$ -4,314.52**

Puppy Luv Pampered Pooch - Your Name
BALANCE SHEET
As of August 10, 2021

	TOTAL
ASSETS	
Current Assets	
Bank Accounts	
Los Angeles City Bank	46,955.73
Savings LACB	10,000.00
Total Bank Accounts	**$56,955.73**
Accounts Receivable	
Accounts Receivable	245.00
Total Accounts Receivable	**$245.00**
Other current assets	
Prepaid Expenses	3,300.00
Undeposited Funds	0.00
Total Other current assets	**$3,300.00**
Total Current Assets	**$60,500.73**
Fixed Assets	
Equipment	16,000.00
Total Fixed Assets	**$16,000.00**
TOTAL ASSETS	**$76,500.73**
LIABILITIES AND EQUITY	
Liabilities	
Current Liabilities	
Accounts Payable	
Accounts Payable	315.80
Total Accounts Payable	**$315.80**
Credit Cards	
City Credit Union	499.45
Total Credit Cards	**$499.45**
Other Current Liabilities	
Loan Payable	5,000.00
Total Other Current Liabilities	**$5,000.00**
Total Current Liabilities	**$5,815.25**
Total Liabilities	**$5,815.25**
Equity	
Owner's Equity	75,000.00
Retained Earnings	
Net Income	-4,314.52
Total Equity	**$70,685.48**
TOTAL LIABILITIES AND EQUITY	**$76,500.73**

Week Ending 8/14/2021

Sadie is feeling really positive about her first week. She made a lot of good contacts and has already scheduled many appointments for the next few weeks. Record the following transactions as appropriate.

Thursday 8/12/2021

- Alison Ball brought both her large dogs, Lucy and Desi, in for Full Pet Grooms; paid with check number 1845. The Sales Receipt numbers should be 1014 and 1015.

- Jesus Moreno brought in his extra-large dog, Sandy, for a Full Pet Groom and a Flea Bath; paid with check number 9855.

- Monty Blayclock brought in a cute medium-sized dog he found for a Bath and Brush and an ear cleaning; paid cash. (Do not set him up as a sub-client.)

- Jerry Lee brought back his large Lab, King, for a Full Pet Groom and a teeth brushing; paid with check number 4887.

- Nancee Ruiz brought in her two small dogs, Ruff and Ralph, for the works today: Full Pet Groom and teeth brushing; paid cash.

- Diovanne Uria brought in her large Pit Bull, Tiny, for a Full Pet Groom; paid with check number 1554.

- Jesse Jones brought in his two medium-sized, very muddy dogs, Billy and Doc, for a quick Bath and Brush; paid cash. The Sales Receipt numbers should be 1022 and 1023.

- Received a bill from Bonni's Dog Biskits for dog treats that Sadie ordered; $26.86 (account: Pooch Supplies).

- Paid for a delivery of a small cooler and some bottled water to keep on hand; $205.19 with City Credit Union credit card (account: Office Supplies and Software).

  Tip! You do not need a Payee on an Expense form.

- Paid for a push broom and bathroom supplies at Office Plus with City Credit Union credit card; $117.55 (account: Office Supplies and Software).

 CHECK FIGURE *Your figures should match those shown here.*

ACCOUNT BALANCE	
Account	**Balance**
City Credit Union	$822.19

Friday 8/13/2021

- Cyndi Kontoes brought in her large Lab, Pal, for a Full Pet Groom and teeth brushing; paid cash. The Sales Receipt number should be 1024.

- Amanda Moreau brought in her medium-sized dog, Pink, for a Full Pet Groom and nails polished a hot pink; paid cash.

- Jefferson Kane brought in both of his medium-sized dogs, Prince and Oscar, for a Mini Pet Groom; paid with check number 58544.

- Asad Ramzanali brought his extra-large dog, Sweetie, for a Bath and Brush and a teeth brushing; paid with check number 7115.

- GreenWay Kennels brought in seven medium-sized dogs for a Bath and Brush and a teeth brushing; on account.

- Received and paid a bill from Consolidated Insurance for August 2021; Liability Insurance; $204; check number 10009. (Create a check.)

- Wrote check number 10010 to City Credit Union for payment of amount due (City Credit Union in the Account field); $110.35.

 CHECK FIGURE *Your figures should match those shown here.*

ACCOUNT BALANCE	
Account	**Balance**
City Credit Union	$711.84

Saturday 8/14/2021

- Received a bill from Atlas Planning for some layout designs for remodeling the grooming room; for $150; due in 15 days (account: Other Business Expenses).

- Received bill number 8858 from the Dollar Saver for weekly advertising (marketing); $85; due in 30 days.

- Donnie Jacobs brought in three small dogs—Lucky, Nancy, and Dolly—for a Full Pet Groom; paid cash.

- John Kannon brought in one extra-large dog, Ruff, for a Bath and Brush; Ears Cleaned and Teeth Brushed; paid with check number 77811.

- Maria Biazus brought in her sweet, medium-sized dog, Puffin, for a Mini Groom and nail polish; paid cash.

- Just at closing time, James King came in asking whether Sadie could clean up a dirty puppy he just found, full of fleas. Sadie gave the little pup a Bath and Brush along with a Flea Bath; James paid cash (do not add sub-client). The Sales Receipt number should be 1035.

- Make the bank deposit into the Los Angeles City Bank checking account for the week's sales; the deposit should be for $1,016.

Create a Report

Prepare a Sales by Client Summary report for Sadie for the week. Total sales should be $1,261.

 CHECK FIGURE *Your figures should match those shown here and on the next page.*

ACCOUNT BALANCE	
Account	**Balance**
Los Angeles City Bank	$47,657.38
City Credit Union	$711.84

A/R AND A/P BALANCES

Statement	Balance
Accounts Receivable	$490
Accounts Payable	$577.66

Prepare Your Deliverables—Set 1 QG

Prepare the following deliverables and export to Excel or PDF as instructed:

- Sales by Client Summary report for the week ending 8/14/2021, saved as: **CH06 Sales by Client Summary 8.14.21**

- Los Angeles City Bank Register report, saved as: **CH06 LA City Bank Register**

- City Credit Union register, saved as: **CH06 City Credit Union Register**

Week Ending 8/21/2021

Sadie is ready for another great week. She has met with another breeder who wants to begin grooming her small dachshunds this week. Record the following transactions as appropriate.

Thursday 8/19/2021

- Andie Garcia's medium-sized dogs, Chester and Mandy, have come home from a run in the woods with fleas. Andie stopped by to see whether Sadie had time for a Flea Bath and a Mini Pet Groom for each; paid with check number 5848. The Sales Receipt numbers should be 1036 and 1037.

- Lu Sinks brought in her large dog, Molly, for a Bath and Brush; paid cash.

- Mami Saunders brought in her large dog, Sam, for a Full Pet Groom; paid with check number 4844.

- Windemere Kennels, 1717 So. Dogwood, Los Angeles, CA 90022, brought in five small dachshunds for a Mini Pet Groom this week; on account; will pay in 15 days.

- Paid for a one-year subscription to *Puppy News Magazine* with debit card; $24.95.

- Paid for some room freshener and a small fan from Office Plus with debit card; $36.96 (account: Office Supplies & Software).

Friday 8/20/2021

- Cindy Craig brought in her large Lab, Foxy, for a Flea Bath, ear cleaning, and teeth brushing; paid cash. The Sales Receipt number should be 1041.

- Dana Davis brought in her medium-size dog, Princess, for a Full Pet Groom and nail polish; paid with check number 14144.

- Jackson Smith brought in two large dogs, Grover and Lincoln, for a Full Pet Groom; paid with check number 774.

- GreenWay Kennels brought in seven medium-sized dogs for a Bath and Brush and teeth brushing; on account; will pay in 15 days.

- Paid all the bills due on or before 8/20/2021. (First check should be number 10011.)
- Make the bank deposit for monies received the last two days; add to the deposit a rebate check from Office Plus for $4 for office supplies. (Deposit should be $382.)

Saturday 8/21/2021

- Wrote check number 10014 for delivery of Pooch Supplies (shampoo and grooming products); $745.45 to Doggies Plus.

- Received payment from GreenWay Kennels for Invoice number 1013; check number 15159. Be sure to deposit to Undeposited Funds.

- Paid Sally Na $45 for washing the front window and door; check number 10015 (account: Other Business Expenses).

- Donated $25 to Sundown District Middle School for fundraiser; check number 10016 (account: Contributions).

- Tomas Sierra brought in his large dog, Kia, for a Full Pet Groom; check number 5811.

- Sara Martin brought in her two large dogs, Joe and King, for a Bath and Brush; paid cash.

- Gina Thomas brought in her two small dogs, Tiny and Ming, for a Full Pet Groom and nail polish; paid with check number 547. The Sales Receipt numbers should be 1049 and 1050.

 CHECK FIGURE *Your figures should match those shown here.*

ACCOUNT BALANCE	
Account	**Balance**
Los Angeles City Bank	$46,846.22
City Credit Union	$711.84

A/R AND A/P BALANCES	
Statement	**Balance**
Accounts Receivable	$615
Accounts Payable	$261.86

Prepare Your Deliverables—Set 2 [QG]

Prepare a Sales by Client Summary report for the week ending 8/21/2021. Export the report to Excel or PDF as instructed, saving it as: **CH06 Sales by Client Summary 8.21.21**

Week Ending 8/28/2021

Sadie met Scott, a representative from Sundown Dog Rescue, this week. She has agreed to give the group a hand at a fundraiser/adoption fair this Friday. The salon will be closed 8/27/2021. Record the following transactions as appropriate.

Thursday 8/26/2021

- Pay all the bills due this month; the first check should be number 10017.

- Deposit all the monies received from last Saturday.

- Amanda Brown found another stray. She brought in the pretty, medium-sized dog for a Bath and Brush; paid cash. The Sales Receipt number should be 1051.

- Windemere Kennels brought in five small dachshunds for a Mini Pet Groom; on account; will pay in 15 days.

Friday 8/27/2021

Salon closed due to Sundown Dog Rescue Fair.

Saturday 8/28/2021

- Sadie gave you check number 6877 for $75 from Sundown Dog Rescue. Sadie had agreed to give dogs an outdoor bath for $15; for each bath, the rescue kept $10 and gave Sadie $5. Along with the check, they sent a thank you letter. The account should be Pooch Services.

- Received check number 15170 from GreenWay Kennels for Invoice number 1029.

- GreenWay Kennels brought in seven medium-size dogs for only a Bath and Brush this week; on account.

- Deposit all monies received; deposit will be $350. This should be handled in a similar manner to how you dealt with the proceeds from the parking lot sale in Develop Your Skills 5-3.

 CHECK FIGURE *Your figures should match those shown here.*

ACCOUNT BALANCE	
Account	**Balance**
Los Angeles City Bank	$47,495.36
City Credit Union	$711.84

A/R AND A/P BALANCES	
Statement	**Balance**
Accounts Receivable	$705
Accounts Payable	$85

Prepare Your Deliverables—Set 3 QG

Prepare a Sales by Client Summary report for the week ending 8/28/2021. Export the report to Excel, saving it as: **CH06 Sales by Client Summary 8.28.21**

Wednesday 9/1/2021

The salon is closed today. You are working from home to reconcile the bank and credit card accounts, catch up on a few things for Sadie, and prepare the month-end financial report.

Sadie sent you a text message about a few things: "Please set up a Chart of Accounts for Conferences expenses. I registered for one on my credit card (Local Pooch Association); sorry, I forgot to mention it. Also, I have been over at Dana's and forgot to get the receipts to you. Enjoy your weekend. Thanks!"

Open the following CSV and PDF files from your **Chapter 06** folder:

- **CH06 Los Angeles City Bank Transactions.csv**
- **CH06 City Credit Union August CC Transactions.csv**
- **CH06 City Credit Union August Statement.pdf**
- **CH06 LA City Bank August Statement.pdf**

Perform the following tasks:

- Set up a Chart of Accounts for conferences, as Sadie mentioned in her text (Conferences is the Expense account type, Office/General Administrative Expenses is the detail type).

- Import the CSV bank feeds into QuickBooks Online and then match or add the bank transactions to the transactions in QuickBooks Online.

- You have noticed several purchases from Dana's Coffee Hut; create a bank rule to save time when entering these purchases in the future. Consider using Meals and Entertainment as the Account Category.

- Use the downloaded bank statements for Los Angeles City Bank and City Credit Union to complete the reconciliations.

Prepare Your Deliverables—Set 4 [QG]

Prepare the following end-of-month deliverables and export to Excel:

- Sales by Client Summary for August 2021, saved as: **CH06 Sales by Client Summary August 2021**

- Balance sheet report for the period ending August 31, 2021, saved as: **CH06 Balance Sheet August 2021**

- Profit and loss statement July 1, 2021 through August 31, 2021, saved as: **CH06 Profit and Loss Statement August 2021**

Look at the Big Picture

Consider these questions:

- Which vendors does Sadie owe as of August 31, 2021?

- Which clients owe Sadie as of August 31, 2021?

7 | Managing Inventory

I nventory is a critical asset to a merchandising business. QuickBooks Online has features to help you manage your inventory. When set up, the accounting is handled for you, from the purchase to the sale of the inventory product. In this chapter, you will learn how QuickBooks Online assists with inventory management. You will learn how to properly set up products, use forms for purchases and sales, and prepare product-related reports.

LEARNING OBJECTIVES

▸ Distinguish between inventory and non-inventory products

▸ Describe first in, first out inventory valuation

▸ Set up and receive products

▸ Create purchase orders

▸ Apply vendor credits

▸ Set up sales tax

▸ Invoice for sale of a product

▸ Create a credit memo for returns

▸ Perform inventory adjustments

▸ Create product-related reports

📂 Project: Craig's Design and Landscaping Services

Craig has been purchasing inventory and selling products to his customers. He frequently purchases special-order products for specific customers and other non-inventory items. He doesn't really understand inventory management principles and the first-in, first-out costing method. He has asked you to set up processes to help him with inventory.

Tracking Inventory

Inventory encompasses purchasing products for sale, stocking and tracking the products, and selling them to customers. Hardware and department stores are examples of businesses in which inventory is of central importance.

BEHIND **THE SCENES**

As you purchase products, the inventory asset account in your balance sheet increases. As you sell products, the inventory asset account in your balance sheet decreases and the Cost of Goods Sold in your profit and loss account increases.

Enabling Tracking

To track inventory in QuickBooks Online, you must enable that feature in the Sales portion of the Account and Settings menu. You cannot disable inventory tracking for an inventory product after it has been enabled, but you can make it inactive. Inactivating an inventory product does not affect the previous transactions that used it.

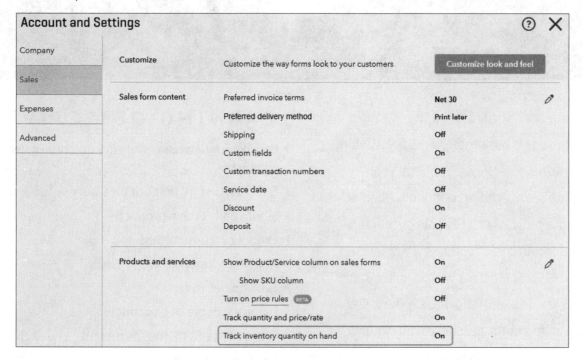

Entering Inventory

Inventory products can be entered individually or imported from Excel, similar to customer and vendor lists. You are not limited to the number of inventory products that you can enter.

After you have set up your inventory product list, you can start purchasing and selling the products on purchase orders, bills, invoices, sales receipts forms, and so on. You can also add new products within the transaction form. When the inventory product is set up correctly, every future transaction will be recorded appropriately from the form used.

First In, First Out

QuickBooks Online uses the first-in, first-out (FIFO) method of inventory valuation. Because product prices fluctuate, the same product may have a different price each time you purchase it. The FIFO method helps you determine what purchase price to apply when you sell each product. FIFO assumes that the first product purchased is the first product sold and adjusts your inventory and cost of goods old (COGS) account appropriately when a sale is made.

Cost of Goods Sold Account

The cost of goods sold (COGS) account records the cost of products that are held in inventory and then sold. Once an item is sold from your inventory, the COGS account increases by the amount you paid for the product when purchased. The difference between the cost and the sales price is income.

DEVELOP YOUR SKILLS 7-1

Some of Craig's inventory products were set up by a previous bookkeeper. Now Craig has asked you to set up a new product that will be a standard inventory item available for sale. In this exercise, you will set up a new inventory item.

Before You Begin: *Access the QuickBooks Online test drive at qbo.intuit.com/redir/testdrive and leave the test drive open for the entire chapter.*

1. Choose Gear ⚙ →**Lists**→**Products and Services**.
2. Click the **New** button and then choose **Inventory** from the list.

3. Complete the fields as follows:

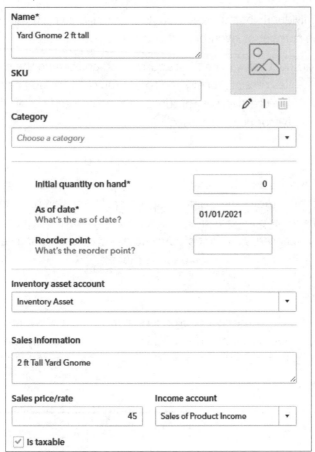

4. Click the **Show More** link or scroll down to expand the list.

5. Complete the purchasing information as shown:

6. Save and close the form.

An inventory product has three Charts of Accounts associated with it. As you purchase inventory, the Inventory Asset amount increases. As you sell inventory, the Inventory Asset amount decreases, while the Cost of Goods Sold and the Sales of Product amounts increase, as shown in the following examples.

Inventory Asset	Checking Account
71.25	71.25

Journal entry for the purchase by check of five Yard Gnomes at $14.25 each

Inventory Asset	Checking Account	Cost of Goods Sold	Sales of Product	Accounts Receivable
71.25	71.25			
28.50		28.50	90.00	90.00

Journal entry for the sale, by invoice, of two of the five Yard Gnomes at $45 each

Non-Inventory Products

Non-inventory products are purchased products whose quantities you don't need to track. An example could be a specific mosaic piece for one customer or nuts and bolts used during an installation. You can set up non-inventory products in QuickBooks Online to capture only sales of the product, only purchases of the product, or both.

DEVELOP YOUR SKILLS 7-2

Craig is going to purchase a product both for business usage and for sale if customers want to purchase it. However, he does not want to keep track of it as an inventory product. In this exercise, you will set up a non-inventory product.

1. Choose **Gear** ⚙ →**Lists**→**Products and Services**.
2. Click **New** and then choose **Non-Inventory**.

3. Complete the fields as indicated:

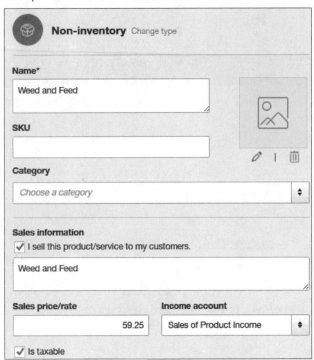

4. Place a checkmark in the **I Purchase this Product/Service from a Vendor** field and then complete as follows:

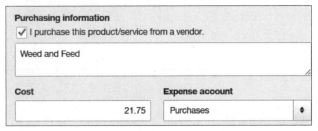

5. Save and close the form.

Set Up a Non-Inventory Product for Special Orders

Craig has decided to offer custom bird feeders to his customers. Each bird feeder will be a different size, color, material, and price, and Craig does not want to create a separate product for each unique order. Now you will set up a non-inventory product for special orders. Each bird feeder will have a different cost and selling price.

6. Choose **Gear→Lists→Products and Services**.

7. Click **New** and then choose **Non-Inventory**.

8. Type **Bird Feeder** in the Name field and then complete as follows:

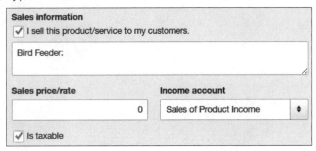

9. Place a checkmark in the **I Purchase this Product/Service from a Vendor** field and then complete as follows:

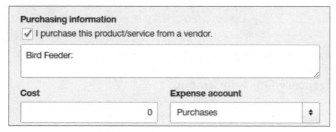

Purchasing information
☑ I purchase this product/service from a vendor.

Bird Feeder:

Cost	Expense account
0	Purchases ◆

10. Save and close the form.

Now Craig can use Bird Feeder as the product or service on the purchases and sales forms. The description of the Bird Feeder can be typed after the colon (:) in the Description field of the form.

Inventory Adjustments

Inventory is an expensive part of your business and needs to be managed frequently. Inventory can become out of sync for many reasons, including spoilage, breakage, theft, and errors in recording products. QuickBooks Online lets you adjust inventory records as needed to reflect what you actually have in inventory.

Craig's Design and Landscaping Services

PHYSICAL INVENTORY WORKSHEET

PRODUCT	DESCRIPTION	QUANTITY	PHYSICAL COUNT
Design:Fountains:Pump	Fountain Pump	25.00	
Design:Fountains:Rock Fountain	Rock Fountain	2.00	
Landscaping:Sprinklers:Sprinkler He...	Sprinkler Heads	25.00	
Landscaping:Sprinklers:Sprinkler Pip...	Sprinkler Pipes	31.00	
Yard Gnome 2 ft tall	2 ft Tall Yard Gnome	2.00	

DEVELOP YOUR SKILLS 7-3

When you took inventory on September 21, 2021, you counted twenty-nine sprinkler pipes in stock. This does not match the record in QuickBooks Online. In this exercise, you will adjust your inventory quantities in QuickBooks Online to match the number you actually have on hand.

1. Choose **Create→Other→Inventory Qty Adjustment**.

2. Type **09/21/2021** in the Adjustment Date field.
3. Choose **Landscaping:Sprinklers:Sprinkler Pipes** in the Product field.
4. Type **29** in the New Qty field.
5. Save and close the form.

   This adjustment will decrease Inventory and increase Inventory Shrinkage (a COGS account).

Tip! You can also adjust inventory from the Products and Services list by choosing Edit→ Adjust Quantity.

Purchase Orders

Purchase orders are documents you send to your vendor/supplier to state your intent to purchase specific products or services. The purchase order describes the product, the quantities, the price, the expected delivery method and date, and other details. You enable the purchase order feature in the Account and Settings menu. You can use this feature for both inventory and non-inventory products.

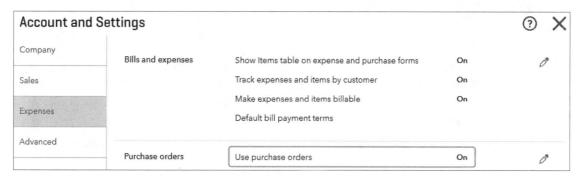

DEVELOP YOUR SKILLS 7-4

In this exercise, you will create a purchase order for some inventory products that Craig has asked you to buy.

1. Choose **Create→Vendors→Purchase Order**.
2. Choose **Tim Philip Masonry** from the Choose a Vendor menu.
3. Type **09/07/2021** in the Purchase Order Date field.
4. Type **UPS** in the Ship Via field.
5. If necessary, click the arrow next to **Account Details** to collapse the rows and hide the section.

6. In Line 1 of the Items Details section, choose **Yard Gnome 2 ft tall** as the product and enter **Yard Gnomes 2 ft tall** as the description.
7. Type **5** in the Qty field.

8. Save and close the form.

			AMOUNT
Tim Philip Masonry ▾	tim.philip@timphilipmasonry.com		**$71.25**
Open ▾			

Mailing address	Ship to	Purchase Order date	Crew #
Tim Philip Tim Philip Masonry 3948 Elm St. Middlefield, CA 94482	*Enter Text* ▾	09/07/2021	
	Shipping address	**Ship via**	**Sales Rep**
	Craig's Design and Landscaping Services 123 Sierra Way San Pablo, CA 87999	UPS	

▶ Account details

▼ Item details

	#	PRODUCT/SERVICE	DESCRIPTION	QTY	RATE	AMOUNT	CUSTOMER	
⠿	1	Yard Gnome 2 ft tall	2 ft Tall Yard Gnome	5	14.25	71.25		🗑
⠿	2							🗑

Add lines	Clear all lines

Your message to vendor

Total **$71.25**

Purchase Order Reports

QuickBooks Online has an Open Purchase Order List report and various other purchase reports in the Reports center on the Navigation bar. The Reports center includes reports for purchases by vendor, by product, and more. These reports allow you to check on the status of purchase orders and take appropriate action. For example, you can follow up on an order with the vendor, or you can verify that goods were not received without applying the receipt of inventory to the purchase order.

DEVELOP YOUR SKILLS 7-5

In this exercise, you will view the Open Purchase Order List report and find various other purchase reports.

1. Open the **Reports** center, click the **All** tab, and then choose **Expenses and Vendors→Open Purchase Order List**. Close any pop-ups that appear.

2. Hover your mouse pointer over the 71.25 amount for purchase order number 1005 and then click.

Craig's Design and Landscaping Services							
OPEN PURCHASE ORDER LIST BY VENDOR							
All Dates							
DATE	NUM	MEMO/DESCRIPTION	CREW #	SALES REP	SHIP VIA	AMOUNT	OPEN BALANCE
▼ Tim Philip Masonry							
03/19/2018	1002					125.00	125.00
09/07/2021	1005				UPS	71.25	71.25
Total for Tim Philip Masonry						**$196.25**	**$196.25**
TOTAL						**$196.25**	**$196.25**

This allows you to access more details about the open purchase order from within the report.

3. Close the purchase order.

4. Return to the **Reports** center and then click the **Purchases by Vendor Detail** report link.

5. Choose **All Dates** in the **Report Period** field and then click **Run Report**.

6. Return to the **Reports** center and then click the **Purchases by Product/Service Detail** report link.

7. Choose **All Dates** in the Report Period field and then click **Run Report**.

8. Go to the **Dashboard**.

Receiving Inventory Against a Purchase Order

To receive the inventory that was ordered on a purchase order and close the purchase order, you have several options:

- Receive the inventory as an expense.

- Receive the inventory and pay by check.

- Create a bill to be paid later.

> **Best Practice**
>
> At this time, QuickBooks Online cannot receive incomplete orders. If a product on the purchase order is short-shipped (i.e., the quantity received is less than the quantity listed) or all items are not received, the best practice is to create a new purchase order for the undelivered products or services.

DEVELOP YOUR SKILLS 7-6

In this exercise, you will receive the inventory on Purchase Order #1005, which has a bill from the vendor that is due in fifteen days.

1. Choose **Create→Vendors→Bill**.

2. Choose **Tim Philip Masonry** in the Choose a Vendor field.

    Notice that a drawer opened on the right with the option to add to the bill.

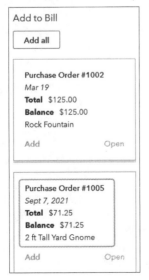

3. In the block for Purchase Order number 1005, click the **Add** link.

4. In the Bill window, set the terms to **Net 15** and set the bill date to: **09/09/2021**

5. Save and close the form.

6. Choose **Gear** ⚙ →**Lists**→**Products and Services**.

7. Scroll to the Yard Gnome 2 ft Tall product and confirm that there are five gnomes available for sale.

8. Return to the **Dashboard**.

Purchase Orders for Non-Inventory Products

You can create purchase orders for all of your products and services, as well as expense items.

DEVELOP YOUR SKILLS 7-7

In this exercise, you will create a purchase order for a non-inventory product. Amy's Bird Sanctuary special-ordered a bird feeder from Craig. You will include this item on the purchase order for Tania's Nursery.

1. Choose **Create**→**Vendors**→**Purchase Order**.

2. Choose **Tania's Nursery** in the Choose a Vendor field.

3. Enter **09/10/2021** in the Purchase Order Date field, tap Tab , and enter **Delivered** in the Ship Via field.

4. Complete row 1 of the Item Details section as indicated:

   • Product/Service: **Weed and Feed**

   • Qty: **15**

   • Rate: **21.75**

5. Complete row 2 of the Item Details as indicated:

   • Product/Service: **Bird Feeder**

   • Description field: Add **Red Barn 24"** after the colon (Bird Feeder: Red Barn 24")

   • Qty: **1**

   • Rate: **28.50**

   • Customer: **Amy's Bird Sanctuary**

6. Save and close the form.

Adding an Expense to a Purchase Order Payment

Vendors frequently add charges to a bill for ordered products or services. These charges are usually for an added delivery or shipping charge that was not included on the purchase order.

DEVELOP YOUR SKILLS 7-8

In this exercise, you will receive and pay for the Weed and Feed on Purchase Order #1006, as well as pay an added delivery fee. You will need to add the delivery fee as a new account.

1. Choose **Create→Vendors→Expense**.
2. Choose **Tania's Nursery** as the payee and **Mastercard** as the account.
3. Enter **09/13/2021** for the payment date and choose **Mastercard** as the payment method.
4. Add **Purchase Order #1006** from the drawer on the right.
5. Click in the **Billable** field to place a checkmark for the bird feeder for Amy's Bird Sanctuary.
6. Click the **trash can** 🗑 icon to the far right of line 1 under Account Details to delete that line.

7. Add the following to line 1 under Account Details (you may need to add the expense account):

- Account: **Delivery Expense**
- Description: **Delivery**
- Amount: **15**

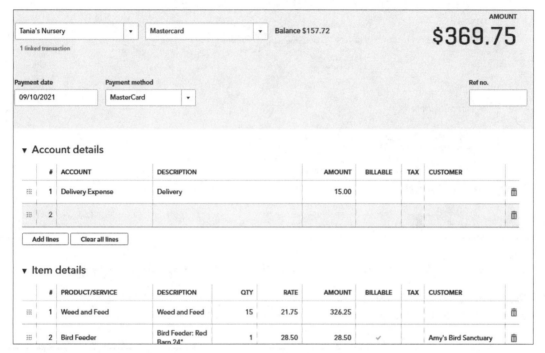

8. Save and close the form.

Purchasing Products and Services Without a Purchase Order

Purchase orders are not a requirement, and many businesses choose not to use them. You can purchase inventory, non-inventory, and service items directly on an expense, check, or bill form. Just use the Item Details portion of the form.

Vendor Credits/Returns

You may need to return products to the vendor because too many items were shipped, the wrong parts were ordered or shipped, or for some other reason. In this case, you can record a vendor credit for expenses and/or for products and services. You can then apply these vendor credits to an unpaid bill prior to payment.

Note! You cannot apply a vendor credit to a bill that has already been paid.

DEVELOP YOUR SKILLS 7-9

One of the gnomes that Craig received in a shipment from Tim Philip Masonry was damaged. In this exercise, you will start by recording a vendor credit for the return of the damaged gnome. Then you will apply the credit to payment for the shipment.

1. Choose **Create→Vendors→Vendor Credit**.
2. Choose **Tim Philip Masonry** as the vendor and enter **09/10/2021** as the payment date field.
3. On line 1 of the Item Details field, enter: **Yard Gnome 2 ft tall**
4. Type **return of damaged item** in the Memo field.
5. Save and close the form.

Apply a Vendor Credit

Now you will apply the credit to the payment.

6. Choose **Create→Vendors→Pay Bills**.
7. Choose **Checking** as the payment account and enter **09/15/2021** as the payment date.
8. Place a checkmark to the left of **Tim Philip Masonry**.

   You can see that QuickBooks automatically applied the credit only to that open balance.
9. Save and print check number 71.
10. Click **Preview and Print** and then click **Print**.

Sales Tax

In some states, you must charge the customer a sales tax when you sell products. QuickBooks Online makes it easy to charge and collect the correct amount of sales tax on the products you sell.

Warning! Be sure to investigate the sales tax laws in your state to set up sales tax appropriately.

When you set up sales tax for the first time, QuickBooks Online will also set up the Sales Tax Payable Liability account. The funds charged on sales forms are held in this account until paid to the appropriate authority.

Warning! If a sales tax rate changes, be sure you set up a new sales tax rate. Do not edit an existing one; doing so will cause the history to change.

DEVELOP YOUR SKILLS 7-10

Craig has already set up sales tax for California, so you will set up a second account to gain experience. In this exercise, you will view the Sales Tax center and set up a new sales tax rate and agency.

1. Open the **Sales Tax** center by clicking **Taxes** on the Navigation bar.

2. In the Related Tasks box, choose **Add/Edit Tax Rates and Agencies**.

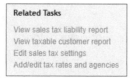

3. Click the **New** button.

4. Verify that the Single Tax Rate option is chosen.

5. Complete the following fields, using Tab to navigate:

   - Tax Name: **2nd California**
   - Agency Name: **State Board of Equalization**
   - Rate: **8.5**

6. Click **Save**.

Return to Sales Tax Owed and Recent Payments

Sales Tax Rates and Agencies

Tax Rate Name	Agency Name	Tax Rate
○ 2nd California	State Board of Equalization	8.50%
◉ California	Board of Equalization	8%
○ Tucson *(Combined rate)*		9.10%
Tucson City	Arizona Dept. of Revenue	2%
AZ State tax	Arizona Dept. of Revenue	7.10%
○ AZ State tax *(Component)*	Arizona Dept. of Revenue	7.10%
○ Tucson City *(Component)*	Arizona Dept. of Revenue	2%

7. Click the **Return to Sales Tax Owed and Recent Payments** link.

8. In the Related Tasks box, choose **Edit Sales Tax Settings**.

9. If necessary, choose **California** in the Default Sales Tax box.

10. Click **Save** and then return to the **Dashboard**.

Inventory and Non-Inventory Products

When you record the sale of inventory, special-order, and non-inventory products on an invoice or sales receipt and then save the form, QuickBooks Online completes the accounting for the sale and cost of sales for you.

DEVELOP YOUR SKILLS 7-11

In this exercise, you will begin by creating a sales form to sell inventory and non-inventory products.

1. Choose **Create→Customers→Invoice**.

2. Create the invoice as indicated:

   - Customer: **Kate Whelan**
   - Terms: **Net 10**
   - Invoice Date: **09/15/2021**
   - Product/Service, line 1: **Yard Gnome 2 ft tall**
   - Qty, line 1: **3**
   - Product/Service, line 2: **Weed and Feed**
   - Qty, line 2: **1**
   - Select a Sales Tax Rate: **California**

   The invoice total should be $209.79.

3. Save the form and then, from the bottom tray, choose **More→Transaction Journal**.

   Now you can see the accounting behind the scenes for this invoice. The COGS has increased, and the Inventory Asset has decreased.

Craig's Design and Landscaping Services

JOURNAL

All Dates

DATE	TRANSACTION TYPE	NUM	NAME	MEMO/DESCRIPTION	ACCOUNT	DEBIT	CREDIT
09/15/2021	Invoice	1038	Kate Whelan		Accounts Receivable (A/R)	$209.79	
				2 ft Tall Yard Gnome	Cost of Goods Sold	$42.75	
				2 ft Tall Yard Gnome	Inventory Asset		$42.75
				2 ft Tall Yard Gnome	Sales of Product Income		$135.00
				Weed and Feed	Sales of Product Income		$59.25
					Board of Equalization Payable		$15.54
						$252.54	$252.54
TOTAL						**$252.54**	**$252.54**

4. Return to the **Dashboard**.

   Now you will create the invoice for the sale of the special-order bird feeder for Amy's Bird Sanctuary.

5. Choose **Create→Customers→Invoice**.

6. Complete the invoice as indicated:

   - Customer: **Amy's Bird Sanctuary**
   - Terms: **Net 10**
   - Invoice Date: **09/16/2021**

7. Add the billable expense from the drawer on the right.

8. Type **75** in the Rate field.

9. Click to add a checkmark in the **Tax** field.

10. Confirm that *California* appears in the Select a Sales Tax Rate field.

    The invoice total should be $81.00.

11. Save and close the form.

Customer Returns and Credits

When customers return products or have been overbilled, you may need to issue a credit memo. The customer Credit Memo form is specifically for this purpose. QuickBooks Online will automatically apply the credit memo to open invoices, reducing the amount due.

DEVELOP YOUR SKILLS 7-12

In this exercise, you will create a credit memo for a Yard Gnome that Kate Whelan returned.

1. Choose **Create→Customers→Credit Memo**.

2. Choose **Kate Whelan** as the customer and enter **09/17/2021** for the credit memo date.

3. Choose **Yard Gnome 2 ft Tall** in the Product/Service field.

4. Type **1** in the Qty field, if necessary.

5. Choose **California** in the Select a Sales Tax Rate field, if necessary.

6. Save and close the credit memo.

    Doing so will add the Yard Gnome back into inventory and reduce the amount due from Kate.

Customer Refunds

Sometimes a customer has paid for a product and returns it (or has paid for a service and is unsatisfied with it), and you must give the customer a refund and issue a refund receipt.

DEVELOP YOUR SKILLS 7-13

Dukes Basketball Camp bought three bags of Weed and Feed but did not need all of them. In this exercise, you will sell a product on a sales receipt. Then you will accept a return and refund the customer.

1. Choose **Create→Customers→Sales Receipt**.

2. Choose **Dukes Basketball Camp** as the customer and enter **09/17/2021** as the sales receipt date.

3. Choose **Check** as the payment method and enter **1545** as the reference number.

4. Choose **Weed and Feed** in the Product/Service field and enter **3** in the Qty field.

5. Save and close the form.

Create a Refund Receipt

Peter Dukes came in on Saturday to return one bag of Weed and Feed and get a refund. Now you will create a refund receipt.

6. Choose **Create→Customers→Refund Receipt**.
7. Complete the fields as indicated:
   - Customer: **Dukes Basketball Camp**
   - Refund Receipt Date: **09/18/2021**
   - Payment Method: **Check**
   - Refund From: **Checking**
   - Product/Service: **Weed and Feed**
   - Qty: **1**
8. In the bottom tray, choose **Print or Preview→Print or Preview**.
9. Click **OK** in the Refund Successfully Issued window.
10. Print check number 72.
11. Return to the **Dashboard**.

Reports

QuickBooks Online has several reports to assist in maintaining accurate inventory quantities and values. The Physical Inventory Worksheet, for example, helps you compare what you actually have in stock with what QuickBooks Online shows as your quantity on hand.

 Reports→All tab→Sales and Customers→Physical Inventory Worksheet

 View the video "Inventory Reports" at: labyrinthelab.com/2017/video/QBO-V0702

DEVELOP YOUR SKILLS 7-14

In this exercise, you will view the various inventory management reports available in QuickBooks Online.

1. Choose **Reports** from the Navigation bar.
2. Click the **All** tab and then click **Sales and Customers**.
3. Choose **Inventory Valuation Summary**.
4. Select **All Dates** in the Report Period field and then click **Run Report**.

   This report provides your total inventory valuation plus the average cost of each product.

5. Return to the **Reports** center and then choose **Sales and Customers→Inventory Valuation Detail**.

6. Select **All Dates** in the Report Period field and then click **Run Report**.

This report gives you information about purchases, sales, and returns of inventory products.

▾ Yard Gnome 2 ft tall								
01/01/2021	Inventory Starting Value	START		0.00	14.25	0.00	0.00	0.00
09/09/2021	Bill		Tim Philip Masonry	5.00	14.25	71.25	5.00	71.25
09/10/2021	Vendor Credit		Tim Philip Masonry	-1.00	14.25	-14.25	4.00	57.00
09/15/2021	Invoice	1038	Kate Whelan	-3.00	14.25	-42.75	1.00	14.25
09/17/2021	Credit Memo	1040	Kate Whelan	1.00	14.25	14.25	2.00	28.50
Total for Yard Gnome 2 ft tall				**2.00**		**$28.50**	**2.00**	**$28.50**

7. Return to the **Dashboard**.

Tackle the Tasks

This is your opportunity to apply some of the skills learned in this chapter to accomplish additional tasks for Craig's Design and Landscaping Services. You will need to add new vendors, customers, and accounts as necessary.

Before You Begin: Close the current test drive window and then open a new test drive window.

Task	Use This Information
Set Up Inventory Products for 9/15/2021	• Large Metal Bird Bath; cost $15.95; selling price $54 • Ground Lights; cost $6.05; selling price $25
Set Up Non-Inventory Products for 9/15/2021	• Pest Control Pellets; cost $1.59; selling price $5 • Custom Glass Bird Bath; cost and selling price vary
Create Purchase Orders	• On 9/16/2021, purchased six Large Metal Bird Baths from Paul's Metal Works at 17 Monty Road, Bayshore, CA; delivered • On 9/17/2021, purchased 20 bags of Pest Control Pellets and 24 Ground Lights from Hicks Hardware; will be shipped via UPS; terms: 15 days • On 9/20/2021, purchased four Custom Glass Bird Baths, two green and two red/orange, from Tania's Nursery; $45.00 each on a special order for Kate Whelan; delivered to you; terms: 10 days
Receive the Products Purchased	• On 9/20/2021, received the products purchased from Paul's Metal Works on 9/16/2021; paid with MasterCard • On 9/20/2021, received the products purchased from Hicks Hardware on 9/17/2021; $6.00 delivery fee added • On 9/29/2021, received the products purchased from Tania's Nursery for Kate Whelan
Sell Products	• On 9/22/2021, sold four Large Metal Bird Baths and 10 Ground Lights to Amy's Bird Sanctuary; terms: net 10 days • On 9/22/2021, sold one Rock Fountain, one bag of Pest Control Pellets, and six Ground Lights to Diego Rodriquez; Diego paid with check number 8595 (Diego has a reseller's permit, so there is no sales tax) • On 9/30/2021, sold Kate Whelan the special-order Bird Baths at $115.00 each; add California sales tax; terms: net 10 days
Adjust Inventory	On 9/25/2021, one of the Large Metal Bird Baths is destroyed by a runaway forklift. Adjust the inventory.
Prepare an Inventory Valuation Detail Report	Prepare report for all dates; balance of Large Metal Bird Baths is $15.95 Export report to Excel; save it in your Chapter 07 folder as: CH07 Inventory Valuation Detail.

Self-Assessment

Check your knowledge of this chapter's key concepts and skills using the Self-Assessment quiz here or in your eLab course.

1. You must have a product or service to create a purchase order.   *True   False*

2. When you purchase inventory, the Purchases account increases.   *True   False*

3. Inventory tracking in QuickBooks Online allows you to define the costing method.   *True   False*

4. A non-inventory product is for supplies only.   *True   False*

5. QuickBooks Online allows for partial shipment against a purchase order.   *True   False*

6. An Inventory Valuation Summary report provides only quantities on hand.   *True   False*

7. Where do you enable the inventory tracking feature in QuickBooks Online?
   A. Products and Services
   B. Reports
   C. Account and Settings
   D. Inventory tracking is always on.

8. What does FIFO mean?
   A. Final Inventory for Others
   B. First in, first out
   C. All the inventory costs are averaged.
   D. None of these options

9. When a customer returns a product for a refund, you should use the _____ form.
   A. Check
   B. Refund Receipt
   C. Credit Memo
   D. Invoice

10. The difference between what you pay for an inventory product and the amount you sell it for is:
    A. Income
    B. Cash made
    C. Cost of goods sold
    D. Purchased amount

11. How can you order a custom product for a specific customer?
    A. Call the vendor to order the product, and handwrite a reminder to yourself about which customer it is for.
    B. Create a non-inventory product.
    C. Create a purchase order with the specific customer; mark it as billable.
    D. Create a non-inventory product and a purchase order with the specific number.

(cont'd.)

12. How would you receive the products and the bill for products on a purchase order?
   A. Choose Expense, select the vendor, add the purchase order, and pay.
   B. Enter a bill.
   C. Enter a bill, select the vendor, add the purchase order, and save for payment later.
   D. None of these options

13. You have received products in full for a purchase order, and the vendor has added a delivery charge. How do you record the charge?
   A. Create another bill for the delivery charge.
   B. Create a product/service item for the delivery charge and add it as an item detail.
   C. Add the delivery charge as an account in the upper portion of the bill.
   D. Refuse to pay for the additional charge.

14. Which report would you prepare to show all details of the inventory?
   A. Purchases by Product/Service Detail
   B. Purchases by Vendor Detail
   C. Physical Inventory Worksheet
   D. Inventory Valuation Detail

15. It's often necessary to make adjustments to inventory quantities. How would you make those adjustments?
   A. Enter a bill to increase quantities.
   B. Choose Create→Other→Inventory Qty Adjustment link.
   C. Edit the quantity from the Products and Services list.
   D. You can either edit the quantity in the Products and Services list or choose Create→Inventory Qty Adjustment.

16. Your company just started selling products, and you need to charge sales tax for products sold to your customers. What should you do?
   A. Choose Gear→Set Up Sales Tax.
   B. Select Taxes from the Navigation bar.
   C. Choose Create→Sales Tax Setup.
   D. QuickBooks Online does not have a sales tax feature.

ℐ Reinforce Your Skills

For these exercises, you will work with Puppy Luv Pampered Pooch, the company account created in your trial subscription to QuickBooks Online.

Sadie has returned from the conference with so many ideas. She is ready to freshen up the reception area and add some items to sell to clients for their pets.

REINFORCE YOUR SKILLS 7-1

Set Up Preferences for Inventory Products and Purchase Orders

In this exercise, you will set up the preferences for inventory products and purchase orders. Sadie has signed a contract to update the reception area by adding shelving and display cases. The work will begin September 7, 2021. Sadie has also given you a list of the products she plans to stock. A few will be for special order only.

Before You Begin: *Access your trial subscription to QuickBooks Online. Read any alerts or reminders that appear and close any unnecessary windows.*

1. Choose **Gear→Your Company→Account and Settings** and then click **Sales** from the menu.
2. Edit the Product and Services section to enable the **Track Inventory Quantity on Hand** option.
3. Save and then click **OK**.
4. Choose **Expenses** from the Account and Settings menu.
5. Edit the Purchase Orders section to enable the **Use Purchase Orders** option.
6. Save your preferences.

REINFORCE YOUR SKILLS 7-2

Set Up Sales Tax Preference

In this exercise, you will set up the sales tax preference for Sadie, so her clients are charged the correct amount of tax on their purchases. Throughout this course, the sales tax rate for Puppy Luv Pampered Pooch will be 9%. You will need to overwrite the sales tax calculated amount on the sales documents.

1. On the Navigation bar, choose **Taxes**.
2. Click the **Set Up Sales Tax** button.
3. Click **Looks Good** in the Is This Your Address window and then click **Next**.
4. Click **No** to indicate that you do not need to collect sales tax outside of California.

5. Complete the screen as indicated (use your current month and year):

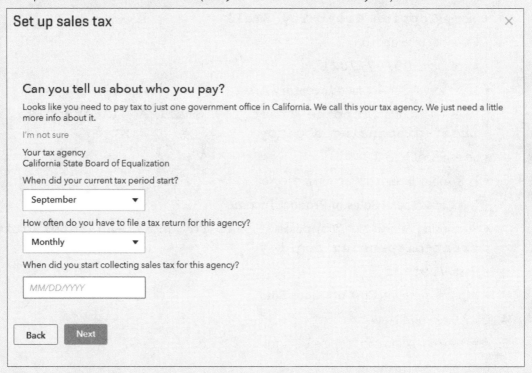

6. Click **Next** and then click **Got It**.

Your Sales tax is automatically set up to charge the current sales tax rate for your zip code. You will need to add the address for Puppy Luv Pampered Pooch to each sales document as the shipping address. You will also need to overwrite the sales tax calculated on each sales form.

REINFORCE YOUR SKILLS 7-3

Set Up Inventory Products

In this exercise, you will use a list Sadie provided to set up the first three inventory products to be purchased from Holly Paw Designs.

Puppy Luv Pampered Pooch
New Inventory Items List

Name	Description		Vendor	Cost	Sales Price
Toppiee Treat Toy	An interactive treat dispensing dog toy	Small	Holly Paw Designs	7.95	19.95
Toppiee Treat Toy	An interactive treat dispensing dog toy	Medium	Holly Paw Designs	9.95	22.95
Toppiee Treat Toy	An interactive treat dispensing dog toy	Large	Holly Paw Designs	10.95	25.95
Uber-Jive Ball	Built for fetch, has a wacky bounce.		Holly Paw Designs	9.95	22.95
Boomers Tug Toy	Built for tug of war or far flung fetch		Holly Paw Designs	9.95	22.95
Zip Flying Disc	Glow in the dark, tougher than a frisbee		Holly Paw Designs	10.95	25.95

Holly Paw Designs
PO BOX 8771
Billings, Montana 59102

1. Choose **Gear→Lists→Products and Services**.

2. Click the **New** button and then choose **Inventory**.

3. Complete the fields as follows:

- Name: **`Toppiee Treat Toy Small`**
- Quantity on Hand: **0**
- As of Date: **09/07/2021**
- Inventory Asset Account: **Inventory Asset**
- Sales Information: **`Toppiee Treat Toy Small-An interactive treat-dispensing dog toy`**
- Sales Price/Rate: **`19.95`**
- Is Taxable: Ensure this option is checked
- Income Account: **Sales of Product Income**
- Purchasing Information: **`Toppiee Treat Toy Small-An interactive treat-dispensing dog toy`**
- Cost: **`7.95`**
- Expense Account: **Cost of Goods Sold**

4. Click **Save and New**.

5. Add the remaining two Toppiee Treat toys.

6. Return to the **Dashboard**.

REINFORCE YOUR SKILLS 7-4

Prepare Purchase Order and Receive the Treat Toys

Sadie sent you a text message to create a purchase order on 9/7/2021 to Holly Paw Designs for fifteen of each size of the Toppiee Treat Toys. They will be shipped via UPS, and fees will be added to the bill. Terms are net 15 days. In this exercise, you will start by creating the purchase order for the treat toys. Then you will receive the products with a bill to be paid later.

1. Choose **Create→Vendors→Purchase Order**.

2. Add **`Holly Paw Designs`** as a new vendor.

3. Set the purchase order date to **09/07/2021** and enter **UPS** in the Ship Via field.

4. In line 1 under Item Details, select **Toppiee Treat Toy Small** as the product/service and **15** as the quantity.

5. Add the two remaining Toppiee Treat Toys to the purchase order.

   The total order should equal $432.75.

6. Save and close the form.

Receive Products

On Friday September 10, UPS delivers the toys on Purchase Order number 1001. The bill from Holly Paw Designs has an added $15 delivery fee. The bill number is 21-9114. Now you will receive the products into QuickBooks Online.

7. Choose **Create→Vendors→Bill**.

8. Fill in the top portion of the bill as indicated:
   - Vendor: **Holly Paw Designs**
   - Bill Date: **09/07/2021**
   - Bill No.: **21-9114**

9. Add **Purchase Order #1001**.

10. Under Account Details, enter **Delivery** in the Account.

    You will need to add this account.

11. Enter **Delivery** in the Description field and **$15** in the Amount field.

    The total bill should be $447.75.

12. Save and close the form.

REINFORCE YOUR SKILLS 7-5 QG

Manage a Non-Inventory Product for a Specific Client

Nancee Ruiz saw the kennel cages that Sadie uses to keep the dogs safe while waiting for their grooming. She has asked Sadie to order three for her own business. Sadie called the vendor and paid with her City Credit Union card. In this exercise, you will start by editing the preference to allow expenses and items to be tracked for a specific client. Then you will create the purchase and the sale of the product.

1. Choose **Gear→Your Company→Account and Settings** and then click **Expenses** in the menu.

2. Edit the Bills and Expenses section to match the boxed items shown:

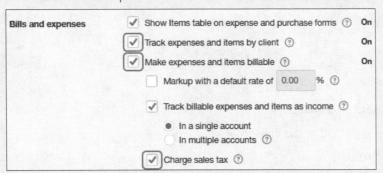

3. Save your preferences and then return to the **Dashboard**.

Record the Purchase

Now you will record the purchase made for the kennels with Sadie's credit card.

4. Choose **Create→Vendors→Expense**.

5. Complete the fields as indicated:
   - Payee: **Ace Groomer and Supply Company**
   - Account: **City Credit Union**
   - Payment Date: **09/10/2021**
   - Payment Method: **Credit Card**

6. In line 1 of the Item Details section, enter **Special Order** as the product/service.

7. Add this non-inventory product and then complete the Product/Service information as noted:

   - Description on Sales Forms: **Special Order:**
   - Description on Purchase Forms: **Special Order:**
   - Income Account: **Sales of Product Income**
   - Place a checkmark in the **Is Taxable** box

8. Save and close the changes.

9. Type **Awesome Folding Kennel Crate Medium** after the colon (:) in the Description field.

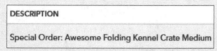

DESCRIPTION
Special Order: Awesome Folding Kennel Crate Medium

10. Type **3** in the Qty field and **45** in the Rate field.

11. Click to add checkmarks in the **Billable** and **Tax** columns.

12. Enter **Nancee Ruiz** in the Client field.

13. Save and close the record.

Create the Invoice

Now you will create the invoice for the sale of the kennel crates. You will need to add the Puppy Luv Pampered Pooch city and state to the shipping address. This is used to calculate the sales tax.

14. Choose **Create→Clients→Invoice**.

15. Use this information to complete the invoice:

    - Client: **Nancee Ruiz**
    - Billing Address: **Los Angeles CA 90051**
    - Invoice Date: **9/16/2021**
    - Add: **Billable Expense**
    - Rate: **120**

      Sales tax will be calculated at the actual current rate, so you will need to overwrite the amount.

    - Click in the **Sales Tax** field.
    - Click **Override this Amount**.
    - Type **9** in the Rate field.
    - Choose **Other** in the Reason field.
    - Click **Confirm Override**.

    The invoice total should be $392.40.

16. Save and close the invoice.

Prepare a Report

17. Prepare a **Purchases by Product/Service Detail** report for **9/01/2021** through **9/10/2021**.

18. Export the report to Excel, saving the file in your **Chapter 07** folder as:
`CH07 Purchases By Product.Service Detail`

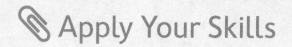 Apply Your Skills

---

Add Remaining Inventory Products

In this exercise, you will add the remaining inventory products for Sadie's business by importing an Excel file.

1. Choose **Gear→Tools→Import Data** and then click **Products and Services**.
2. Click **Browse**, navigate to your **Chapter 07** folder, select the **CH07 Inventory Import** file, and click **Next**.
3. Click **Next**.
4. Verify there are three records to import and then click **Import**.
5. Prepare and export a Product/Service List report, saving it in Excel to your **Chapter 07** folder as: **CH07 Product-Service List**
6. Return to the **Dashboard**.

APPLY YOUR SKILLS 7-2

Purchase Remaining Inventory Products

Sadie found products in stock from a different vendor. In this exercise, you will create a purchase order and receive the remaining inventory products. You may need to create the inventory products and terms as you create the purchase order.

1. Create a purchase order on 9/10/2021 to Ace Groomer and Supply Company for these items, shipped via UPS:
   - 10 Boomers Tug Toys
   - 20 Uber-Jive Balls
   - 10 Zip Flying Discs
2. Receive all products and a bill for PO number 1002 on 9/14/2021; terms are net 10 and $13 was added for delivery.

   The total should be $421.
3. Return to the **Dashboard**.

Sell Services and Products and Manage Returns

In this exercise, you will create sales receipts and/or invoices for dog grooming services and products. All customers will be charged California sales tax for the products. You will also manage customer returns. Remember to overwrite the sales tax to 9%.

1. Record these transactions:

   - 9/9/2021; Arlene Garrison brought her small dog, Joe, in for a Mini Pet Groom; bought one Small Toppiee Treat Toy; paid with check number 4544. Total $46.75 (the Sales Receipt should be number 1055).

   - Bonnie Zoe brought Missy in for a Full Groom, Small; bought three Small Toppiee Treat Toys; paid with check number 8977.

   - 9/10/2021; GreenWay Kennels brought in seven dogs for Bath and Brush, Medium; bought 14 Medium Toppiee Treat Toys; on account.

   - 9/16/2021; Alison Ball was walking by and noticed the colorful display of toys; purchased two Zip Flying Discs; paid with cash.

   - 9/16/2021; GreenWay Kennels brought in seven dogs for Bath and Brush, Medium; they wanted to return four of the Medium Toppiee Treat Toys, still in package, unused; on account. Invoice total $109.94.
     Hint: Type a -4 in the Qty field for the return.

   - 9/17/2021; Windemere Kennels brought in five dogs for Mini Pet Groom, Small; purchased five Uber-Jive Balls; on account.

2. Prepare an Inventory Valuation Detail report for all dates; export the report to Excel, saving the file in your **Chapter 07** folder as: **CH07 Inventory Valuation Detail**

Return a Purchase for Credit and Pay the Bill

In this exercise, you will return some of the products purchased for a credit and then apply the credit when paying.

2. On 9/20/2021, record a vendor credit for the return of 10 Large Toppiee Treat Toys.

3. On 9/22/2021, pay all the bills due on or before 9/22/2021; starting check number 10019.

4. Print the checks.

5. Create a Sales by Product/Service Summary for 9/01/2021 through 9/17/2021; export it to Excel, saving the file in your **Chapter 07** folder as: **CH07 Sales By Product-Service Summary**
   Notice the Gross Margin columns in this report. They display, in both dollars and percentage, the profit on each inventory product.

CHECK FIGURE *Your figures should match those shown here.*

ACCOUNT BALANCES	
Account	**Amount**
Los Angeles City Bank	$47,002.39
City Credit Union	$1,153.44

OTHER BALANCES	
Statement	**Amount**
Inventory Asset	$528.30
Accounts Receivable	$2,017.64
Accounts Payable	$421

8 | Working with Balance Sheet Accounts and Budgets

The balance sheet uses information from the assets, liabilities, and equity accounts in the Chart of Accounts to provide a snapshot of your business's financial position at a specific moment in time. Transactions in these accounts—as well as uncollectible debts, petty cash, and transfers of funds—must be recorded properly for the balance sheet to accurately reflect your company's financial position. Budgets also play an important part in business analysis. Once created, they allow you to measure how well the business performed compared to the plan or budget. In this chapter, you will set up and record balance sheet transactions. You will also set up a budget and compare it to actual income and expenses.

LEARNING OBJECTIVES

- Manage other current assets
- Prepare journal entries
- Create recurring entries
- Set up fixed-asset purchases
- Set up long-term liabilities
- Transfer funds between accounts
- Set up and manage petty cash
- Write off uncollectible receivables (bad debts)
- Set up budgets and view budget reports

Project: Craig's Design and Landscaping Services

Craig has been chatting with his insurance broker about the high cost of vehicle insurance. The broker has suggested that, if Craig could pay for insurance six months in advance instead of monthly, he could get a better rate. Craig has also decided to purchase two new trucks for the business. He plans to take a three-year loan on each one. Finally, Craig wants to take a look at the budget features available in QuickBooks Online so that he can get a better picture of how his business is doing and start making more informed decisions in the future.

Recording Other Current Assets

In accounting, assets refer to what the business owns. Other current assets refer to what the business plans to use within a one-year period; examples of other current assets include prepaid insurance, prepaid rent, and security deposits. Businesses usually record other current assets (for example, prepaid insurance) at the time of purchase. Then, for each period that a portion of the asset (for example, insurance) is used, another entry is made to decrease the asset and increase the expense. This process helps ensure that the balance sheet remains accurate.

BEHIND THE SCENES

These illustrations provide an example of journal entries made for a prepaid expense.

	Prepaid Insurance		Checking	
1/1/2021	5,000.00			5,000.00

On January 1, 2021, you write a check for $5,000 for the next six months of insurance (January through June).

	Prepaid Insurance		Checking		Insurance Expense
1/1/2021	5,000.00			5,000.00	
1/31/2021		833.33			833.33

On January 31, 2021, you will record a decrease in Prepaid Insurance and an increase in Insurance Expense for one-sixth of the prepayment.

	Prepaid Insurance		Insurance Expense	
1/1/2021	5,000.00			
1/31/2021		833.33	833.33	
2/28/2021		833.33	833.33	
3/31/2021		833.33	833.33	
4/30/2021		833.33	833.33	
5/31/2021		833.33	833.33	
6/30/2021		833.35	833.35	
Acount balance at 6/30/2021	0		5,000.00	

You will continue this process for each month through June, at which point Prepaid Insurance will be $0.00 and Insurance Expense will be $5,000.

DEVELOP YOUR SKILLS 8-1

On August 1, 2021, Craig wrote a check for $3,500 to the insurance broker for six months of auto insurance. He used check number 10071. In this exercise, you will set up a prepaid expense account to manage the prepaid asset.

Before You Begin: *Access the QuickBooks Online test drive at qbo.intuit.com/redir/testdrive and leave the test drive open for the entire chapter.*

> **Note!** Remember, the user interface for QuickBooks Online is updated frequently, so some of the names and features in course exercises may differ from what you see on your interface.

1. Choose **Gear→Your Company→Chart of Accounts** and then click the **New** button.
2. Select **Other Current Assets** as the Account Type and **Prepaid Expenses** as the Detail Type.

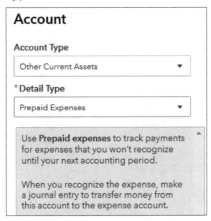

3. Type **Prepaid Insurance** in the Name field.
4. Click **Save and Close**.
5. Choose **Create→Vendors→Check**.
6. Complete the check as shown:

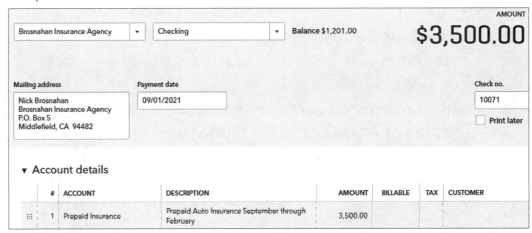

7. Save and close the form.

Journal Entries and Recurring Transactions

QuickBooks Online is a form-based accounting program, meaning it uses forms like checks, invoices, bills, and deposits to create a balanced transaction that is then recorded in the financial reports. QuickBooks Online does not have a form for adjustments; for example, allocations of prepaid expenses. In this case, you can use a journal entry form. A journal entry form requires you to know the specific accounts that will be increased and decreased with debits and credits.

If you have multiple months of entries to make, and they are the same each month, you can save a lot of time and reduce the potential for errors with a recurring journal entry.

The three recurring transaction types are:

- **Scheduled**—This type records the transaction you create according to a fixed schedule. It is useful for payments that have amounts that do not vary (for example, loans).

- **Reminder**—This type proposes you record transactions based on a schedule that you set. It is useful for monthly bills that have a varying amount (for example, utility bills).

- **Unscheduled**—This type is a template with incomplete data that is used when needed. It is useful for irregular transactions

Most transaction types can be made recurring, including those shown in this partial list.

DEVELOP YOUR SKILLS 8-2

In this exercise, you will create a journal entry to record the insurance expense for September and then make that journal entry recur for six months. You will start by adding an account for the auto insurance expense.

1. Choose **Create→Other→Journal Entry**.
2. Type **9/01/2021** in the Journal Date field and tap ⎯Tab⎯ twice.
   The journal number will stay consecutive if left alone.
3. In line 1 of the Account field, type **Auto Insurance** and tap ⎯Tab⎯.
4. Type **583.33** in the Debits field and then tap ⎯Tab⎯ twice.
5. Type **to expense one month of prepaid insurance** in the Description field and tap ⎯Tab⎯ twice.
6. In the Account field for line 2, type **Prepaid Insurance** and tap ⎯Tab⎯.
   QuickBooks Online should automatically populate the Credits and Description fields.
7. Confirm that **583.33** appears in the Credits field; if it doesn't appear, enter it.

8. Confirm that the description from line #1 also appears on line #2; if not, type it in.

Your completed journal entry should appear similar to this image. You can see that the Debits equal the Credits, which is a requirement. If the journal entry does not balance, you will not be able to save it.

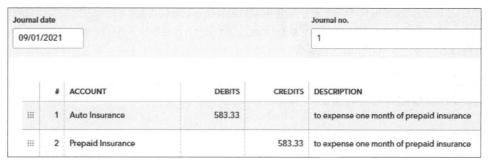

	#	ACCOUNT	DEBITS	CREDITS	DESCRIPTION
⠿	1	Auto Insurance	583.33		to expense one month of prepaid insurance
⠿	2	Prepaid Insurance		583.33	to expense one month of prepaid insurance

Make a Recurring Journal Entry

Now you will make this journal entry recur for the next six months.

9. Click **Make Recurring** in the tray at the bottom of the window.

10. Complete the fields as shown and then click **Save Template**.

This journal entry will be recorded automatically for the next six months.

View Recurring Transactions

Now you will view all of the recurring transactions.

11. Choose **Gear→Lists→Recurring Transactions**.

Two bills and this one journal entry will appear on your list. You can edit a transaction, delete it, or use it to create a new one.

12. Return to the **Dashboard**.

Fixed Assets and Long-Term Liabilities

Fixed assets are usually a company's tangible assets with a useful life of more than one year. Examples include buildings, office equipment, vehicles, and machinery. Long-term liabilities are frequently the loans for the fixed assets that have been purchased; for example, when you have a financing contract to repay over more than one year. Both are balance sheet accounts that reflect assets owned and liabilities owed.

DEVELOP YOUR SKILLS 8-3

Craig has decided it's time to purchase additional trucks for delivering products and moving equipment from worksite to worksite. He has found two 2022 Ford Super Duty trucks for a total of $45,000 each, with $1,000 down for each and the balance financed for three years.

In this exercise, you will start by creating the fixed asset and long-term liability accounts for the two new trucks. Then you will record the purchase and the liability for them. You may need to add vendors and accounts.

1. Choose **Gear→Your Company→Chart of Accounts** and then click the **New** button.
2. Complete the fields as indicated to create the fixed asset:
    - Account Type: **Fixed Assets**
    - Detail Type: **Vehicles**
    - Name: `2022 Ford Super Duty`
    - Description: `2 Ford Super Duty Trucks`
3. Click **Save and New**.
4. Complete the fields as indicated to create the long-term liability:
    - Account Type: **Long Term Liabilities**
    - Detail Type: **Other Long Term Liabilities**
    - Name: `Ford Trucks Loan`
5. Click **Save and Close**.

Record the Purchase

6. Choose **Create→Vendors→Check**.
7. Complete the fields as indicated:
    - Payee: `Holiday Ford Finance Company`
    - Account: **Checking**
    - Date: `9/01/21`
    - Check No: `10072`
    - Account, line 1: **2022 Ford Super Duty**
    - Description, line 1: `2 2022 Ford Super Duty Trucks`
    - Amount: `90000.00`
    - Account, line 2: **Ford Trucks Loan**

- Description, line 2: `2 2022 Ford Super Duty Trucks`
- Amount: `-88000.00`

This action will record the down payment check for $2,000 as well as the increases to the asset and liability accounts.

8. Save and close the form.

Transferring Funds Between Accounts

Businesses often transfer funds from one asset account to another asset or liability account. For example, they may transfer monies from a checking account to a savings account, or they may transfer monies from a checking account to pay a credit card or loan installment. QuickBooks Online makes it simple to record such transactions by providing a specific form for transfers. You can also make recurring transfers if necessary.

DEVELOP YOUR SKILLS 8-4

Craig has authorized Holiday Ford Finance Company to automatically withdraw the monthly payment on the truck loan for the next three years. He has asked you to set up the accounting in QuickBooks Online.

In this exercise, you will create the transfer to record the monthly payment to Holiday Ford Finance Company. Then you will make it recurring.

1. Choose **Create→Other→Transfer**.

2. Choose **Checking** in the Transfer Funds From field and tap ⌷Tab⌷.
3. Choose **Ford Trucks Loan** in the Transfer Funds To field and tap ⌷Tab⌷.
4. Type **2445** in the Transfer Amount field and tap ⌷Tab⌷.
5. Type **10/01/2021** in the Date field and tap ⌷Tab⌷.
6. Type **Monthly Payment** in the Memo field.
7. Click **Make Recurring** at the bottom of the window.

8. Complete the fields as follows:

Recurring Transfer

Template name		Type			
Truck Loan Payment		Scheduled ▾	Create 3	days in advance	

Interval							Start date		End		
Monthly ▾	on	day ▾	1st ▾	of every 1	month(s)		10/01/2021		After ▾		36

9. Click **Save Template**.

Petty Cash

Many businesses keep small amounts of cash available to make change or to pay for small and last-minute expenses. This is called petty cash or cash on hand. Petty cash is funded by withdrawing cash from a bank account, establishing a petty cash account, and then replenishing it as needed. In QuickBooks Online, you set up a bank account in your Chart of Accounts to track usage and replenishment of funds.

BEHIND THE SCENES

These illustrations provide an overview of what happens behind the scenes.

Petty Cash		Checking Account	
200.00			200.00

When you establish the petty cash account by withdrawing monies from a checking account, the debit to Petty Cash increases and the credit to Checking Account decreases.

Petty Cash		Supplies	
200.00			
	21.00	21.00	

As you spend petty cash, the debit to supplies, postage, or other miscellaneous expenses increases and the credit to Petty Cash decreases.

DEVELOP YOUR SKILLS 8-5

Craig is looking at opportunities to have a small cash box available for C.O.D. deliveries, postage, and occasional reimbursement of office or field expenses. You have decided a small locking box in the office can hold the cash and receipts.

In this exercise, you will establish a petty cash account (cash on hand) and reimburse an employee for a permit that he paid for.

1. Choose **Create→Vendors→Check**.
2. Type **Cashier** in the Choose a Payee field (add the vendor) and tap [Tab] three times.

3. Type **09/06/2021** in the Payment Date field and tap [Tab].

4. Type **10073** in the Check No. field (unless it already appears) and tap [Tab] twice.

5. Type **Petty Cash** in the line 1 Account field (you will need to add the bank account) and tap [Tab].

6. Type **to establish petty cash** in the Description field and tap [Tab].

7. Type **150** in the Amount field and tap [Tab].

8. Save and close the form.

Reimburse for Expenses

An employee paid out of his own pocket for a permit for one of the landscaping jobs. He brought you the receipt to get reimbursed. You gave him the monies from the petty cash box and placed the receipt in the box. Now, you will record the transaction.

9. Choose **Create→Vendors→Expense**.

   Expense forms do not require a payee name. This allows you to keep your Vendors list free of one-time vendors that you don't need to keep a record of. Because you don't want to add Craig's employee as a vendor, you will not add a payee name to this form.

10. Type **Petty Cash** in the Choose an Account field and tap [Tab].

11. Type **9/8/2021** in the Payment Date field and tap [Tab] three times.

12. Type **Permits** in the line 1 Account field and tap [Tab].

13. Type **reimbursement for permits on Smith job site** in the Description field and tap [Tab].

14. Type **26** in the Amount field and tap [Tab].

15. Save and close the form.

Handling Uncollectible Receivables/Bad Debts

An uncollectible account receivable refers to a sale made on account that you do not expect to collect payment for. An account becomes uncollectible for many reasons: a bankruptcy, an inability to locate a customer, a product or service dispute, and so on. You should not void or delete an invoice for a bad debt because you need to maintain a record of the sale in the proper accounting period. Instead, you should create a product or service and an expense account in your Chart of Accounts and then record a credit memo.

BEHIND THE SCENES

When you record a credit memo for uncollectible receivables, the asset amount in Accounts Receivable decreases, and the Bad Debt Expense in the current period increases.

Bad Debt Expense		Accounts Receivable
75.00		75.00

DEVELOP YOUR SKILLS 8-6

Craig has notified you that Kookies by Kathy has gone out of business and will not be paying the $75 due from Invoice number 1016.

In this exercise, you will start by setting up the service/product and the account for the bad debt.

1. Choose **Gear→Your Company→Chart of Accounts**.
2. Click the **New** button and then complete the Account fields as indicated:
   - Account Type: **Expenses**
   - Detail Type: **Bad Debts**
   - Name: **Bad Debts**
3. Click **Save and Close**.
4. Choose **Gear→Lists→Products and Services**.
5. Choose **New→Service** and then complete the form:
   - Name: **Bad Debt**
   - Description on Sales Forms: **Write off uncollectible:**
   - Sales Price/Rate: **0**
   - Income Account: **Bad Debts**
   - Is Taxable: **Uncheck**
6. Click **Save and Close**.

Create a Credit Memo

Now you will create a credit memo for the uncollectible invoice amount.

7. Choose **Create→Customers→Credit Memo**.
8. Complete the fields as follows:
   - Customer: **Kookies by Kathy**
   - Credit Memo Date: **9/10/21**
   - Product/Service: **Bad Debt**
   - Description (add after existing text): **Invoice number 1016**
   - Amount: **75**
9. Save and close the form.

   QuickBooks Online automatically applies this credit memo to the open invoice.

Creating and Reviewing Budgets

Many businesses want to budget for the coming months or year in order to predict future expenses and income and measure performance against the prediction. QuickBooks Online allows you to create a budget by account and month—and, if needed, by customer—for all your profit and loss accounts. You can create a new budget based on amounts from a previous year, or you can start from scratch. Once you have created a budget, you can view various budget reports to see whether your business is on track.

The Budgeting feature in QuickBooks Online is under the Tools menu.

Tools
Import Data
Export Data
Reconcile
Budgeting
Audit Log
Order Checks ↗

 Gear→Tools→Budgeting

DEVELOP YOUR SKILLS 8-7

Craig gave you his predictions for the last quarter of the year. He has asked you to create a budget for this period so he can track actual income and expenses against his forecast. In this exercise, you will create a budget from scratch for October through December of 2021.

1. Choose **Gear→Tools→Budgeting**.
2. Click **Add Budget**.

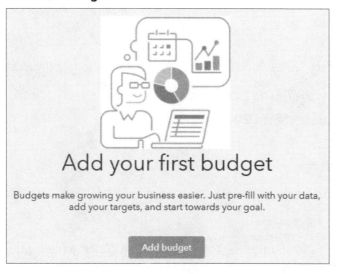

3. Type **4th Qtr 2021** in the Name field.

4. Choose **FY2021 (Jan 2021-Dec 2021)** in the Fiscal Year field.

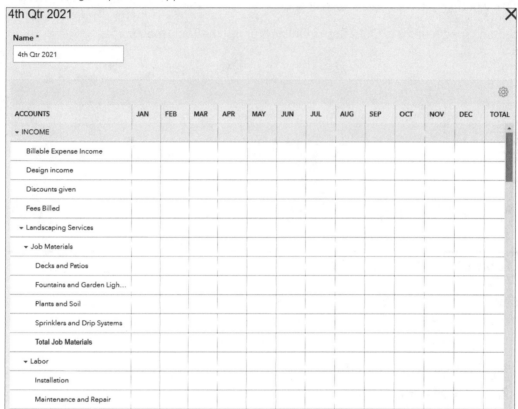

5. Click **Next**.

The New Budget input form appears.

Create a Budget

Now you will enter the amounts for the selected account in the fields at the bottom of the window.

6. Click any of the month fields in the Design Income row to activate that row.

7. Type **5000** in the Oct and Nov fields and **2000** in the Dec field.

OCT	NOV	DEC
5,000.00	5,000.00	2,000.00

Note! Don't worry if you make a mistake. Just select the account and click the Clear (X) button on the right end of the row and then re-enter the correct amount. Click Save & Next and move forward. Or, you can select the account and type over the values.

8. Following the same process you used for Design Income, enter the amounts shown for the indicated accounts.

Line Item	October	November	December
Cost of Goods Sold	1500	1500	700
Advertising	100	150	150
Automobile	450	400	400
Purchases	500	400	250

If you were performing these steps for a real business, you would continue until the budget were completed. In this demonstration, you can consider the budget finished.

9. Click **Save and Close**.

Review Budget Reports

Now that you have entered the budget, you will review the resulting reports with Craig to be sure this is the information he is looking for.

10. Open the **Reports** center; click the **All** tab, and then choose **Business Overview→ Budget Overview**.

    Hint: You may need to scroll down to find Budget Overview.

11. Verify that the report period is 01/01/2021 to 12/31/2021.

12. Verify that the Budget field shows **4th Qtr 2021 – FY21 P&L**.

    This report displays only the budget. It's a good place to verify the data entry and to remind the business owner of the projection.

13. Click the **< Back to Report List** link.

14. Choose **Business Overview→Budget vs. Actuals**.

15. Set the From Date to **10/01/2021** and then click **Run Report**.

    This report displays the actual income or expense amount and the predicted budget amount, as well as the over or under amount and percentage. It's a great tool for measuring performance.

16. Return to the **Dashboard**.

Tackle the Tasks

This is your opportunity to apply some of the skills learned in this chapter to accomplish additional tasks for Craig's Design and Landscaping Services. To refresh your memory, refer to the concepts and Develop Your Skills exercises as needed. You will need to add new vendors, customers, and accounts as necessary.

Before You Begin: Close the current test drive window and then open a new test drive window.

Task	Use This Information
Set Up an Account for Prepaid Rent and Create the Payment	Craig paid $900 in advance for six months' rent on a storage unit for some equipment; 10/01/2021; check number 10075 to Downtown Storage
Record the Prepaid Rent Expense and Make It Recurring	One-sixth (1/6) of the prepaid rent should be transferred to the Rent expense on 10/31/2021; recurring payment; six months in total
Create a New Fixed Asset and a New Long-Term Liability Account	Craig has just purchased a small Bobcat S150 for $22,000. He made a $5,000 down payment and will finance the rest.
Record the Purchase	Craig wrote check number 10076 on 10/3/2021 to WF Finance for $5,000.
Transfer the Funds for the Payment of the Bobcat Loan and Make the Payment Recurring for 36 Months	The payment on the Bobcat loan will be automatically deducted from Craig's bank account on the 25th of every month for 36 months, beginning November 2021. Payment amount is $473.
Print a Recurring Transaction List in PDF Format	Craig would like to review the recurring transactions list. He may want to add more transactions to streamline the data entry process. Print the list in PDF format; save it as Recurring Template List.
Set Up a Petty Cash Account **Fund Petty Cash** **Use Petty Cash to Reimburse an Employee**	Craig requested a petty cash fund of $100 for making change and paying for small purchases. Check number 10077 to the cashier for $100; on 10/1/2021 Fuel purchased with personal funds for business-related errands; $24.25
Create a Budget for Income Only	Craig just handed you his sales projections for the fourth quarter of 2021: • Design Income: Oct: 4,500, Nov: 4,500, Dec: 2,500 • Landscaping Services: Oct: 7,000, Nov: 7,000, Dec: 5,000 • Pest Control Services: Oct: 7,000, Nov: 2,000, Dec: 1,500
Create a Budget Overview Report	Use the income budget just prepared; fourth quarter only; export to Excel; save the file in your Chapter 08 folder as: Budget Overview

Self-Assessment

Check your knowledge of this chapter's key concepts and skills using the Self-Assessment quiz here or in your eLab course.

1. You must use a vendor name to create an expense.   *True   False*

2. When a previous sale on account is uncollectible, the best way to remove the amount from your balance sheet is to delete the invoice.   *True   False*

3. You have paid for three months of storage on the first month. How should you record the payment?
   A. Rent expense
   B. Prepaid rent
   C. Asset
   D. Credit card

4. Which type of accounts might you find in the Other Current Assets category of the Chart of Accounts?
   A. Expenses
   B. Credit cards
   C. Equipment
   D. Security deposits and prepaid expenses

5. What is the purpose of a journal entry?
   A. To streamline form creation
   B. To record transactions that don't have a specific form
   C. You cannot use journal entries in QuickBooks Online.
   D. To record all the money spent

6. You have signed a two-year lease on an office rental at $300/month to be electronically deducted from your bank account. What is the most efficient way to record the automatic withdrawal each month?
   A. Put a note on your computer to remind you to record the rent expense each month.
   B. Wait for the bill and then record the expense each month.
   C. Create a recurring expense for the next 24 months.
   D. None of these is correct.

7. Which type of account would you use for the purchase of an expensive piece of equipment that has a useful life of more than one year?
   A. Equipment expense
   B. Asset
   C. Fixed asset
   D. Liability

(cont'd.)

8. You want to view all the recurring transactions. Where would you find them?
   A. Reports→Recurring Reports
   B. Gear→Account and Settings
   C. Transactions→Recurring Transactions
   D. Gear→Recurring Transactions

9. What is a petty cash account?
   A. Money the owner takes out of his pocket to pay for purchases
   B. Petty or small purchases
   C. An expense account
   D. A bank account that is set up to provide on-hand cash

10. When creating a budget in QuickBooks Online, you can:
    A. use actual amounts from previous years
    B. use previous budget amounts
    C. start from scratch
    D. All of these are correct.

11. If you make a mistake when creating a budget in QuickBooks Online, you can:
    A. start over
    B. select the account, click Clear, and then re-enter the correct amounts
    C. select the account and overwrite the amounts
    D. use the Clear button to overwrite the amounts

12. You want to see the results of the budget to confirm the data is correct. Which report should you select?
    A. Profit and Loss Statement
    B. Budget Overview
    C. Company Snapshot
    D. Budget Summary

13. You want to compare your actual income and expenses to the predicted amounts. Which report should you select?
    A. Budget vs. Actual
    B. Budget Summary
    C. Company Snapshot
    D. Budget Overview

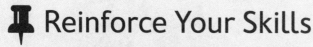 Reinforce Your Skills

For these exercises, you will record the prepaid storage rent, record payment of the remodel (a fixed asset), set up a petty cash account, and set up a budget.

The contractor has completed the remodel of the Puppy Luv Pampered Pooch reception area to accommodate displays of the merchandise Sadie plans to sell and allow for an additional grooming room in the new year. Sadie has rented a storage container for three months to store the merchandise and new grooming equipment while she waits to install the shelving and display posters.

REINFORCE YOUR SKILLS 8-1

Record a Prepayment

Sadie left a rental agreement on your desk. It is for the storage container for three months. She used check number 10021 to pay $225 to Torrez Lock and Stor. In this exercise, you will record the payment for the storage container. (Add a vendor and/or account as needed.)

Before You Begin: *Access your trial subscription to QuickBooks Online. Read any alerts or reminders that appear and close any unnecessary windows.*

1. Choose **Create→Vendors→Check**.
2. Complete the fields as follows:
   - Payee: **Torrez Lock and Stor**
   - Account: **Los Angeles City Bank**
   - Date: **9/22/2021**
   - Check No.: **10021**
   - Account: **Prepaid Storage (Other Current Asset)**
   - Description: **Three months Oct – Dec storage rent**
   - Amount: **225**
3. Save and close the form.

REINFORCE YOUR SKILLS 8-2

Record a Fixed Asset Purchase

Sadie left you the contract with Shilo Construction for the remodel that began on 9/07/2021, along with check number 10022, dated 9/22/2021. In this exercise, you will record the payment for the fixed asset purchase. (Add a vendor and account as needed.)

1. Choose **Create→Vendors→Check**.
2. Complete the fields as follows:
   - Payee: **Shilo Construction**
   - Account: **Los Angeles City Bank**
   - Date: **9/22/21**
   - Check No.: **10022**
   - Account: **Remodel (Fixed Asset-Leasehold Improvement)**

- Description: **Remodel of reception area**
- Amount: **$5,000**

3. Save and close the form.

Set Up a Petty Cash Account

Sadie would like you to set up a petty cash fund of $50 to make change and pay for small purchases.

In this exercise, you will establish a petty cash account for Puppy Luv Pampered Pooch. (Add a vendor and account as necessary.)

1. Choose **Create→Vendors→Check**.
2. Complete the fields as follows:
   - Payee: **Cashier**
   - Date: **9/23/21**
   - Check No: **10023**
   - Account: **Petty Cash**
   - Description: **to establish petty cash**
   - Amount: **50**
3. Save and close the form.

Set Up a Budget

Sadie would like to set up a budget in QuickBooks Online for the next three months of the year. She has a budget draft in Excel and has asked you to get the budget set up. She will email you the figures next week. In this exercise, you will complete the budget setup for the year 2021.

1. Choose **Gear→Tools→Budgeting**.
2. Read the **Creating a Budget** pop-up note and click **Add Budget**.
3. Type **4th Quarter Budget** in the Name field.
4. Select **FY2021 (Jan 2021–Dec 2021)** in the Fiscal Year field.
5. Select **Monthly** in the Interval field.
6. Select **No** in the Pre-Fill Data? field.
7. Select **Don't Subdivide** in the Subdivide By field.
8. Click **Next** and then click **Save**.

   You may need to refresh your screen to view the budget setup.

9. Return to the **Dashboard**.

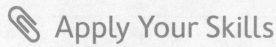

Apply Your Skills

The Apply Your Skills exercises give you a chance to figure out things on your own. You will apply critical thinking skills to prepare the remaining sales receipts and the bank deposit for the grand opening of Puppy Luv Pampered Pooch.

Sadie has left on your desk notes about items she needs recorded in QuickBooks.

- Prepaid salon rent; expense September's rent, and set up for remaining five months. (Paid with check number 10005 on 7/30/2021.)

- Prepaid storage rent. Set up the three months' expense; October through December.

- Los Angeles City Bank will begin to automatically deduct for the loan payments on 9/25/2021; please record $209 for September and set up the next 22 months.

- You have the budget figures; enter them into the budget and create a report.

APPLY YOUR SKILLS 8-1

Create a Journal Entry and Recurring Transaction

In this exercise, you will create the journal entry to expense the prepaid rent on Sadie's salon and make it recurring for six months. You will also create a recurring transaction for prepaid storage.

1. Record the September expense by creating a journal entry for one-sixth of the prepaid salon rent, which was $3,300 paid in July 2021.

2. Create a recurring expense journal entry for $550 for the last day of each month for October 2021 through February 2022.

3. Create a recurring expense journal entry for one-third of the prepaid storage, which was paid on September 22, 2021. Make it for the last day of each month for the following three months.

APPLY YOUR SKILLS 8-2

Set Up to Record the Automatic Transfer of Funds

In this exercise, you will record the automatic payment of the loan payable for September. (You should have a $5,000 loan payable from 8/7/2021.)

1. Record the first transfer on 9/25/2021 for $209.00.

2. Create the recurring transfer for the following twenty-two months.

3. Create a **Recurring Template List**.

4. Print the list as a PDF, saving it to your **Chapter 08** folder as: **CH08 Recurring Template List**

Enter Budget Values

In this exercise, you will populate Sadie's budget and create a budget report.

1. Open **CH08 Budget Worksheet.xlsx** from your **Chapter 08** folder.

2. Enter the values from Sadie's worksheet into the budget in QuickBooks Online.

3. Create a **Budget Overview** report for the 4th quarter of 2021 and export it to Excel, saving it in your **Chapter 08** folder as: **CH08 Budget Overview 2021**

QUICKBOOKS ONLINE

9 Customizing, Fine-Tuning, and Extending Capabilities

As you become familiar with basic features in QuickBooks Online, you may want to fine-tune and expand its capabilities to meet the unique needs of your business. In this chapter, you will create custom reports and save them for future use. You will find out how to customize sales forms to save data entry time and use keyboard shortcuts to streamline navigation. You will also control who sees confidential information. Finally, you will learn about applications that you can use to extend your capabilities with QuickBooks Online.

LEARNING OBJECTIVES

▸ Customize reports
▸ Save and send customized reports
▸ Add custom fields to sales forms
▸ Enable Privacy mode
▸ Set user permissions
▸ Use keyboard shortcuts
▸ Search for QuickBooks apps
▸ Access QuickBooks Labs

📂 Project: Craig's Design and Landscaping Services

Craig wants to use more of the reports in QuickBooks Online. He would like you to create some custom reports and keep them for the future, not just for one-time viewing. Craig is also concerned about the security and privacy of the data that appears in QuickBooks Online. He does not want anyone walking behind you to be able to view bank balances or other financial information. In addition, he wants to control which employees can access, edit, or otherwise interact with the data. Finally, Craig is curious about how he can extend the capabilities of QuickBooks Online and has suggested learning more about the QuickBooks App center and QuickBooks Labs.

Customizing Reports

When accounting has been completed on the forms prepared during the business day, the information on those forms can be used to create reports. QuickBooks Online has nine categories of predefined reports that you can customize to meet your unique business needs. Customizing saves time and makes month-end or weekly reports consistent.

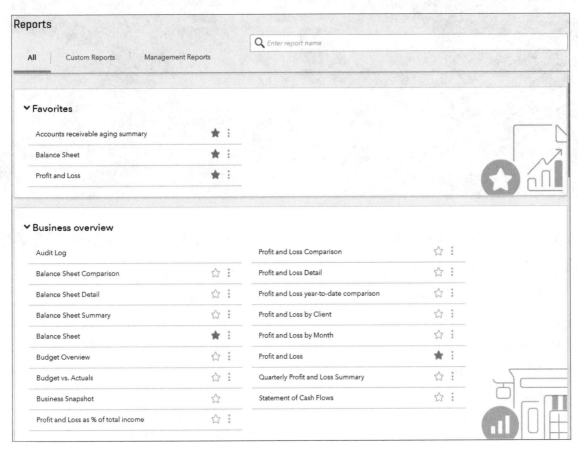

In this exercise, you will customize and save a report so you can use it again without having to complete the same tasks.

Before You Begin: *Access the QuickBooks Online test drive at qbo.intuit.com/redir/testdrive and leave the test drive open for the entire chapter.*

1. Open the **Reports** center and click the **All** tab.
2. Choose **Business Overview→Profit and Loss**.
3. Complete the fields as shown:

4. Click **Run Report**.

   This report shows what your income and expenses were for the period selected, on an accrual basis. Your net income should be $1,642.46.

Customize the Report

At the top of the report header, you'll see a row of icons. Now, you will use these icons to collapse and sort the list, add a note, and edit the header.

5. Click **Collapse** at the top of the report to collapse all sub-accounts into the account.

   The collapsed version has the same information but in summary format.

6. Choose **Sort→Total in Ascending Order**.

   Now all the sections of the statement are in ascending order.

7. Click **Add Notes**.

8. In the notes section, type: **This is a preliminary report.**

   You will now see a footnote at the bottom of the report.

9. Click **Edit Header**.

10. Type **Income Statement** over the words *Profit and Loss* to change the name of the report.

Craig's Design and Landscaping Services

INCOME STATEMENT

All Dates

Notice the familiar icons above the heading that allow to email, print, and export to Excel or PDF.

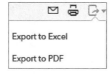

Export to Excel

Export to PDF

11. At the top of the window, choose **Cash** as the Accounting Method and then click **Run Report**.

   This version of the report shows your income and expenses as the monies were received and spent in the period. It shows that Craig has a loss of $1,904.12.

Save the Report for Future Use

Craig has asked you to save this report as it is for future use. Doing so will save steps the next time you use the report.

12. Click the **Save Customization** button.

13. Change the report name to: **Summary Income Statement/Cash Basis**

14. Click **Save**.

   The report is now saved in the My Custom Reports folder.

Sending Reports

You can schedule customized reports to be emailed automatically to yourself, your boss, shareholders, accountants, or others on a specific day of each period. Doing so helps you stay organized, saves steps, and ensures that information gets to the right people in a timely manner.

DEVELOP YOUR SKILLS 9-2

In this exercise, you will schedule the report you just customized to be emailed automatically to Craig each month.

1. Go to the **Reports** center and click the **Custom Reports** link.

2. On the Summary Income Statement/Cash Basis line, click the **Edit** link.

3. Turn the Set Email Schedule button to **On** and then set the fields as follows:

   • Repeats: **Monthly**

   • Every: **1**

   • On: **Day, 5th**

   • End: **None**

4. Enter your email address.

5. Type the subject line as follows: **Monthly Reports**

6. Type this message: **Attached are the monthly reports.**

7. Save and close the form and then return to the **Dashboard**.

Adding a Custom Field to Sales Forms

Businesses often want to add special identifying information to sales forms. On an invoice, for example, this information could be the name of the person who made the sale, the crew that completed the work, or the order number. QuickBooks Online allows you to create up to three custom fields on each type of sales form (i.e., invoice, sales receipt, or estimate).

DEVELOP YOUR SKILLS 9-3

Craig would like to know who has made the sale when a customer buys something in the store. He has asked you to add a field for the salesperson's ID to each invoice. Currently only the crew number is listed.

In this exercise, you will customize the current default invoice.

1. Choose **Create→Customers→Invoice**.
2. Click the **Gear** 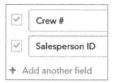 button at the top right to open the customization screen.

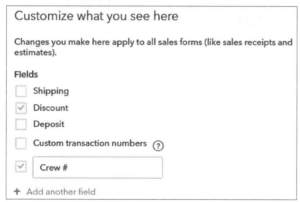

3. Click the **Add Another Field** link and type: `Salesperson ID`

   To remove a custom field, uncheck the field and then click Save. For this exercise, leave the Crew # field as is.

4. Click the **Close** button at the top-right corner of the drawer.

   The new field now appears on the form.

Crew #	Salesperson ID

5. Return to the **Dashboard**.

Protecting Confidential Information

It is a good practice to limit the number of people who can view and manipulate the data you enter in QuickBooks Online. The most effective way to do so is by setting user permissions; however, you can also use Privacy mode to quickly hide financial information on the Dashboard.

Enabling Privacy Mode on the Dashboard

When you are on the Dashboard of QuickBooks Online, bank and credit card balances, open accounts receivable and payable, and other confidential details are displayed. If people are behind you in the office or at a public location, all that information is visible to them. You can use Privacy mode to easily hide this data. Keep in mind that this feature currently conceals data only on the Dashboard, so even if you enable it, financial data will still appear on other pages.

DEVELOP YOUR SKILLS 9-4

In this exercise, you will enable Privacy mode.

1. On the Dashboard, click the Privacy setting to **On**.

All the financial information disappears from the Dashboard.

2. Change the Privacy setting back to **Off**.

Setting User Permissions

QuickBooks Online allow you to set up different users with different levels of access:

- Regular users with narrowly defined access

- Company administration users with all rights

- Reports-only users

- Time-tracking users

- Your accountant

Setting up each person as a specific type of user allows you to review that person's activity in the Audit Log and limit access to portions of QuickBooks Online.

DEVELOP YOUR SKILLS 9-5

Craig would like you to set up the sales manager as a user of sales data only. In this exercise, you will set up Don Martinez as a Regular user with restrictions.

Note! At the time of this writing, the Manage Users feature is intermittently available. If the Manage Users link is not present or active in step 1, just read through this exercise to get a sense of how the feature works. And remember that QuickBooks Online is updated constantly, so the feature may become active at any time. Try again later.

1. Choose **Gear→Your Company→Manage Users→New**.

   A Mini Interview box appears. It describes various types of users and their permission levels.

2. Select **Regular or Custom User** and click **Next**.

3. Select **Limited, Customers and Sales** and click **Next**.

4. Complete the fields as indicated:

   • User Management: **No**

   • Company Information: **View Only**

   • Subscription & Billing: **No**

   • Click **Next**

5. Enter your email address, confirm your address, and then click **Next**.

   If you click Finish, you will get an error message because you are in a sample file.

6. Click **Cancel**.

Keyboard Shortcuts

QuickBooks Online has many keyboard shortcuts to speed up navigation. When you press
$\boxed{\text{Ctrl}}$+$\boxed{\text{Alt}}$+$\boxed{?}$ for Windows or $\boxed{\text{Command}}$+$\boxed{\text{Option}}$+$\boxed{?}$ for Mac, a pop-up window appears
with your Company ID and a list of keyboard shortcuts. Once you get accustomed to using the
shortcuts, you will notice how quickly you can get around in QuickBooks Online.

Your Company ID is 1231 4584 2839 957 H23

Keyboard Shortcuts

To take advantage of shortcuts, simultaneously press
[ctrl] and **[alt or option]** and one **[key from the list below]**

REGULAR PAGES - HOMEPAGE, CUSTOMERS, AND SO ON		TRANSACTION PAGES - INVOICE, EXPENSE, AND SO ON	
SHORTCUT KEY	ACTION	SHORTCUT KEY	ACTION
i	Invoice	x	Exit transaction view
w	Check	c	Cancel out
e	Estimate	s	Save and New
x	Expense	d	Save and Close
r	Receive Payment	m	Save and Send
c	Customers	p	Print
v	Vendors		
a	Chart of Accounts		
l	Lists		
h	Help		
f	Search Transactions		
? or /	This dialog		

Extending Capabilities with Apps

QuickBooks Online is accounting software. It can't do everything. One of the distinctive features of QuickBooks Online's being cloud- or web-based, however, is the robust system of third-party application plug-ins that extend QuickBooks Online capabilities and automatically sync data with QuickBooks Online. These plug-ins are called apps.

More than 300 apps are available to provide users with tools to manage their businesses and integrate with QuickBooks Online for financial reporting. By searching for or typing in a category, you can view the current apps for that category and even read reviews. For example, you can find apps for inventory management, customer relationship management (CRM), merchant processing, and billing. A mobile app for your smart phone and mobile devices allows you to create sales receipts and take credit card payments on the spot. You can also snap a picture of a receipt and upload it directly to QuickBooks Online.

Also be sure to explore the QuickBooks apps for Windows and Mac. They let you run QuickBooks Online on your desktop instead of a browser. Some of the benefits of doing so are that you stay signed in, the page does not time out, pages load faster, it's easy to have multiple open windows, and there is a dropdown toolbar. You can access these apps at: https://quickbooks.intuit.com/apps/

Whether users have a PC or a Mac, or they access QuickBooks Online via the Chrome or the Safari browser, all users access the same data.

The Apps center link is at the bottom of the Navigation bar.

Currently, the Sample Company (Craig's Design and Landscaping Services) does not allow you to link to the apps, but you will have an opportunity to view them in the end-of-chapter exercises.

The QuickBooks Community

Providing user feedback and trying experimental QuickBooks Online software are important ways of letting Intuit know what your business needs, what works best for you, and what could be improved.

Submitting User Feedback

QuickBooks Online provides a direct link to the QuickBooks Online development staff to report bugs in the software or to recommend added features. You can even attach a picture of the bug or a report you would like Intuit to create. This feature is in the Gear menu under Profile.

QuickBooks Labs

The software for QuickBooks Online is ever-changing. QuickBooks Lab is a testing ground for new or improved features. It's where QuickBooks Online developers place the best experimental plug-ins so that users can try, test, and provide feedback on them.

Craig and you have been looking around in QuickBooks Online and have discovered a link for QuickBooks Labs. You are curious and want to find out what this is all about. In this exercise, you will view the QuickBooks Online Labs link.

1. Choose **Gear**→**Your Company**→**QuickBooks Labs**.
2. Scroll through the *high-tech playground*.

Come play in our high-tech playground

Be the first to try our best QuickBooks experimental plug-ins. Check back often to see what's new!

Note: Sometimes experiments break or disappear. (And sometimes they grow up to be real, live features!)

Have ideas for new features? We'd love to hear them.
Tell us!

---

3. Read what some of the experimental plug-ins do, watch a video, and enable a few to see what happens to your data.
4. Return to the **Dashboard**.

Tackle the Tasks

This is your opportunity to apply some of the skills learned in this chapter to accomplish additional tasks for Craig's Design and Landscaping Services. To refresh your memory, refer to the concepts and Develop Your Skills exercises as needed. You will need to add new vendors, customers, and accounts as necessary.

Before You Begin: Close the current test drive window and then open a new test drive window.

Task	Use This Information
Create a Custom Report	Create a cash-basis balance sheet for all dates; collapse the rows and then run the report. Net income should be –$1,904.12.
Save the Custom Report and Schedule It	Save the custom report as Customized Cash Basis Balance Sheet. Arrange to have the report emailed monthly to craig@email.net; the subject line should be Monthly Balance Sheet.
Remove and Add a Custom Field on the Sales Receipt Template	Remove the Crew # field and add a Rep ID field.
Set Up a New User Permission	Add Roger Adams, the new purchasing manager, as a new QuickBooks Online user for Vendors and Purchases only. Use your email address.
Explore What's New in Quickbooks Labs	Check the plug-ins available in QuickBooks Labs, try one, and then write a brief description of the feature.

Self-Assessment

Check your knowledge of this chapter's key concepts and skills using the Self-Assessment quiz here or in your eLab course.

1. QuickBooks Online allows you to customize only some of the predefined reports.　　　　　　　　　　　　　　　　　　　　　　　　　　　*True　False*

2. You CANNOT add notes to QuickBooks Online reports.　　　　　　　　　*True　False*

3. To access the QuickBooks Online keyboard shortcuts in Windows, you tap `Ctrl`+`Alt`+`!`.　　　　　　　　　　　　　　　　　　　　　　　　*True　False*

4. How can you hide/collapse some rows on a report without changing the totals?
   A. Create the report, right-click each row you want to collapse, and then click Hide.
   B. Create the report and then click the Collapse icon.
   C. Create the report, click Edit, and then click Hide.
   D. You cannot hide or collapse rows.

5. How can you create a custom report and have it automatically emailed to your Board of Directors every month?
   A. Customize the report from scratch each month and use the email icon on the report to send it.
   B. Customize and save the report. Each month, choose it from the Custom Reports folder and email it.
   C. Create the report, export it to PDF or Excel, and email it each month.
   D. Customize and save the report and set an email schedule within the My Custom Reports folder.

6. How can you adjust your sales form to keep track of sales made by each salesperson?
   A. Change one of the existing fields to Salesperson.
   B. Customize the form by choosing Header→Custom and then adding a Salesperson field.
   C. Customize the form by choosing Activity Table→Custom and then adding a Salesperson field.
   D. You cannot change the form in QuickBooks Online.

7. You're doing some work in QuickBooks Online at a local coffee shop using your laptop. How can you prevent others from seeing your financial information on the screen?
   A. Place a shade over the top of your monitor to hide it from others.
   B. Turn on the Privacy mode from the Dashboard.
   C. Dim the brightness of your monitor to make it difficult for others to see.
   D. Don't work on your business in public.

(cont'd.)

8. When using keyboard shortcuts, what happens when you simultaneously press Ctrl + Alt + ? or Command + Option + ??
   A. A pop-up window offers keyboard shortcut options to choose from.
   B. A new invoice opens on your monitor.
   C. The Save and Close action is performed.
   D. The Find feature opens on your monitor.

9. How can you learn about new ideas or upcoming features in QuickBooks Online?
   A. Check the Intuit website for a listing of new features for QuickBooks Online.
   B. Check your email for any updates.
   C. Choose Gear→Your Company→QuickBooks Labs.
   D. Choose Gear→What's New?

10. Where would you go in QuickBooks Online to learn about other applications that plug in to QuickBooks Online?
    A. Account and Settings
    B. User Profile
    C. Dashboard
    D. Navigation bar→Apps

Reinforce Your Skills

For these exercises, you will work with Puppy Luv Pampered Pooch, the company account created in your trial subscription to QuickBooks Online.

Sadie has asked you to fine-tune some things related to accounting. She would like to have a field on the sales receipt form that indicates the breed of each dog groomed. She would also like to change some of the reports and have some of them emailed to her each week. She has also asked you to set up a new user to view reports only.

REINFORCE YOUR SKILLS 9-1

Customize a Report

Sadie would like her profit and loss report changed to a Cash basis. She also wants to change the name of the report to Income Statement. In this exercise, you will customize the profit and loss report and then save the customization.

1. Open the **Reports** center and choose the **Profit and Loss** report.
2. Set the Report Period range to **07/01/2021** to **09/30/2021** and then run the report.
3. Change the accounting method to **Cash**.
4. Click **Edit Header** and change the report title to: `Income Statement`
5. Run the report.
6. Click the **Save Customization** button and then set the Custom Report Name to: `Cash Basis Income Statement`
7. Save the customization and then return to the **Reports** center.

REINFORCE YOUR SKILLS 9-2

Schedule a Report to Be Emailed

In this exercise, you will schedule the Cash Basis Income Statement to be automatically emailed to Sadie at the end of each week.

1. Click the **Custom Reports** tab in the Reports center.
2. Click the **Edit** link for the Cash Basis Income Statement.
3. Set the email schedule to **On**.
4. Set the schedule to repeat **Weekly** on **Friday**.
5. In the Email To field, enter: `Sadie@qbmail.net`
6. In the Subject field, enter: `Weekly Income Statement`
7. Save and close the form. If you get a warning about the date, click **OK**.

REINFORCE YOUR SKILLS 9-3

Add a Custom Field

In this exercise, you will add a custom field to the sales receipt form for the breed of dog groomed.

1. Choose **Gear→Your Company→Custom Form Styles**.
2. Click **Edit** for the Pink Sales Receipt.
3. Select **Content**, click on the upper portion of the form, and click **+ Custom Field** in the lower-left corner of the window.
4. Place a checkmark next to the first **Custom Name** field in the Header folder.
5. Type **Breed** in the first Custom Name field.
6. Click **Done**.

REINFORCE YOUR SKILLS 9-4

Set Up User Permissions

In this exercise, you will set up Don Marshall to view only reports. You will also invite Sadie's accountant to view reports.

1. Set up Don Marshall to view reports only, using the email address:
   DMViewer@qbmail.net
2. Click **Invite Accountant** to send an invitation to Sadie's accountant at:
   SamTax@qbmail.net

   You may need to refresh your browser to view the added users.

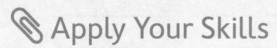# Apply Your Skills

You and Sadie have been discussing the growth of Puppy Luv Pampered Pooch. You've made a list of items you want to research as potential add-ons to QuickBooks. In these exercises, you will investigate some apps that may be appropriate for Sadie to consider.

APPLY YOUR SKILLS 9-1

Review Payroll Apps

Sadie is considering hiring an employee or two so that she can open the salon another two days a week, but she doesn't want the hassle of doing payroll. She has asked you for help! In this exercise, you will review the payroll apps and summarize your findings.

1. Choose **App→Find Apps→Or Browse by Category→Payroll**.

2. Review two of the top-rated apps (indicated by the number of stars).

3. Write a brief summary of your findings that mentions at least one feature for each app and then make a recommendation to Sadie.

4. Save your summary and recommendation as a Word file in your **Chapter 09** folder named: `CH09 App Recommendations`

APPLY YOUR SKILLS 9-2

Review Appointment Management Apps

Sadie would like you to look at some apps to use to schedule grooming appointments. In this exercise, you will review the scheduling apps and write a summary and recommendation.

1. Choose **Apps** at the top of the window and then type **Scheduling** in the search bar.

2. Review two apps that would be suitable for Sadie.

3. Write a brief summary of your findings that mentions at least one feature for each app and then make a recommendation to Sadie.

4. Save your summary and recommendation as a Word file in your **Chapter 09** folder named: `CH09 Scheduling Apps`

APPLY YOUR SKILLS 9-3

Review Credit Card Processing Apps

Sadie has decided to begin accepting credit cards as payment for grooming. In this exercise, you will review credit card processing apps and write a summary and recommendation.

1. Type **Credit Card Processing** in the search bar.

2. Review an app that might be suitable for Sadie.

3. Write a brief summary of your findings that mentions at least one feature for the app and then make a recommendation to Sadie.

4. Save your summary and recommendation as a Word file in your **Chapter 09** folder named: `CH09 CC Processing Apps`

APPLY YOUR SKILLS 9-4

Review the Mobile App

In this exercise, you will learn about the mobile app available for QuickBooks Online.

1. Type **Mobile** in the search bar.
2. Select the **QuickBooks Online Mobile** app.
3. Learn about the features and then write a brief review of the app that discusses three of its features.
4. Save your review as a Word file in your **Chapter 09** folder named: **CH09 QBO Mobile App Review**

APPLY YOUR SKILLS 9-5

Explore QuickBooks Labs

In this exercise, you will try an experimental plug-in offered in QuickBooks Labs.

1. Choose **Gear→Your Company→QuickBooks Labs**.
2. Select at least one of the plug-ins and write a brief review of the use of the plug-in. Be sure to indicate whether you would recommend it, and why or why not.
3. Save your review as a Word file in your **Chapter 09** folder named: **CH09 QBO Plug-Ins**

APPLY YOUR SKILLS 9-6 QG

Export the Report

In this exercise, you will export the report created in Reinforce Your Skills 9-1.

1. Open the **Reports** center and choose **My Custom Reports→Cash Basis Income Statement**.
2. Export the report to Excel and save it in your **Chapter 09** folder as: **CH09 Cash Basis Income Statement**

 CHECK FIGURE *Your figures should match those shown here.*

Statement	Balance
Net Loss	$5,204.35

10 | Staying on Track: The Accounting Cycle, Classes, and Locations

Every business needs to ensure that it is keeping proper track of transactions and following good business practices. Following Generally Accepted Accounting Principles (GAAP) and the accounting cycle are a good starting point. In this chapter, you will focus on the first three steps of the accounting cycle and learn how to use class and location tracking to gain deeper insight into specific areas of your business. You will also learn how to keep track of charges or credits that you haven't added to an invoice or credit memo yet.

LEARNING OBJECTIVES

▸ Identify steps of the accounting cycle

▸ Enable class and location tracking

▸ Record transactions using class and location tracking

▸ Create reports using class and location tracking

▸ Prepare delayed charges and credits

Generally Accepted Accounting Principles and the Accounting Cycle

Sound accounting practices and accurate financial data are critical for any business. Financial data may be used for many purposes and by many different individuals. Business owners use this data to understand how their business is doing. Banks and other lending institutions depend on accurate financial data when considering loans. Government tax agencies require information about business income or losses.

Following the GAAP principles and the accounting cycle provides consistency and helps ensure accurate records throughout any industry.

GAAP

GAAP refers to the underlying guidelines that accountants must adhere to for consistency, fairness, and honesty in accounting procedures. GAAP principles are set by the Financial Accounting and Standards Board (FASB). They include revenue recognition, consistency, prudence, and objectivity. Publicly owned companies are required by law to follow these principles. Many private businesses also adopt these principles as part of their best practices.

Accounting Cycle Steps

The accounting cycle is the sequence of procedures used for accurately recording business transactions for a period of time—usually called a fiscal year. There are also fiscal periods, such as a month or quarter of the fiscal year. These steps help keep the business's accounting records in line with GAAP and ensure that financial information is accurate.

The five steps of the accounting cycle are shown here.

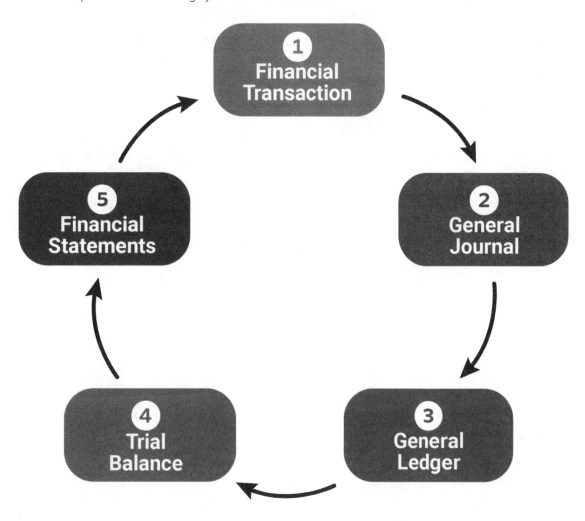

1. Analyze the business transaction to determine the next appropriate action.
2. Record the business transaction in the general journal.
3. Post the transaction to the general ledger.
4. Prepare a trial balance report to analyze all account balances.
5. Prepare the financial statements for the fiscal period.

DEVELOP YOUR SKILLS 10-1

Craig has left a few documents on your desk, along with a note that reads, "Please take care of these in QuickBooks Online." In this exercise, you will start by performing the first step in the accounting cycle: analyzing transactions.

Before You Begin: *Access the QuickBooks Online test drive at qbo.intuit.com/redir/testdrive and leave the test drive open for the entire chapter.*

1. Analyze each transaction to determine which accounts will be affected and what action to take.

Transaction	Accounts Affected	Action to Take
Example: A receipt, dated 9/20/2021 and paid on Craig's Visa account, from Bob's Burger Joint	*Meals and Entertainment expense: Increase* *Visa credit card liability: Increase*	*Record an expense transaction.*
A bill for $45.16 from Hicks Hardware, dated 9/21/2021, for various job expenses; due in 15 days		
A note from Craig: Invoice Dukes Basketball Camp for the 2 pumps we replaced on 9/22/2021		
Copies of checks from: • Amy's Bird Sanctuary for $239 • Jeff's Jalopies for $81 • A deposit slip for $320 dated 9/23/2021		

Record the Transaction

Recording is the second step in the accounting cycle. Now you will record the transactions that you just analyzed.

2. Record the bill for $45.16 from Hicks Hardware, dated 9/21/2021; terms Net 15 days.

	#	ACCOUNT	DESCRIPTION	AMOUNT	BILLABLE	TAX	CUSTOMER	
⠿	1	Job Expenses	various job expenses	45.16				🗑

3. Record the invoice for Dukes Basketball Camp for two pumps on 9/22/2021.

Dukes Basketball Camp — Dukes_bball@intuit.com

☐ Send later   Cc/Bcc

BALANCE DUE
$32.40

Billing address
Peter Dukes
Dukes Basketball Camp
25 Court St.
Tucson, AZ 85719

Terms Net 30
Invoice date 09/22/2021
Due date 10/22/2021

Crew #

	#	PRODUCT/SERVICE	DESCRIPTION	QTY	RATE	AMOUNT	TAX	
⠿	1	Design:Fountains:Pump	Fountain Pump	2	15	30.00	✓	🗑
⠿	2							🗑

[Add lines] [Clear all lines] [Add subtotal]

Message displayed on invoice
Thank you for your business and have a great day!

Statement memo

Subtotal	$30.00
Taxable subtotal $30.00	
California ▾ 8%	2.40
Discount percent ▾	$0.00
Total	$32.40
Balance due	$32.40

4. Record payments received: Amy's Bird Sanctuary check for $239 on 9/22/2021.

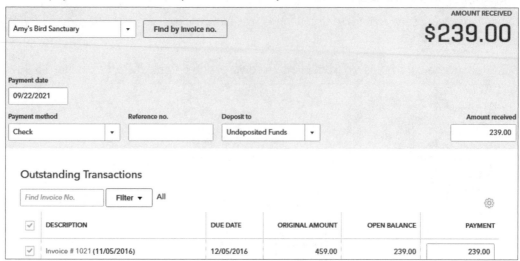

5. Record payments received: Jeff's Jalopies check for $81 on 9/22/2021.

6. Record the deposit for both checks.

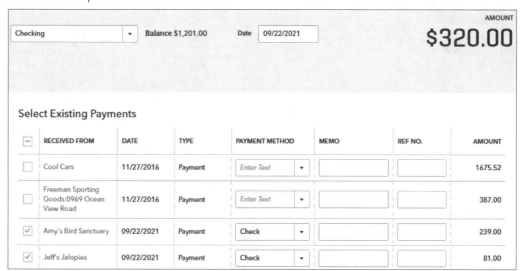

Congratulations! You have just completed the first two steps in the accounting cycle!

QuickBooks Online completes the third step in the accounting cycle for you. Each time you save a form, the transactions are posted to the general ledger.

Class Tracking

Class tracking allows you to keep track of income and expenses by department, project, event, or some other segment. By tracking income and expenses for individual classes, you can focus more closely on particular areas of your business and assess what is profitable or not. Financial reports by class give you a picture of each segment as part of the total.

Here are some examples of the classes that different industries may create:

- Retail: Clothes, hardware, electronics

- Construction: New construction, remodeling

- Non-profit: Programs, overhead

- Salon: Retail, services

Warning! After you decide to use class tracking, it is important to use it for every transaction, meaning you must include a class on each line of the transaction.

DEVELOP YOUR SKILLS 10-2

Craig has asked you to organize his business by retail jobs, contract jobs, and business overhead. In this exercise, you will start by enabling class tracking for Craig's business.

1. Choose **Gear→Your Company→Account and Settings** and then click the **Advanced** tab.

2. Click **Categories** to enable editing in this section and then add a checkmark to the **Track Classes** checkbox to enable classes.

3. Add a checkmark to the **Warn Me When a Transaction Isn't Assigned a Class** checkbox to enable this option.

4. In the Assign Classes field, choose **One to Each Row in Transaction**.

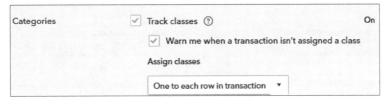

5. Click **Save** and then return to the **Dashboard**.

Create Class Categories

Now you will create the classes for the different areas of Craig's business.

6. Choose **Gear→Lists→All Lists** and then click the **Classes** link.

7. Click the **New** button, type **Retail** in the Name field, and click **Save**.

8. Create two more new classes: **Contract Jobs** and **General Overhead**

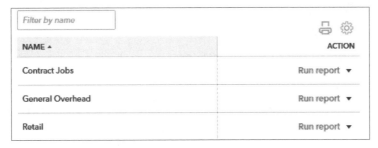

After you have created a class, you can add it to a sales receipt, invoice, bill, or other form by selecting the class name, as shown here.

#	PRODUCT/SERVICE	DESCRIPTION	QTY	RATE	AMOUNT	TAX	CLASS	
1	Landscaping:Gardening	Weekly Gardening Service	2	55	110.00		Contract Jobs	

Create Forms with Classes

Now you will create some income and expense forms that use classes and then run a Profit and Loss by Class report.

> **Note!** If your business decides to use class tracking after you have already completed many transactions, you can easily edit the transactions to add the appropriate class.

9. Create a sales receipt for a taxable retail sale of six sprinkler heads on October 3, 2021, paid with cash; add the Retail class. (Be sure to add sales tax.)

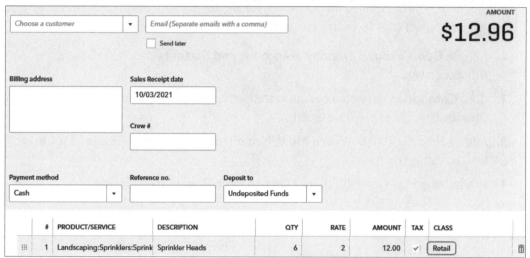

10. Create an invoice for a landscape contract job for Kate Whelan for gardening for two weeks at $55 per week, dated October 3, 2021; add the Contract Jobs class.

11. Create a bill for $345 from Tania's Nursery for miscellaneous general plants and soil for contract jobs, dated October 3, 2021; terms Net 10 days; add the Contract Jobs class.

12. Record a $180 expense for advertising from Lee Advertising, paid with Visa card on October 3, 2021; add the General Overhead class.

Create a Report by Class

Now you will produce a Profit and Loss by Class report to view how the preceding transactions are segmented on the financial report.

13. Open the **Reports** center and switch to the **All** tab.

14. Choose **Business Overview→Profit and Loss by Class**.

15. Set the date range to **10/01/2021** through **10/03/2021**.

16. Run the report.

Craig's Design and Landscaping Services				
PROFIT & LOSS BY CLASS				
October 1-3, 2021				
	CONTRACT JOBS	GENERAL OVERHEAD	RETAIL	TOTAL
▾ INCOME				
Landscaping Services	110.00			$110.00
Sales of Product Income			12.00	$12.00
Total Income	**$110.00**	**$0.00**	**$12.00**	**$122.00**
▾ COST OF GOODS SOLD				
Cost of Goods Sold			4.50	$4.50
Total Cost of Goods Sold	**$0.00**	**$0.00**	**$4.50**	**$4.50**
GROSS PROFIT	**$110.00**	**$0.00**	**$7.50**	**$117.50**
▾ EXPENSES				
Advertising		180.00		$180.00
▾ Job Expenses				$0.00
▾ Job Materials				$0.00
Plants and Soil	345.00			$345.00
Total Job Materials	345.00			$345.00
Total Job Expenses	345.00			$345.00
Total Expenses	**$345.00**	**$180.00**	**$0.00**	**$525.00**
NET OPERATING INCOME	$ -235.00	$ -180.00	$7.50	$ -407.50
NET INCOME	$ -235.00	$ -180.00	$7.50	$ -407.50

This report provides a complete profit and loss total but segments by class as well. This could be valuable for measuring income and expenses over time.

Location Tracking

Location tracking allows you to produce financial information reports by location. A business might use location tracking for different regions, store locations, properties, departments, or territories. Location tracking differs from class tracking in that it is limited to one location per transaction form. Classes are tracked per line item on a form.

Account and Settings			
Company	Accounting	First month of fiscal year	January
		First month of income tax year	Same as fiscal year
Sales		Accounting method	Accrual
		Close the books	Off
Expenses			
Advanced	Company type	Tax form	Not sure/Other/None
	Chart of accounts	Enable account numbers	Off
		Discount account	Discounts given
		Billable expense income account	Billable Expense Income
	Categories	Track classes	On
		Track locations	Off

🔧 Gear→Your Company→Account and Settings→Advanced→Categories→Track Locations

Craig has opened a second retail store location called Craig's Two. In this exercise, you will start by enabling the location feature to track sales for each store.

1. Choose **Gear→Your Company→Account and Settings** and then click the **Advanced** tab.
2. Click the **Edit** icon in the Categories section.
3. Add a checkmark to the **Track Locations** checkbox.
4. Choose **Store** from the Location Label menu.
5. Save your changes.

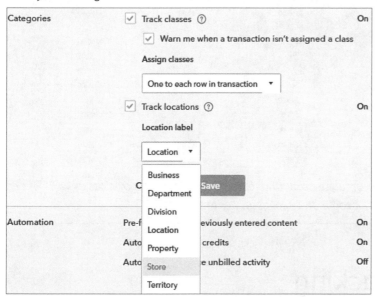

6. Choose **Gear→Lists→All Lists** and then click the **Stores** link.
7. Click the **New** button, type **Craig's One** as the store name, and then click **Save**.
8. Repeat step 7, but this time use **Craig's Two** as the store name.

NAME ▲	ACTION
Craig's One	Run report ▼
Craig's Two	Run report ▼

(cont'd.)

Create Transactions by Class and Location

Now you will create several transactions with class and location tracking and then create a Sales by Store report.

9. Create a sales receipt for a taxable (California) cash sale at Craig's Two for seven bags of soil, on October 4, 2021; Retail class.

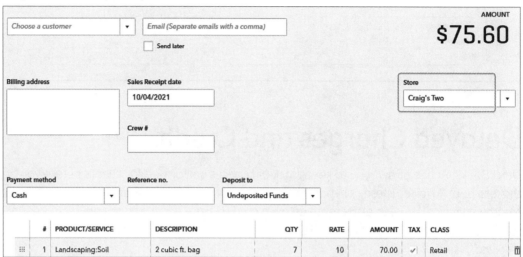

10. Create a sales receipt for a taxable (California) cash sale at Craig's One for one rock fountain on October 4, 2021; Retail class.

> **Note!** When location tracking is enabled and each location makes its deposits individually, you can also track banking deposits by location. Define the deposits by selecting Show Payments for this Store and then choosing which store made the deposit.

Create a Sales by Store Report

Now you will create a Sales by Store Summary report for October 4, 2021. By creating different reports for each store, Craig will have a way to measure sales growth at each location.

11. Open the **Reports** center and switch to the **All** tab.

12. Choose **Review Sales→Sales by Store Summary**.

13. Set the report period dates to **10/04/2021** through **10/04/2021**.

14. Run the report.

Craig's Design and Landscaping Services	
SALES BY STORE SUMMARY	
October 4, 2021	
	TOTAL
Craig's One	275.00
Craig's Two	70.00
TOTAL	**$345.00**

Delayed Charges and Credits

QuickBooks Online allows you to keep track of services performed for clients before you add the charges to an invoice. These non-posting entries serve as a placeholder until you are ready to create an invoice. You can also create delayed credits. For example, if you have a potential sales return, you can create a delayed credit that is then converted to a credit memo after the return is received.

DEVELOP YOUR SKILLS 10-4

Craig is tired of using sticky notes to keep track of weekly landscaping hours for customers. He has asked you to find a way to keep track of all the hours and then create one monthly invoice for each gardening customer.

In this exercise, you will create the delayed charges as submitted each week and then add them to a monthly customer invoice.

1. Choose **Create→Customers→Delayed Charge**.

2. Choose **Freeman Sporting Goods:55 Twin Lane** as the customer and tap [Tab].

3. Type **09/03/2021** in the Delayed Charge Date field and tap [Tab] twice.

4. Choose **Landscaping:Gardening** in the Product/Service field and tap [Tab] twice.

   Now you will enter the number of hours worked.

5. Type **2** in the Qty field and tap [Tab].

6. Type **25** in the Rate field and tap [Tab] three times.

7. Choose **Contract Jobs** in the Class field.

8. Save and close the form.

   Now you will add the delayed charges for another week of gardening for Freeman Sporting Goods.

9. Repeat **steps 1–8** using the date **09/10/2021**.

Create the Invoice for the Delayed Charge

It's time to create the monthly invoice and add the two delayed charges.

10. Choose **Create→Customers→Invoice**.

11. Choose **Freeman Sporting Goods:55 Twin Lane**.

12. Click **Add** in both of the charges shown in the drawer on the right.

13. Save and close the form.

Tackle the Tasks

This is your opportunity to apply some of the skills learned in this chapter to accomplish additional tasks for Craig's Design and Landscaping Services. To refresh your memory, refer to the concepts and Develop Your Skills exercises as needed. You will need to add new vendors, customers, and accounts as necessary.

Before You Begin: Close the current test drive window and then open a new test drive window.

Task	Use This Information
Enable Class Tracking	Classes: Retail, Landscaping Services, and General Overhead
Enable Location Tracking	Stores: Store One and Store Two
Apply Class and Location to Transactions	Write check number 72 to Tania's Nursery for various plants and soil for Landscaping Services totaling $143 and miscellaneous supplies for Retail Store One totaling $16.85 on October 4, 2021. (Hint: Use two lines with different classes.)
	Create a taxable (California) sales receipt for Retail Store Two for a cash sale to Diego Rodriguez on October 4, 2021, for 12 sprinkler heads.
	Create a bill from Cal Telephone for telephone charges dated October 4, 2021, for Retail Store Two for $112.52.
	Record a $150 Visa credit card expense on October 4, 2021, to Books by Bessie for bookkeeping services for both stores; Class: General Overhead; leave the Store field blank.
Create a Class Report	Create a Profit and Loss by Class report for October 4, 2021.
Create a Store Report	Create a Profit and Loss by Store report for October 4, 2021.

Self-Assessment

Check your knowledge of this chapter's key concepts and skills using the Self-Assessment quiz here or in your eLab course.

1. The accounting cycle consists of a series of steps to record accurate business transactions.   *True   False*

2. Banks, tax agencies, and business owners depend on accurate financial information consistent with GAAP.   *True   False*

3. When using the class tracking feature, you must use only one class per form.   *True   False*

4. To create a delayed charge, you choose Gear→Customer→Delayed Charge.   *True   False*

5. What does the acronym GAAP stand for?
   A. Good Acceptable Accounting Practices
   B. Generally Adopted Accounting Practices
   C. General Acceptable Accounting Practices
   D. Generally Accepted Accounting Principles

6. What is the first step in the accounting cycle?
   A. Record the transaction.
   B. Analyze the transaction to determine what the appropriate action is.
   C. Add a new account to the Chart of Accounts.
   D. Post to the general ledger.

7. You are analyzing a bill received from a vendor for $800 for a multimedia marketing campaign that is to be paid in fifteen days. Which accounts will be affected?
   A. Checking will increase, and Marketing will decrease.
   B. Accounts Receivable will decrease, and Marketing will increase.
   C. Accounts Payable will decrease, and Marketing will increase.
   D. Accounts Payable will increase, and Marketing will increase.

8. You are analyzing a bill received from a vendor for $800 for a multimedia marketing campaign that is to be paid in fifteen days. What action would you take?
   A. Record an expense transaction.
   B. Record an invoice transaction.
   C. Record a sale receipt transaction.
   D. Record a bill transaction.

9. How does QuickBooks Online complete a step in the accounting cycle for you?
   A. It records each transaction into the general ledger each time you save the form.
   B. It reconciles all the accounts.
   C. It only allows you to record, not post.
   D. It does not complete anything for you.

(cont'd.)

10. Why would you use class tracking?
   A. To keep track of different bank and credit card accounts
   B. To track different departments of the business
   C. To track customers' multiple addresses
   D. To track different vendor types

11. Your business has multiple store branches. Which feature would you use to track the income and expenses for each branch?
   A. Accounts
   B. Lists
   C. Locations
   D. Reports

12. What are the steps to enable class or location tracking?
   A. Gear→Your Company→Account and Settings→Advanced→Track Classes
   B. Gear→Your Company→Account and Settings→Advanced→Categories
   C. Gear→Lists→All Lists
   D. Transactions→Chart of Accounts→Categories

13. Which sales reports would be helpful if you are trying to analyze sales by class or location?
   A. Sales by Class Summary and Detail
   B. Sales by Location Summary and Detail
   C. Monthly Sales Report
   D. Profit and Loss
   E. Both Sales by Class Summary and Detail, and Sales by Location Summary and Detail

14. What would be a good example of a delayed charge?
   A. Sale of inventory products on an invoice
   B. Sale of inventory and services paid for at the time of sale
   C. Purchase of parts and services to be paid for later
   D. Services or sales that are completed but won't be immediately invoiced

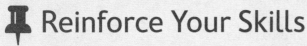

Reinforce Your Skills

For these exercises, you will work with Puppy Luv Pampered Pooch, the company account created in your trial subscription to QuickBooks Online.

REINFORCE YOUR SKILLS 10-1

Analyze and Record Transactions

Sadie has left a stack of miscellaneous paperwork in your inbox. In this exercise, you will sort through it to determine what is affected and what action to take. Then, you will create and record the required transactions.

1. Analyze these transactions, noting the accounts affected and the appropriate action.

Transaction	Accounts Affected	Action to Take
A deposit slip dated September 17, 2021, for $208.56		
Copies of checks from: • Windemere Kennels: Check number 18871 for $250 for August 2021 invoices • GreenWay Kennels: Check number 15205 for August 2021 invoices • A copy of a deposit slip dated September 27, 2021, for $705		
A City Credit Union credit card receipt from Office Plus for printer paper and toner, dated September 27, 2021, for $158.14		

2. Record the transactions.

REINFORCE YOUR SKILLS 10-2

Set Up Class Tracking and Add New Classes

1. Choose **Gear→Your Company→Account and Settings** and then click **Advanced**.

2. Edit the Categories setting to turn on classes and enable the option to **Warn Me When a Transaction Isn't Assigned to a Class**; click **Save** and then click **Done**.

3. Click in the checkbox to assign **One class to each row** in a transaction and then save your changes.

4. Add these classes: **Becky D.**, **Andy G.**, and **Kennel**

Prepare Forms Using the Class Field

In this exercise, you will prepare the sales receipts for the day using the appropriate groomer in the Class field. Then you will prepare an invoice for work that Sadie did at Windemere Kennels.

1. Prepare the sales receipts using this information:

	Becky D.	Andy G.
10/1/2021 Appointment 1	Benny Stewart brought his small dog, Maggie, in for a Bath and Brush and a teeth brushing; paid with check number 4844.	Julie Walton brought in her two large dogs, Alice and Suzy, for Full Pet Grooms; paid with check number 2521.
10/1/2021 Appointment 2	Bonnie Zoe brought her small dog, Missy, in for a Mini Groom and nail polishing; paid with cash.	Mami Saunders brought her large dog, Sam, in for a Bath and Brush; paid with check number 6551.
10/1/2021 Appointment 3	Jamee Thompson had his small dog, Peaches, in for a Full Pet Groom; paid with check number 8741.	Dana Davis brought in her medium dog, Princess, for a Mini Pet Groom and ear cleaning; paid cash.
10/1/2021 Appointment 4	Arlene Garrison brought her small dog, Joe, in for a Bath and Brush; paid with check number 981.	Doug Sherrill brought in his extra-large dog, Skeeter, for a Bath and Brush; paid with check number 3354.
10/1/2021 Appointment 5	Jesus Moreno brought in Sandy, an extra-large dog, for a Full Pet Grooming; paid with check number 5854.	Gina Thomas stopped by with her small dog, Tiny, for a quick Mini Pet Groom; paid cash.

2. Sadie worked onsite at Windemere Kennels. She did Mini Pet Grooms for five small dogs and cleaned all their ears. Record the invoice for this service.

Apply Your Skills

APPLY YOUR SKILLS 10-1

Delayed Charges

In this exercise, you will set up delayed charges for a new client: Johnson-Smith Kennels, breeders of large Basset Hounds. Puppy Luv Pampered Pooch will perform grooming for five dogs each Friday. Invoicing will be at the end of the month. Terms are Net 15 days.

1. Create a delayed charge for five large dogs: Bath and Brush each Friday as follows:

   A. October 1, 2021

   B. October 8, 2021; add teeth brushing

   C. October 15, 2021

   D. October 22, 2021; add ear cleaning

   E. October 29, 2021

2. Create the invoice for the delayed charges on October 29, 2021.

3. Save and close the form.

APPLY YOUR SKILLS 10-2 QG

Create Reports by Class

In this exercise, you will create reports for Sadie.

1. Prepare a sales report to display the classes for October 1, 2021, through October 31, 2021. Export the report to Excel and save it in your **Chapter 10** folder as: **CH10 Sales Report By Class**

2. Prepare a Profit and Loss by Class report for October 1, 2021, through October 31, 2021.

3. What is the income for Becky D.? _____

4. Export the report to Excel and save it in your **Chapter 10** folder as: **CH10 Profit and Loss By Class**

 CHECK FIGURE *Your figure should match the one shown here.*

Total Sales by Class	$1,773

11 | Completing the Accounting Cycle, Closing the Books, and Reviewing Changes

As an accounting period ends, you must ensure that all financial records are accurate and close the books for the period. In many cases, you will prepare presentations for executives and other decision-makers. And in some cases, you may need to review forms and transactions to track down an error or see what other users have done. In this chapter, you will complete the last two steps of the accounting cycle, making adjusting journal entries and inventory adjustments as needed. You will create preformatted management reports and close the books at a specific date. You will also use the audit log and audit history features.

LEARNING OBJECTIVES

▸ Complete the accounting cycle

▸ Create a trial balance report

▸ Create adjusting journal entries

▸ Adjust inventory quantities

▸ Create financial statements and management reports

▸ Close the books in QuickBooks Online

▸ Review the audit log and audit history

📂 Project: Craig's Design and Landscaping Services

Craig's Design and Landscaping Services is getting ready to close the books for the year to date. To begin, you will need to create a Trial Balance report, do a bit of analysis, and prepare any adjusting journal entries that may be necessary. Then, you will create the year-end financial statements and close the books in QuickBooks Online. Along the way, you and Craig will take a look at the audit trail.

Completing the Accounting Cycle

The final tasks in the accounting cycle are:

- Create a trial balance report, analyze it, and make adjustments as needed.

- Prepare financial statements.

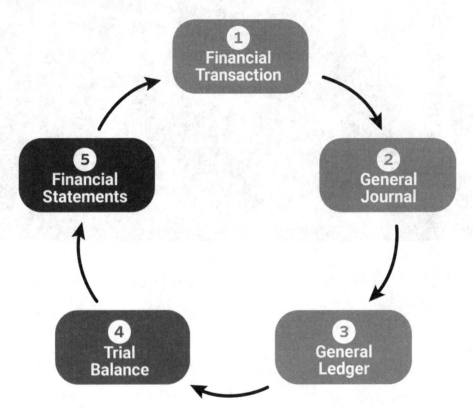

Creating the Trial Balance Report and Making Adjustments

The fourth step in the accounting cycle is creating a trial balance report. A trial balance report is a listing of all the accounts in your Chart of Accounts and their balances on the date selected. It allows you to analyze your balances and make adjustments as needed to ensure that all data is accurate.

DEVELOP YOUR SKILLS 11-1

Craig would like to go through the trial balance for the current year-to-date with you and discuss any adjustments that need to be made. In this exercise, you will create a trial balance for the current quarter. Note that the trial balance in this exercise displays the current year-to-date of 2018. Yours will be different.

Before You Begin: *Access the QuickBooks Online test drive at qbo.intuit.com/redir/testdrive and leave the test drive open for the entire chapter.*

Craig's Design and Landscaping Services
Trial Balance
As of April 25, 2018

	Debit	Credit
Checking	1,201.00	
Savings	800.00	
Accounts Receivable (A/R)	5,281.52	
Inventory Asset	596.25	
Undeposited Funds	2,062.52	
Truck:Original Cost	13,495.00	
Accounts Payable (A/P)		1,602.67
Mastercard		157.72
Arizona Dept. of Revenue Payable		0.00
Board of Equalization Payable		370.94
Loan Payable		4,000.00
Notes Payable		25,000.00
Opening Balance Equity	9,337.50	
Retained Earnings		91.25
Design income		2,250.00
Discounts given	89.50	
Landscaping Services		1,287.50
Landscaping Services:Job Materials:Fountains and Garden Lighting		2,246.50
Landscaping Services:Job Materials:Plants and Soil		2,220.72
Landscaping Services:Job Materials:Sprinklers and Drip Systems		138.00
Landscaping Services:Labor:Installation		250.00
Landscaping Services:Labor:Maintenance and Repair		50.00
Pest Control Services		40.00
Sales of Product Income		912.75
Services		503.55
Cost of Goods Sold	405.00	
Advertising	74.86	
Automobile	113.96	
Automobile:Fuel	349.41	
Equipment Rental	112.00	
Insurance	241.23	
Job Expenses	155.07	
Job Expenses:Job Materials:Decks and Patios	234.04	
Job Expenses:Job Materials:Plants and Soil	353.12	
Job Expenses:Job Materials:Sprinklers and Drip Systems	215.66	
Legal & Professional Fees	75.00	
Legal & Professional Fees:Accounting	640.00	
Legal & Professional Fees:Bookkeeper	55.00	
Legal & Professional Fees:Lawyer	100.00	
Maintenance and Repair	185.00	
Maintenance and Repair:Equipment Repairs	755.00	
Meals and Entertainment	28.49	
Office Expenses	18.08	
Rent or Lease	900.00	
Utilities:Gas and Electric	200.53	
Utilities:Telephone	130.86	
Miscellaneous	2,916.00	
TOTAL	**$ 41,121.60**	**$ 41,121.60**

1. Open the **Reports** center and switch to the **All** tab.
2. Choose **For My Accountant→Trial Balance**.
3. Set the Report Period field to **This Year-to-Date**. `This Year-to-date ⬍`
4. Run the report.

Adjusting Journal Entries

Adjusting journal entries are typically used to adjust for depreciation, allocation of prepaid expenses, and corrections to inventory. They are made just prior to the issuance of the period's financial statements (for example, at the end of a month, quarter, or year).

When you create adjusting journal entries or any other form, you can enter an equation into an amount field, and the Quick Math feature will perform the calculation for you. You can use the ☐ key to add values together, the ☐ key to subtract, the ☐ key to multiply, and the ☐ key to divide. For example, if you wanted to divide $13,000 by 18 months, you would enter 13000/18. This feature will save you a lot of time and help prevent computational errors.

DEVELOP YOUR SKILLS 11-2

You and Craig used the trial balance report in the previous exercise to review all accounts. You have reconciled the bank statements and have verified that all the Accounts Receivable are collectible and the inventory is accurate. The two tasks remaining are to record the depreciation on the truck purchased for $13,495 and to take a physical inventory and make adjustments as needed.

You and Craig decide that the truck has a useful life of three years (thirty-six months) with no residual value. In this exercise, you will create the journal entry for one month's depreciation and make it recurring for the following thirty-five months.

1. Choose **Create→Other→Journal Entry**.

2. Complete the fields as indicated:

    • Journal Date: [use today's date]

    • Journal No.: **to adj for depr**

    • Account, line 1: **Depreciation**

    • Debits, line 1: **13495/36** (press [Tab] to calculate)

    Quick Math performs the calculation for you, and the monthly amount (374.86) appears in the Debits field.

    • Description: **to adjust for depreciation**

3. Choose **Truck:Depreciation** in the line 2 Account field; enter the Credits amount and the Description if the fields do not fill in automatically.

4. Save your changes.

	#	ACCOUNT	DEBITS	CREDITS	DESCRIPTION
⁞⁞⁞	1	Depreciation	374.86		to adjust for depreciation
⁞⁞⁞	2	Truck:Depreciation		374.86	to adjust for depreciation

5. Click **Make Recurring** in the bottom tray.

6. Enter **Truck Depreciation** in the Template Name field.

7. Complete as follows; your dates will differ from the figure but should span **thirty-five** months:

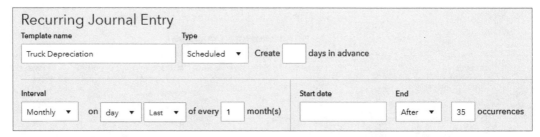

8. Save the template. (You will need to adjust the dates, depending on what year you are actually working in.)

Comparing Inventory Quantities and Making Adjustments

Inventory must be counted at fixed intervals during the year to be sure you have sellable product on hand. When taking inventory, you will often find that some inventory is missing, broken, or obsolete. If this happens, you will need to adjust your on-hand inventory quantity and value. Doing so will decrease your asset value and increase your expenses.

DEVELOP YOUR SKILLS 11-3

Craig wants to be sure his on-hand inventory value matches the trial balance report (see Develop Your Skills 11-1). In this exercise, you will create a report to compare QuickBooks Online inventory values to those in the trial balance report. Then you will create a worksheet to use to take the physical inventory.

1. Open the **Reports** center and choose **Accountant Reports→Trial Balance** on the All tab.

2. Return to the **Reports** center and choose **All tab→Sales and Customers→Inventory Valuation Summary**.

3. Select **This Year-to-Date** in the Report Period field.

4. Verify the Asset Value column total is the same as on the trial balance report.

   The total should be $596.25.

5. Click **Back to Report List**.

6. Select **Physical Inventory Worksheet**.

This worksheet lists the quantities recorded in QuickBooks Online and provides a place for you to record the actual quantities in physical inventory.

<table>
<thead>
<tr><th colspan="6">Craig's Design and Landscaping Services</th></tr>
<tr><th colspan="6">PHYSICAL INVENTORY WORKSHEET</th></tr>
<tr><th>PRODUCT</th><th>DESCRIPTION</th><th>QTY ON HAND</th><th>REORDER POINT</th><th>QTY ON PO</th><th>PHYSICAL COUNT</th></tr>
</thead>
<tbody>
<tr><td>Design:Fountains:Pump</td><td>Fountain Pump</td><td>25.00</td><td></td><td></td><td></td></tr>
<tr><td>Design:Fountains:Rock Fountain</td><td>Rock Fountain</td><td>2.00</td><td></td><td></td><td></td></tr>
<tr><td>Landscaping:Sprinklers:Sprinkler Heads</td><td>Sprinkler Heads</td><td>25.00</td><td></td><td></td><td></td></tr>
<tr><td>Landscaping:Sprinklers:Sprinkler Pipes</td><td>Sprinkler Pipes</td><td>31.00</td><td></td><td></td><td></td></tr>
</tbody>
</table>

7. Leave the worksheet open.

Adjust Inventory Quantities and Value

Craig has taken the physical inventory and compared it to the worksheet. He has discovered that seven of the sprinkler heads have been damaged and are not sellable. Now you will adjust the quantity and value of the sprinkler heads.

8. Choose **Create→Other→Inventory Qty Adjustment** and then complete the fields as indicated:

   • Adjustment Date: [use today's date]

   • Inventory Adjustment Account: [leave this field blank; QBO will create an Inventory Shrinkage account]

   • Product: **Landscaping:Sprinklers:Sprinkler Heads**

   • New Qty: **18**

9. Save and close the form.

   The Physical Inventory Worksheet is now updated to reflect the correct quantity of sprinkler heads.

Adjusted Trial Balance Report

After all of the adjusting entries have been completed, you must also prepare an Adjusted Trial Balance report. This report is used to verify that all of the balances are correct and that debits and credits are still equal.

DEVELOP YOUR SKILLS 11-4

You have made all of the adjusting entries for the quarter. In this exercise, you will create an adjusted trial balance report.

1. Open the **Reports** center and choose **All tab→For My Accountant→Trial Balance**.
2. Select **This Year-to-Date** in the Report Period field.

   You have now completed step 4 of the accounting cycle. Your adjusted trial balance should look similar to the one here.

Craig's Design and Landscaping Services
Trial Balance
As of April 25, 2018

	Debit	Credit
Checking	1,201.00	
Savings	800.00	
Accounts Receivable (A/R)	5,281.52	
Inventory Asset	591.00	
Undeposited Funds	2,062.52	
Truck:Depreciation		374.86
Truck:Original Cost	13,495.00	
Accounts Payable (A/P)		1,602.67
Mastercard		157.72
Arizona Dept. of Revenue Payable		0.00
Board of Equalization Payable		370.94
Loan Payable		4,000.00
Notes Payable		25,000.00
Opening Balance Equity	9,337.50	
Retained Earnings		91.25
Design income		2,250.00
Discounts given	89.50	
Landscaping Services		1,287.50
Landscaping Services:Job Materials:Fountains and Garden Lighting		2,246.50
Landscaping Services:Job Materials:Plants and Soil		2,220.72
Landscaping Services:Job Materials:Sprinklers and Drip Systems		138.00
Landscaping Services:Labor:Installation		250.00
Landscaping Services:Labor:Maintenance and Repair		50.00
Pest Control Services		40.00
Sales of Product Income		912.75
Services		503.55
Cost of Goods Sold	405.00	
Inventory Shrinkage	5.25	
Advertising	74.86	
Automobile	113.96	
Automobile:Fuel	349.41	
Equipment Rental	112.00	
Insurance	241.23	
Job Expenses	155.07	
Job Expenses:Job Materials:Decks and Patios	234.04	
Job Expenses:Job Materials:Plants and Soil	353.12	
Job Expenses:Job Materials:Sprinklers and Drip Systems	215.66	
Legal & Professional Fees	75.00	
Legal & Professional Fees:Accounting	640.00	
Legal & Professional Fees:Bookkeeper	55.00	
Legal & Professional Fees:Lawyer	100.00	
Maintenance and Repair	185.00	
Maintenance and Repair:Equipment Repairs	755.00	
Meals and Entertainment	28.49	
Office Expenses	18.08	
Rent or Lease	900.00	
Utilities:Gas and Electric	200.53	
Utilities:Telephone	130.86	
Depreciation	374.86	
Miscellaneous	2,916.00	
TOTAL	**$ 41,496.46**	**$ 41,496.46**

Creating Financial Statements

The final step in the accounting cycle is the preparation of financial statements and any associated management reports.

The two basic financial reports used by most businesses are the profit and loss statement (or income statement) and the balance sheet.

- The profit and loss statement reports the income for the period, less all the cost of goods sold and expenses for the period. If income is greater than expenses, the result is a net income. If expenses exceed income, the result is a net loss.

- The balance sheet is a statement of the business's assets, liabilities, and equity; it reflects the business's financial position on a stated date.

QuickBooks Online has standard reports as well as reports that display ratios or trends. You can customize these reports to display exactly what the business owner wants to see. Many businesses also add a few management reports to financial statements. Examples of these reports include an Accounts Receivable Aging report, a Sales report, a statement of expenses by vendor, and more.

DEVELOP YOUR SKILLS 11-5

Craig has asked for a profit and loss statement with percentage of income for each line item. He has also requested a balance sheet report. In this exercise, you will create both reports for the year to date.

1. Open the **Reports** center and choose **All tab→Business Overview→Profit and Loss**.
2. Select **This Year-to-Date** in the Report Period field.
3. Click the **Collapse** link just above the report.

   All the sub-accounts collapse, making a much more compact report. Notice that the Collapse link changes to Expand.

4. Click the **Expand** link.
5. Click the **Customize** button in the top-right corner of the window.
6. Click the **Rows/Columns** link to expand the section.
7. Add a checkmark to the **% of Income** checkbox.

% of Row	% of Column
✓ % of Income	% of Expense

8. Run the report.

   Craig's Design and Landscaping Services percent of Net Income for the period is 11.94%.

9. Export the report to a PDF file or Excel, saving the file in your **Chapter 11** folder as:
   CH11 Craig's Profit and Loss

10. Return to the **Reports** center and choose **All tab→Business Overview→Balance Sheet**.

11. Select **This Year-to-Date** in the Report Period field and then run the report.

    The balance sheet shows that Craig's Design and Landscaping Services has $23,056.18 in assets and $31,131.33 in liabilities.

    Congratulations! You have just completed the accounting cycle!

Assembling Management Reports

Predesigned management reports in QuickBooks Online let you assemble a package of professional-looking financial reports for presentation to executives, business partners, and others. The packages include a cover page and table of contents, and they can be customized with the company's logo. You can also add comments and preliminary pages.

 View the video "Customize Management Reports" at: labyrinthelab.com/2017/video/QBO-V1101

DEVELOP YOUR SKILLS 11-6

Craig would like a package of financial reports that he can take to his banker and Board of Directors to discuss growth opportunities. He has asked you for a balance sheet, a profit and loss statement, an A/R Aging Summary, and a Sales by Product/Service Summary. In this exercise, you will view a management report package, edit the package, and send it via email.

1. Open the **Reports** center and click the **Management Reports** tab.

2. In the Company Overview row, click **View**.

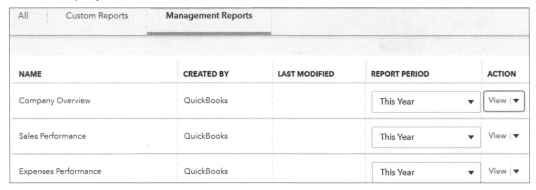

NAME	CREATED BY	LAST MODIFIED	REPORT PERIOD	ACTION
Company Overview	QuickBooks		This Year	View | ▼
Sales Performance	QuickBooks		This Year	View | ▼
Expenses Performance	QuickBooks		This Year	View | ▼

    The Print Preview screen appears.

3. Scroll through the report.

    Notice that the profit and loss statement and balance sheet already appear in the report package. Now you will edit the report package to add the other two reports that Craig would like to include.

4. Close the report.

5. In the Company Overview row, click the **Action menu** ▼ button and choose **Edit**.

6. Click **Reports** in the left pane. (You may need to scroll down the list.)

The Management Report window appears.

7. Click **Add New Report** and then select **A/R Aging Summary** from the Select a Report menu.

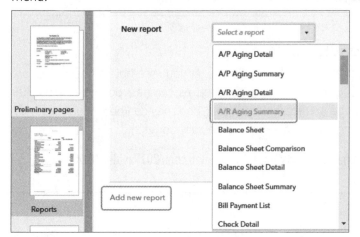

8. Click **Add New Report** again and, this time, select **Sales by Product/Service Summary**.

Note! The table of contents is automatically updated as you add new reports.

9. Change the Template Name to: `Company Overview with AR and Sales`

10. Change the Cover Page date by selecting the **Cover Page** and then typing the period ending date in the Report Period field (use the current date).

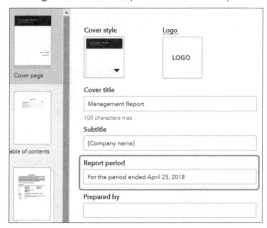

11. Save and close the form.

The added management report package is on your list now, ready for you to edit, send, export, copy, or delete.

12. Email the report package to yourself or export it to PDF or Excel, saving the file in your **Chapter 11** folder as: `CH11 Craig's Management Report Package`

Note! You can edit each page of the management report package by selecting the page and then making the edits.

Closing the Books

Closing the books refers to preparing financial statements and performing other tasks as part of month-end and year-end closing procedures. If you were closing the year for Craig's Design and Landscaping Services, QuickBooks Online would transfer all the income and expense accounts to the Retained Earnings account.

> ✔ *Best Practice*
> To prevent any entries after a period has ended, close the books after each period.

When you close the books in QuickBooks Online, the software prevents you from inadvertently adding entries to a closed period. It also includes a feature that allows you to change transactions in a closed period after a warning is displayed or you enter a password.

DEVELOP YOUR SKILLS 11-7

Craig wants to ensure that changes cannot be made to the accounting prior to the end of the quarter. In this exercise, you will close the books at a specific date and require a password to add or change a transaction in that period.

1. Choose **Gear→Your Company→Account and Settings** and then click **Advanced**.
2. Click the **Edit** icon in the Accounting section.
3. Place a checkmark before **Close the Books**.
4. Type the last day of the quarter you are in (for example, 09/30/2016) in the Closing Date field.
5. Select **Allow Changes after Viewing a Warning and Entering Password** in the next box.
6. Type a password (make it up) in the Password field and the Confirm Password field.
7. Click **Save** and then click **Done**.

The Audit Log and Audit History

QuickBooks Online has two auditing features to help you track changes to forms and transactions: the audit log and the audit history.

> **Note!** Each user must have a unique login and password for log information to be accurate.

Audit Log

The audit log provides a chronological list of activities performed. It tracks who logged in, when, and what each user added, edited, voided, or deleted. You can use filters to focus on a specific user, date range, or type of event.

In this exercise, you will access the audit log and apply a filter.

1. Choose **Gear→Tools→Audit Log**.

   Notice all the logins and logouts for Craig Carlson and what the event was.

2. Click the **Filter** button.

3. Add a checkmark in the **Sign In/Sign Out** checkbox to enable this option.

4. Click **Apply** and then view the time each user logged in and logged out.

Audit History

The audit history feature lets you track changes to customer and vendor transactions, including who made the change and when.

In this exercise, you will access the audit history for a transaction.

1. From the Customers list, click the link for **Amy's Bird Sanctuary**.

2. Click in the row for **Invoice # 1001**.

3. Click the **More** button in the bottom tray and choose **Audit History**.

You can review what was added or edited, when the change was made, and by whom.

4. Click **Compare** to view the changes side by side.

5. Click the **Back** button in your browser window (top-left corner of the screen) to return to the previous window.

6. Choose **Show All**.

   Changes are now highlighted, allowing you to more easily identify them.

Self-Assessment

Check your knowledge of this chapter's key concepts and skills using the Self-Assessment quiz here or in your eLab course.

1. QuickBooks Online allows you to close the books by entering a password only.　　　　　　　　　　　　　　　　　　　*True　False*

2. You can make a journal entry that is automatically entered for only twelve months.　　　　　　　　　　　　　　　　　　*True　False*

3. When you collapse a report, the sub-accounts become hidden and only summary totals display.　　　　　　　　　　　　　*True　False*

4. A trial balance is a statement of:
   A. The Chart of Accounts
   B. Profit and loss
   C. Transactions
   D. The Chart of Accounts and balances on a specific date

5. Which form is used to create adjusting entries?
   A. A transfer
   B. A journal entry
   C. A statement
   D. An expense

6. Why would you adjust inventory?
   A. The business did not sell enough of an item.
   B. Some items are no longer used or are obsolete.
   C. Some items are damaged.
   D. Some items are no longer used, are obsolete, or are damaged.

7. If you have an adjusting entry that will be the same and continue for many months, what would be the most efficient way of making it repeat?
   A. Create a recurring journal entry.
   B. Create an automatic reminder to create a journal entry each month.
   C. Create a transfer each month.
   D. Create a delayed journal entry.

8. The basic financial statements in QuickBooks Online are:
   A. Trial Balance
   B. Profit and Loss Statement and Balance Sheet
   C. Income Statement
   D. A/R Aging report and A/P Aging report
   E. Trial Balance and Income Statement

(cont'd.)

9. To customize a profit and loss statement to show the percentage of income for each line, you choose:

   A. Collapse

   B. Customize→Rows/Columns→Check % of Row

   C. Customize→Lines/Columns→Check % of Expense

   D. Customize→Rows/Columns→Check % of Income

10. Management reports allow you to:

    A. use preformatted reports for managers

    B. create a professional-looking set of reports in a package with a cover page and table of contents

    C. customize the look and contents of a report package

    D. All of these options

11. Why is the audit log used?

    A. To track users' logins and logouts

    B. To track added or edited transaction history

    C. To audit the books

    D. To track users' logins/logouts and to track added/edited transaction history

12. You can view the history of a transaction by viewing the:

    A. audit log's History column

    B. trial balance history report

    C. Audit History

    D. None of these; you cannot view the history of a transaction.

13. By closing the books in QuickBooks Online you:

    A. separate each month so no additional transactions can occur in prior months

    B. close a period so no new transactions can be entered in that period or a prior period without entering a password

    C. lock a period to prevent any updates

    D. None of these; you cannot close the books in QuickBooks Online.

⚲ Reinforce Your Skills

For these exercises, you will work with Puppy Luv Pampered Pooch, the company account created in your trial subscription to QuickBooks Online.

REINFORCE YOUR SKILLS 11-1

Prepare Reports

Sadie is really excited about the growth of her salon, but she knows she is a little behind in looking at her financial statements. She has asked you to prepare a report that displays all the accounts and their balances as of September 30, 2021, and then meet with her for a review. In this exercise, you will create two reports for Sadie.

1. Create a Trial Balance report for the period ending September 30, 2021.

2. Create an Inventory Valuation Summary report for September 30, 2021.

3. Verify that the Inventory Valuation Summary report total is the same as the Inventory Account on the Trial Balance report.

REINFORCE YOUR SKILLS 11-2

Create Depreciation Entries

Upon review of the trial balance, you and Sadie agree that you need to record the depreciation for the equipment purchased for $16,000. In this exercise, you will create the journal entry for September for the depreciation and then make it recurring. You will need to add two accounts: an Other Expense account for depreciation and a Fixed Asset account for the accumulated depreciation.

1. Create a journal entry for September for one month's depreciation expense on the equipment with a five-year life, dated September 30, 2021. (Be sure to use Kennel for the class.)

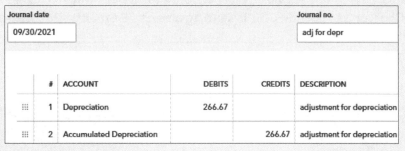

Journal date					Journal no.	
09/30/2021					adj for depr	

	#	ACCOUNT	DEBITS	CREDITS	DESCRIPTION
⁝⁝⁝	1	Depreciation	266.67		adjustment for depreciation
⁝⁝⁝	2	Accumulated Depreciation		266.67	adjustment for depreciation

2. Save the form.

3. Make the entry recurring for fifty-nine months.

REINFORCE YOUR SKILLS 11-3

Adjust for Inventory

You have taken a physical inventory and have discovered that only eleven Uber-Jive Balls are in stock. In this exercise, you will create an inventory adjustment.

1. Make the inventory adjustment, dated September 30, 2021.

    Hint: Be sure to use the Kennel class.

2. Create a Trial Balance report that reflects the changes made.

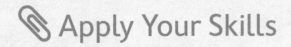 Apply Your Skills

Create Financial Statements

In this exercise, you will create the profit and loss statement and balance sheet reports for Sadie.

1. Create a Balance Sheet report for September 30, 2021; export the report to Excel, saving the file in your **Chapter 11** folder as: **CH11 Balance Sheet**

 CHECK FIGURE *Your figures should match those shown here.*

Statement	Balance
Total Assets	$77,991.42
Total Liabilities	$6,598.83

2. Create a Profit and Loss Statement for the year-to-date ending September 30, 2021, with percentage of income for each row; export the report to Excel, saving the file in your **Chapter 11** folder as: **CH11 Profit and Loss Statement**

 CHECK FIGURE *Your figures should match those shown here.*

Net Loss	Percentage
−$3,607.41	−73.71%

3. Create a management report package that includes the balance sheet, profit and loss statement, and Sales by Product/Service Summary reports all for July 1, 2021, through September 30, 2021.

4. Send the report package to yourself via email or export it to PDF or Word (DOCX), saving the file in your **Chapter 11** folder as: **CH11 Management Report Package**

Close the Books

In this exercise, you will close the books in QuickBooks Online to prevent any changes to the current or prior periods.

1. Close the books for Puppy Luv Pampered Pooch as of September 30, 2021.

2. Select **Allow Changes After Viewing a Warning and Entering Password**.

3. Enter and confirm the password. (Write it down. You may need it!)

4. Save your changes.

12 Using Payroll in QuickBooks Online

Payroll processing is a critical function of your business, and payroll is a key feature in QuickBooks Online. However, payroll is a separate add-on in QuickBooks Online. In this chapter, you will learn how to add and pay employees, pay payroll taxes, and file the payroll tax forms for Craig's Design and Landscaping.

LEARNING OBJECTIVES

▸ Set up new employees

▸ Pay employees

▸ File payroll tax forms

▸ Create employee and payroll reports

📂 Project: Craig's Design and Landscaping Services

Craig Carlson currently has three active employees, and he pays them every Friday. Craig is using the QuickBooks Online payroll service to process payroll, process payroll tax payments, and complete and file the quarterly and annual payroll tax forms required.

Introducing Payroll

Payroll is an intricate part of the accounting function, and QuickBooks Online offers some great tools to guide you through the setup and management of employees' wages and tax filings. There are additional fees involved. Subscribers can choose from two payroll offerings:

- **Enhanced** lets you enter the hours worked and then receive instant paycheck calculations. You can choose to print paper checks or use direct deposit.

- **Full Service** includes all the enhanced features plus federal and state tax form filing, W-2 filing, and support.

Payroll Setup

When you first subscribe to the QuickBooks Online payroll service, you will complete a series of forms to indicate your preferences regarding electronic services, pay policies, tax setup, deductions, and other settings.

To view your payroll preferences, you can click the Gear icon and select Payroll Settings under Your Company. You can then click the links for any of the options to view or edit your preferences.

Note! Keep in mind that the payroll tax withholdings and employer taxes are frequently updated, so the figures in this chapter may not reflect updates.

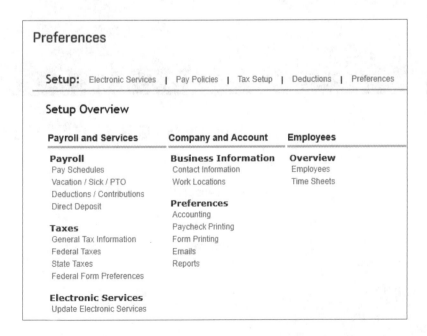

The Workers/Employees Center

The Workers/Employees center, located on the Navigation bar, provides information about your employees and your transactions with them in a single place. It allows you to perform payroll-related tasks such as adding employees, viewing the previous paycheck list, editing employee information, and making terminated employees inactive.

The Employees center shows a list of each employee along with that person's pay rate, pay method, and status. In the upper-left corner you'll find information on the total payroll cost for the current year and a breakdown of employee and employer costs. In the upper-right corner you'll see the next payroll due date and a link to the paycheck list. Also in the upper-right corner is the icon to Run Payroll, with options to add or edit employee information.

DEVELOP YOUR SKILLS 12-1

In this exercise, you will first turn on payroll for Craig's Design and Landscaping. Then you will add a new part-time employee whom Craig just hired to assist with some yard maintenance, as well as edit another employee's withholding allowance.

Before You Begin: *Access the QuickBooks Online test drive at qbo.intuit.com/redir/testdrive and leave the test drive open for the entire chapter.*

1. Open the **Workers/Employees** center from the Navigation pane.
2. Click **Get Started**.

Enter a New Employee

3. Click the **Add an Employee** button.

4. Tapping [Tab] to navigate the cells, fill in the employee's name:

   • First Name: **Shawn**

   • M.I.: **K**

   • Last Name: **Banta**

The lower half of the window shows a series of numbered questions related to payroll for an employee. You will now answer some of the questions.

5. Under step #1 ("What are Shawn's withholdings?"), click **Enter W-4 Form**.

6. Complete the W-4 as shown:

7. Click **Done** in the lower-right corner.

8. Under step 3, enter **$16.00** as the hourly rate and then click **Done**.

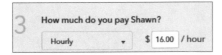

Return to the Employees list.

Edit an Existing Employee

9. Click **Lucchini, Bill** to open the details for this employee and then click **Edit Employee** (at top of screen) to edit Bill's taxes.

10. Click **Enter W-4 Form** under step 1.

11. In box 4, enter **1** for the total number of allowances Bill is claiming and then click **Done** twice.

Return to the Employees list.

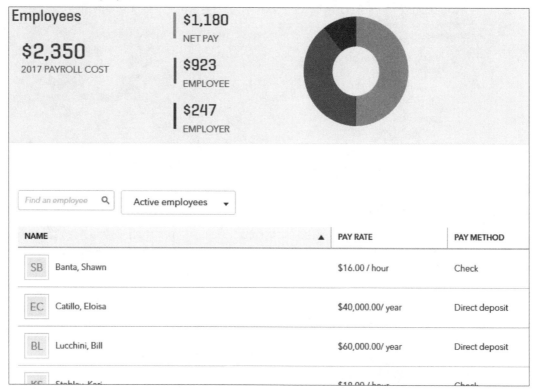

You are now ready to run the next payroll for all four employees.

Run Payroll

Before processing payroll, it's important to make any edits to employee records, including changes in pay rate, employment status, and address. Updating the employee information ensures that the employee will receive the correct wage, tax withholdings, and W-2 delivery at the end of the year.

QuickBooks Online payroll does all the calculations for gross pay each pay period based on the W-4 information provided. Calculations for the federal and state taxes to be withheld along with the employer taxes are automatic, based on the information provided for each employee. After the payroll has been submitted, the entry into the check register is automatically created.

In this exercise, you will run the payroll for all employees. Shawn worked 18 regular hours, while Kari worked 40 regular hours and 2 overtime hours. Eloisa and Bill are paid annual salaries, and their total salaries have been divided by the number of weeks in the year. Unless they work overtime, there is no need to enter any hours or amounts.

1. Click the **Run Payroll** button.

2. Enter the regular and overtime ("OT") hours for the employees as shown:

	EMPLOYEE		SALARY	REGULAR PAY HRS	OT HRS
☑	SB	Banta, Shawn K $16.00 / hour		18.00	
☑	EC	Catillo, Eloisa $40,000.00 / year	$769.23		
☑	BL	Lucchini, Bill $60,000.00 / year	$1,153.85		
☑	KS	Steblay, Kari $18.00 / hour		40.00	2.00
		TOTAL	$1,923.08	58.00	2.00

3. Click the **Preview Payroll** button.

   The payroll data should be reviewed for accuracy before submitting. If you need to make any changes, you can click the Edit icon to the right of the net pay for each employee.

4. Click the **Submit Payroll** button in the lower-right corner.

   In a true business environment, you would now print the payroll checks for Shawn and Kari and print the direct deposits stubs for Eloisa and Bill. For this exercise, you will not print.

5. Click **Finish Payroll**.

   A pop-up box regarding tax payments due appears.

6. Read the message and then click **Review and Pay**.

   Here you have an opportunity to view the payroll taxes due.

7. Return to the **Dashboard**.

Payroll Taxes

Along with payroll processing for each employee, every business must also pay the payroll taxes associated with each payday. QuickBooks Online calculates the employee and the employer payroll taxes on each payday and sets up reminders for the employer to pay the taxes on time and in the correct amount. If you are enrolled in the electronic services with the taxing authority, your payments will be paid to the federal and state agencies directly from your banking account, upon your approval. If you are not required to be enrolled in electronic services, QuickBooks will prefill payment coupons for you to attach to your payments.

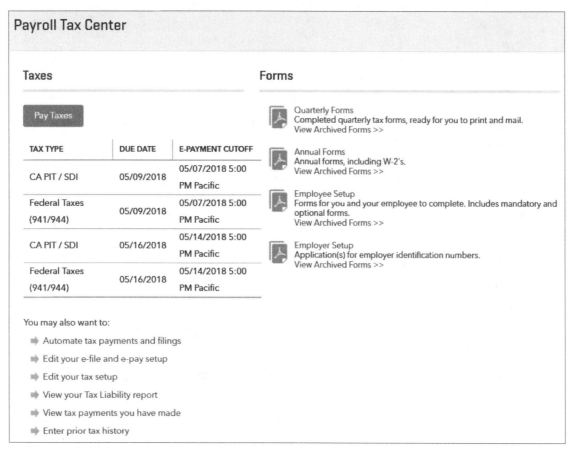

Within the Payroll Tax Center you can edit your tax setup and view many payroll tax reports and forms. After the tax payment has been created, the payment will automatically be recorded in the banking account register.

DEVELOP YOUR SKILLS 12-3

In this exercise, you will review and pay the payroll taxes associated with the prior payroll period.

1. Click **Taxes** on the Navigation pane and then choose **Payroll Tax**.

   The Payroll Tax Center opens.

2. Click the **Pay Taxes** button.

3. On the CA PIT / SDI row for last week's payroll (due date closest to today), click the **Create Payment** link. You may get a warning message if you are paying the tax early. If so, click **OK**.

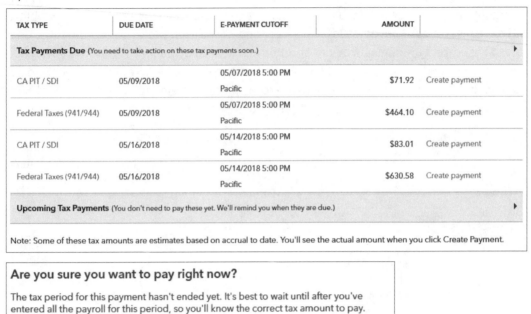

TAX TYPE	DUE DATE	E-PAYMENT CUTOFF	AMOUNT	
Tax Payments Due (You need to take action on these tax payments soon.)				▶
CA PIT / SDI	05/09/2018	05/07/2018 5:00 PM Pacific	$71.92	Create payment
Federal Taxes (941/944)	05/09/2018	05/07/2018 5:00 PM Pacific	$464.10	Create payment
CA PIT / SDI	05/16/2018	05/14/2018 5:00 PM Pacific	$83.01	Create payment
Federal Taxes (941/944)	05/16/2018	05/14/2018 5:00 PM Pacific	$630.58	Create payment
Upcoming Tax Payments (You don't need to pay these yet. We'll remind you when they are due.)				▶

Note: Some of these tax amounts are estimates based on accrual to date. You'll see the actual amount when you click Create Payment.

Are you sure you want to pay right now?

The tax period for this payment hasn't ended yet. It's best to wait until after you've entered all the payroll for this period, so you'll know the correct tax amount to pay.

[Cancel]   [OK]

4. This tax will be paid electronically, so click **E-Pay** at the bottom-right corner.

5. Click **Done** in the Payment Confirmation window.

   You are returned to the Pay Taxes window.

6. Click the **Create Payment** link for the **Federal Taxes (941/944)** from the previous week's payroll (due date closest to today).

   If a warning message appears because you are paying the tax early, click OK or ignore the warning.

7. This tax will also be paid electronically, so click **E-Pay**.

8. Click **Done** in the Payment Confirmation window.

9. Return to the **Dashboard**.

Payroll Tax Forms

Employers are required to file payroll tax forms to the federal and state (if applicable) tax agencies. The forms are submitted quarterly and annually, depending on the tax being reported. QuickBooks Online completes the forms so they are ready for the employer to review and submit at the end of each quarter or year. Annual reports include Form 940, Form 944, and Form W-2.

Quarterly reports required and the frequency with which they are due can vary from state to state. In California, for example, the reports include Form 941 (federal), DE9 (state of California), and DE9C (state of California).

Tip! Know the payroll forms required by employers in your state.

DEVELOP YOUR SKILLS 12-4

In this exercise, you will view the tax forms required for Craig's Design and Landscaping. You will not complete any tax forms, though, because there is not enough test data provided in QuickBooks Online to do so.

1. Open the Payroll Tax Center by choosing **Taxes→Payroll Tax**.
2. Under the Forms heading on the right, click **Quarterly Forms**.

   This is the list of forms due at the end of each quarter. They need to be reviewed and submitted by the employer.

3. Return to the Payroll Tax Center.
4. Click **Annual Forms** to view the list of forms due at the end of the year and then return to the Payroll Tax Center.
5. Click the links for the remaining forms (Employee Setup and Employer Setup) and then return to the Payroll Tax Center.

Payroll Reports

QuickBooks Online creates many payroll-related reports for the employer to use for managing the various payroll costs.

DEVELOP YOUR SKILLS 12-5

In this exercise, you will view one of the payroll reports available in QuickBooks Online.

1. Open the **Reports** center from the Navigation bar.
2. Choose **All tab→Payroll→Payroll Summary**.

   This report provides information on each employee, including total (gross) pay, deductions, and net pay. It also shows the employer taxes associated with each employee and the total payroll costs.

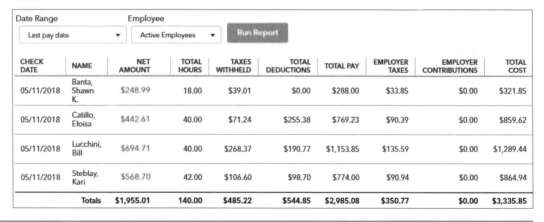

CHECK DATE	NAME	NET AMOUNT	TOTAL HOURS	TAXES WITHHELD	TOTAL DEDUCTIONS	TOTAL PAY	EMPLOYER TAXES	EMPLOYER CONTRIBUTIONS	TOTAL COST
05/11/2018	Banta, Shawn K.	$248.99	18.00	$39.01	$0.00	$288.00	$33.85	$0.00	$321.85
05/11/2018	Catillo, Eloisa	$442.61	40.00	$71.24	$255.38	$769.23	$90.39	$0.00	$859.62
05/11/2018	Lucchini, Bill	$694.71	40.00	$268.37	$190.77	$1,153.85	$135.59	$0.00	$1,289.44
05/11/2018	Steblay, Kari	$568.70	42.00	$106.60	$98.70	$774.00	$90.94	$0.00	$864.94
	Totals	$1,955.01	140.00	$485.22	$544.85	$2,985.08	$350.77	$0.00	$3,335.85

Tackle the Tasks

This is your opportunity to apply some of the skills learned in this chapter to accomplish additional tasks for Craig's Design and Landscaping Services. To refresh your memory, refer to the concepts and Develop Your Skills exercises as needed.

Before You Begin: Close the current test drive window and then open a new test drive window.

Task	Use This Information
Turn on payroll and add an employee	• Arlin King, 7844 Main Road, Mountain View, CA 94043 • Social Security Number: 555-55-5599 • Married with 1 allowance for federal and state • Pay rate: $21.00 per hour • Pay with a paper check
Edit an employee	On Kari Steblay's W-4, change the number of allowances to 1.
Run payroll	Run payroll for the next payroll due date using these hours: Arlin King, 30 regular; Kari Steblay, 40 regular and 1 overtime. The total pay should equal $3,300.08.
Pay payroll taxes	Create the tax payments for the previous payroll period for CA PIT/SDI and Federal Taxes (941/944).
Create a payroll report	Create a Payroll Summary report for the last pay date. If directed, export your report to Excel or PDF, or print it manually.

Your report should look similar to this.

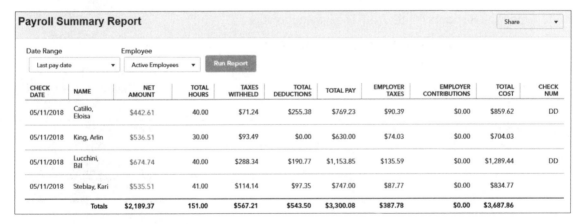

CHECK DATE	NAME	NET AMOUNT	TOTAL HOURS	TAXES WITHHELD	TOTAL DEDUCTIONS	TOTAL PAY	EMPLOYER TAXES	EMPLOYER CONTRIBUTIONS	TOTAL COST	CHECK NUM
05/11/2018	Catillo, Eloisa	$442.61	40.00	$71.24	$255.38	$769.23	$90.39	$0.00	$859.62	DD
05/11/2018	King, Arlin	$536.51	30.00	$93.49	$0.00	$630.00	$74.03	$0.00	$704.03	
05/11/2018	Lucchini, Bill	$674.74	40.00	$288.34	$190.77	$1,153.85	$135.59	$0.00	$1,289.44	DD
05/11/2018	Steblay, Kari	$535.51	41.00	$114.14	$97.35	$747.00	$87.77	$0.00	$834.77	
	Totals	$2,189.37	151.00	$567.21	$543.50	$3,300.08	$387.78	$0.00	$3,687.86	

Self-Assessment

Check your knowledge of this chapter's key concepts and skills using the Self-Assessment quiz here or in your eLab course.

1. Which payroll taxes does QuickBooks Online Payroll calculate on each payday?
   A. Business taxes
   B. Employer taxes
   C. Employee and Employer taxes
   D. Employee and Business taxes

2. QuickBooks Online offers _____ payroll services for additional fees.
   A. Basic and Deluxe
   B. Enhanced and Full Service
   C. Regular and Assisted
   D. Regular and Deluxe

3. What employee information is required to set up and process payroll?
   A. Employee full name only
   B. Employee full name, address, and Social Security number
   C. Employee full name, address, and withholding allowances
   D. Employee full name and pay rate

4. QuickBooks Online payroll allows an employer to change:
   A. the taxes withheld
   B. an employee's address, wage, and withholding allowances
   C. the date taxes are due
   D. the amount of employer taxes due

5. QuickBooks Online payroll allows the employer to process payroll for _____ on the same pay date.
   A. regular and overtime employees
   B. hourly and salaried employees
   C. administration and hourly employees
   D. only salaried employees

6. After beginning payroll processing by clicking Run Payroll, an employer:
   A. enters the regular and overtime hours worked
   B. can add the employees
   C. can make changes to employee information
   D. can verify the accuracy of the payroll information

(cont'd.)

7. What are the steps to process payroll in QuickBooks Online?

   A. Run, submit, and finish payroll

   B. Start, review, and finish payroll

   C. Run, preview, submit, and finish payroll

   D. Start, review, submit, and finish payroll

8. QuickBooks Online payroll sets up reminders for employers to pay payroll taxes on time and to the right agency. Where would the employer go to pay those taxes?

   A. Taxes→Payroll Tax

   B. Gear→Account and Settings

   C. Payroll Tax Center

   D. Employees→Pay Taxes

9. Does QuickBooks Online payroll create all the required payroll tax forms?

   A. Yes, but the employer must enter the payments made.

   B. Yes, but the employer needs to review and submit them.

   C. No, it only creates the federal forms.

   D. No, the employer must prepare them from the available reports.

10. Where are the payroll reports located?

   A. Reports→Payroll

   B. Employees→Payroll

   C. Employees→Reports→Payroll

   D. Reports→All tab→Payroll

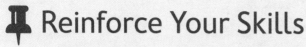

Reinforce Your Skills

For these exercises, you will work with Puppy Luv Pampered Pooch, the company account you created in your trial subscription to QuickBooks Online.

QuickBooks Online payroll must process the payroll and taxes on the current date. Use the current date in these exercises, even if that doesn't coincide with the Puppy Luv dates.

REINFORCE YOUR SKILLS 12-1

Set Up Payroll

Sadie has decided to purchase and use QuickBooks Online payroll to pay her two employees. In this exercise, you will turn on payroll and complete the employee setup for Sadie. All groomers receive hourly compensation plus commissions and are paid weekly with a paper check.

1. Open the **Employees** center and click **Choose Your Plan**.

2. Select **Automatic Tax Calculations**, **Unlimited Payroll Runs**, and **Free Direct Deposits & W-2s**.

3. Click the **Try Now** button under Enhanced Payroll.

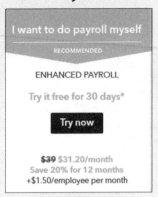

4. Click **Get Set Up**.

5. Click in the circle next to the **No** option to indicate that you have not paid any employees in the current year and then click **Continue**.

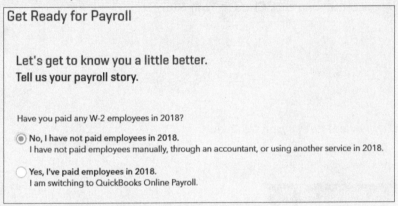

6. Click in the **Yes** circle to indicate that you have completed the W-4 forms and then click **Continue**.

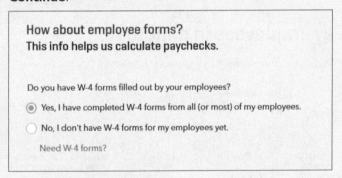

7. Click the **Add an Employee** link.

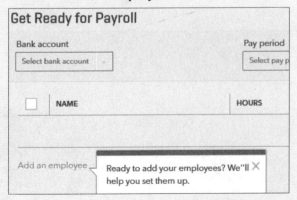

8. On the next screen, enter the information for Becky Douglas.

    Hint: Remember to click Done to complete screens.

    - Under step #1: Fill in the W-4 form.
    - Under step #2: Click **Enter a Pay Schedule** to review the information but leave the defaults.
    - Under step #3: Enter the hourly rate in the box and then click **Add Additional Pay Types** and add a checkmark next to **Commission**.
    - Under step #4: Leave *No (most common)*.
    - Under step #5: Choose **Paper Check**.

Employee Name	Becky Douglas
Address	115 Oldwood Los Angeles, CA 90051
Social Security Number	548-85-9999
W-4 Allowance	Single, 1
Pay Rate	$12.50 per hour, plus 15% of all groomings

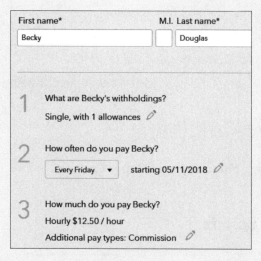

9. Return to the Employees list.

10. Continue with Andy Gomez.

Employee Name	Andy Gomez
Address	8774 Connee Ln. #281 Los Angeles, CA 90049
Social Security Number	123-44-9944
W-4 Allowance	Single, 0
Pay Rate	$12.50 per hour, plus 15% of all groomings
Deductions	No

11. Close the window and return to the **Dashboard**.

    You may need to refresh your browser.

Set Up Payroll Taxes

In this exercise, you will complete the payroll tax setup for Sadie.

1. Open the Payroll Tax center by choosing **Taxes→Payroll Tax**.

2. Read the information and click **Continue**.

3. Enter the birthdates and hire dates for Becky and Andy and then click **Continue**.

   Becky's birthday is 03/13/1999 and Andy's is 11/01/2001. Use 01/01/20xx (current year) as the hire date for each employee.

4. On the Payroll Taxes Setup and Compliance screen:

   You may receive only some of the questions shown here or different ones. That's okay! Answer the questions as appropriate.

   - Verify the business name and address.
   - Choose the appropriate quarter under "When will you first be running payroll with QuickBooks Online Payroll?"
   - Choose **Yes** under "Did you hire your first employee within the last six months?"
   - Choose **No** under "Did you buy your business from a previous owner?"
   - Choose **No** under "Would you like a workers' comp insurance quote?"

5. Click **Continue**, read the contents of the pop-up window, and then click **OK**.

6. On the next window, enter the Federal and State Employer Identification numbers and click **Save**.

   The Federal Employer Identification number is 10-1111100 and the State Employer Account number is 114-4567-8.

7. On the E-Pay and E-File Setup screen, select **Manually with Paper Coupons** and click **Next**.

   > ### All set! Thanks for entering your tax info.
   >
   > Now that we have your info, we can help prepare your payroll taxes and notify you when it's time to take action.

8. Click **Done** and then return to the **Dashboard**.

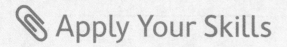 Apply Your Skills

Process Payroll

In this exercise, you will process the first payroll for Sadie. The information needed for Becky's and Andy's hours and commissions follows.

- *Becky Douglas: First day of the week, 5 hours; second day of the week, 5 hours; Grooming Sales equals $193.00*

- *Andy Gomez: First day of the week, 7 hours; second day of the week, 5 hours; Grooming Sales equals $280.00*

Before You Begin: *Deselect the closing date by choosing Gear→Your Company→Account and Settings→Advanced and unchecking Close the Books. Click Done.*

1. Open the **Employees** center and click the **Run Payroll** button.

2. Select both employees by placing checkmarks in the boxes and then enter their hours and commission amounts.

☑	EMPLOYEE		REGULAR PAY HRS...	COMMISSION	MEMO	TOTAL PAY
☑	BD	Douglas, Becky $12.50 / hour	10.00	$ 28.95		$153.95 ✎
☑	AG	Gomez, Andy $12.50 / hour	12.00	$ 42.00		$192.00 ✎
		TOTAL	22.00	$70.95		$345.95

3. Click **Preview Payroll**.

   The Total Pay should be $345.95.

4. Click **Submit Payroll**.

5. Enter check number **10024** for Becky and check number **10025** for Andy and then click **Finish Payroll**.

   Congratulations! You have successfully processed your first payroll.

6. Return to the **Dashboard**.

Pay Payroll Taxes

In this exercise, you will pay the payroll taxes due for the payroll just paid.

1. Open the **Payroll Tax Center**.
2. Click **Pay Taxes**.
3. Click **Record Payment** for the CA PIT / SDI you want to pay right now. (If a warning box appears, click **OK**.)
4. Click **Record Payment**.
5. Review the pop-up window and then click **View and Print Form**.
6. View the form and then close the window to return to the Payroll Tax Center.

Tip! The forms may not be available, depending on where you are in the current year.

7. Click **Pay Taxes**.
8. Click **Record Payment** for the Federal Taxes (941/944) you want to pay right now. (Accept the warning if it appears.)
9. Click **Record Payment**.
10. Review the pop-up window and then click **View and Print Form**.
11. View the report and then close the window.

APPLY YOUR SKILLS 12-3 QG

Run Payroll Reports

In this exercise, you will produce a summary of the payroll for Sadie.

1. Open the **Reports** center and choose **All tab→Payroll→Payroll Summary**.
2. In the Date Range box, choose **Last Pay Date**, if necessary.
3. In the top-right corner of the screen, choose **Share→Export to Excel** and save the file in your **Chapter 12** folder as: **CH12 Payroll Summary**

 CHECK FIGURE *Your figures should match the one shown here.*

Total Pay	$345.95

13 | Bringing It All Together!

I n this chapter, you will work on a project to demonstrate all you have learned about QuickBooks Online. You will analyze the information provided to set up a new auto detailing business and then process transactions, reconcile accounts, make adjusting entries, and prepare reports.

📂 Project: Raincross Auto Detailing Case Study

Brothers Chris and Eric Christian are going to open a small automobile detailing business in a converted vintage gasoline station. They are using Raincross in their name to help connect their business to the community, which uses the Raincross symbol in its flag and other civic institutions. They will open on December 1, 2021. You will set up and keep the books for this first month. As you work in the company file, you will add new customers, vendors, and other information as needed. You will use your own problem-solving skills to complete the project. Throughout the project, you will produce deliverables for evaluation. You are welcome to use help and the information in this course to accomplish all the tasks.

Before You Begin

Remember that QuickBooks Online allows only one company file per license. This means that you cannot use the trial subscription that you have been using in the previous chapters. Instead, you will access the free, 30-day trial of QuickBooks Online to complete this chapter.

You must access the free trial and register with your name, email address, and phone number. You may need to set up a new email account specific to this project, as you cannot use the email address used for the trial software that came with your textbook.

Access the QuickBooks Free Trial and Set Up a Company

Before beginning the project, access a free, 30-day trial of QuickBooks Online and set up the Raincross Auto Detailing company.

The following sequence of steps begins by guiding you to the free trial. Remember that websites can change! If steps 2-4 don't work exactly, try searching the page for "free trial."

1. In your web browser, go to: **quickbooks.intuit.com /try-for-free-accounting-software/**

2. Click **Start Now for Free**.

3. Click **FREE TRIAL** to the right of the toggle button to show the no-cost offerings.

4. Click the **Try It Free** button for the Plus version under Small Businesses.

5. Complete the registration by filling in all fields, keeping in mind the following notes and tips:
   - Enter a phone number that allows for the receipt of text messages.
   - Do not use the same email address you used for the trial version of the software used in previous chapters. Intuit requires a different email address.
   - Click in the **Password** box and notice the list of required password attributes.

Tip! To avoid Intuit marketing, try using the words *Test* or *Student* in your email address.

6. Click **Create Account** at the bottom of the form.

7. If you get a pop-up message, click **Continue with Trial**.

   You should see a "Welcome to QuickBooks" message. You can now set up the Raincross Auto Detailing project and complete this chapter.

New Company Set Up

Chris has been operating a mobile automobile detailing business for a few months. He and his brother, Eric, decide to rent a garage to offer onsite auto detailing and retail some products. They will use Chris's existing customer base. You are responsible for creating the new company file and adding details about customers, vendors, products, services, and more.

8. Use this information to create the new company data file:

Business Name	Raincross Auto Detailing (Add your name)
Business Address	1807 Hamburg Ave., Riverside, CA 92501
Phone	951-555-1114
Industry	Automotive Repair and Maintenance
What Do You Sell?	Products and Services
Business Type	Partnership
What Would You Like to Do in QuickBooks?	Invoicing, Expenses, Inventory, Sales, Bills, Sales Tax
Employer Tax ID	99-9999991
Purchase Orders	Turn on feature
Tax Year	January
Tax Form	Form 1065
Accounting Method	Accrual
Default Sales Term	Net 15
Logo	Add **CH13 Raincross Logo.png**, located in your **Chapter 13** folder.

9. Use this information to create the bank and credit card accounts:

Account Name	Opening Balance	Opening Date
Checking - Raincross Business Bank 4673	$13,000	November 30, 2021
Savings - Raincross Business Bank	$5,000	November 30, 2021
Credit Card – Visa	$0	November 30, 2021

10. Delete **Billable Expense Income** from the Chart of Accounts.

11. Change the names of the following accounts in the Chart of Accounts:

From	To
Sales	Services
Advertising & Marketing	Advertising/Promotional
Other Business Expenses	General Operating Expenses
Job Supplies	Service Supplies

12. Regarding sales tax:

- All customers will be taxable; all products (but not services) will be taxable
- There are no sales outside of California
- Tax Period Start: [use the current month]
- Frequency to File Tax Return: select **Monthly**
- Start Date for Collecting Sales Tax: [use the current date]
- Tax rate: 8.5% (you will override the sales tax amount on each sales document that has a product sold)

13. Set up or import existing customers.

*You can use this information to create entries one at a time or use the Import Customers feature to import all the customers at once (**CH13 Customer List.xls**).*

Customer Name	Company	Email	Phone	Street	City	State	ZIP
John McNay		jmcnay@email.com	951-555-2195	2118 Hagen St.	Riverside	CA	92502
Dan Greany		dgreany@email.com	951-555-6103	102 Copper Rd.	Riverside	CA	92503
Dan Thomas		dthomas@email.com	951-555-1245	147 West 4th St.	Riverside	CA	92503
Annette Helsper		ahelsper@email.com	951-555-5928	1305 West 3rd St.	Riverside	CA	90504
Pam Swanson		pswanson@email.com	951-555-6203	246 Birch St.	Riverside	CA	92502
Mike McCollough		mmccollough@email.com	951-555-1093	955 Eagle Mountain Dr.	Riverside	CA	92507
Larry Bloodneck		lbloodneck@email.com	951-555-3397	1104 East Park St.	Riverside	CA	92502
Mark Biggs		mbiggs@email.com	951-555-5981	496 Mt Baldy Rd.	Riverside	CA	92502
Sean Murphy		smurphy@email.com	951-555-1942	1106 West Park St.	Riverside	CA	92502
Lesli McGrevy		lmcgrevy@email.com	951-555-8851	507 West 3rd St.	Riverside	CA	92504
Mike Carson	Carson Auto Sales	mcarson@email.com	951-555-9441	4201 East 6th St.	Riverside	CA	92502
Ericka Jenson	Jenson Auto Wholesalers	ejenson@email.com	951-555-7344	331 Pine St.	Riverside	CA	92502

14. Set up or import existing vendors.

*You can use the following information to create entries one at a time or use the Import Vendors feature to import vendors all at once (**CH13 Vendor List.xls**).*

Name	Company	Email	Phone	Street	City	State	ZIP
Colleen Johnson	Johnson Insurance Co	cjohnson@email.com	951-555-2195	206 West 4th St.	Riverside	CA	92504
Raincross Power and Gas	Raincross Power and Gas	rcpg@email.com	951-555-4431	201 West 3rd St.	Riverside	CA	92502
Scheideman Property Management	Scheideman Property Management	spm@email.com	951-555-7534	4213 Salem St.	Riverside	CA	92502
City Water Works	City Water Works	cww@email.com	951-555-3842	1104 West 4th St.	Riverside	CA	92504
District Waste Management	District Waste Management	dwm@email.com	951-555-4982	666 Hellsgate Ln.	Riverside	CA	92505
Patsy's Automotive Supplies	Patsy's Automotive Supplies	patsy@email.com	800-555-2235	1900 Butte Hill Re	Phoenix	AZ	85001
GLJ Car Detail Supplies	GLJ Car Detail Supplies	glj@email.com	951-555-9988	24567 Danny Boy Way	Corona	CA	92877
PriceCo							

15. Set up the Products and Services list by adding or importing the following non-taxable services and non-inventory products (**CH13 Services and Noninventory.xls**):

Product/Service Name	Sales Description	Type	Sales Price	Income Account	Expense Account
Rock Chip Windshield Repair	Rock Chip Windshield Repair	Service	55.00	Services	
Automotive Paint Sealant Repair	Automotive Paint Sealant Repair	Service	125.00	Services	
Paint Over Spray Removal Repair	Paint Over Spray Removal Repair	Service	25.00	Services	
Paint Touch Up Repair	Paint Touch Up Repair	Service	20.00	Services	
Hand Wash	Hand Wash	Service	20.00	Services	
Hand Wash with Interior	Hand Wash with Interior	Service	35.00	Services	
Electronic Odor Elimination	Electronic Odor Elimination	Service	25.00	Services	
Shampoo Carpet	Shampoo Carpet	Service	60.00	Services	
Shampoo Upholstery	Shampoo Upholstery	Service	50.00	Services	
Engine Clean	Engine Clean	Service	45.00	Services	
Exterior Polish and Wax	Exterior Polish and Wax	Service	75.00	Services	
Exterior Wax	Exterior Wax	Service	45.00	Services	
Water Spot/Tar Removal	Water Spot/Tar Removal	Service	15.00	Services	
Vinyl/Leather Treatment	Vinyl/Leather Treatment	Service	25.00	Services	
Tire/Bumper Dressing	Tire/Bumper Dressing	Service	15.00	Services	
Shampoo Trunk	Shampoo Trunk	Service	25.00	Services	
Paint Protection Small Car	Paint Protection Small Car	Service	90.00	Services	
Paint Protection Large Car	Paint Protection Large Car	Service	125.00	Services	
Full Interior/Exterior Detailing Small Car	Car	Service	180.00	Services	
Full Interior/Exterior Detailing Large Car	Car	Service	225.00	Services	
Full Exterior Detailing Small Car	Full Exterior Detailing Small Car	Service	160.00	Services	
Full Exterior Detailing Large Car	Full Exterior Detailing Large Car	Service	180.00	Services	
Interior Detailing Small Car	Interior Detailing Small Car	Service	100.00	Services	
Interior Detailing Large Car	Interior Detailing Large Car	Service	140.00	Services	
Brushes	Brushes	Noninventory			Service Supplies
Rags	Rags	Noninventory			Service Supplies
Buckets	Buckets	Noninventory			Service Supplies
Water Hoses	Water Hoses	Noninventory			Service Supplies
Paper Hand Towels	Paper Hand Towels	Noninventory			Service Supplies
Mimi's Upholstery and Carpet Cleaner	Cleaner	Noninventory			Service Supplies
Jack's Superior Exterior Car Wash Cleaner	Cleaner	Noninventory			Service Supplies

16. Add or import (**CH13 Inventory.xlsx**) the following inventory products:

- All items have zero inventory on the current date.
- Use Sales of Product Income as the Income account, Cost of Goods Sold as the Expense account, and Inventory Asset as the Inventory Asset account.
- All inventory products are taxable.

Product Name	Sales/Purchase Description	Sales Price	Purchase Cost
Wash Mitts	Micro Fiber Wash Mitts, 3 pack	12.00	7.00
Dry Towels	Micro Fiber Dry Towels, 3 pack	10.00	5.25
Window Cleaner	Jasper's 14 oz Window Cleaner	4.00	1.75
Glass Polish	Jasper's 8 oz Glass Polish	5.00	2.59
Paste Wax	Rosey's Exterior Paste Wax	13.00	7.25
Interior Cleaner	Jasper's 16 oz Interior Cleaner	8.00	3.89
Vinyl Rubber Dressing	Rosey's 8 oz Vinyl/Rubber Dressing	7.00	3.55
Leather Conditioner	Rosey's 6 oz Leather Conditioner	11.00	6.27
Wheel Rim Polish	Rosey's 16 oz Wheel-Rim	9.00	4.50
Rubbing Compound	Rosey's 12 oz Rubbing Compound	9.00	5.03

Prepare Your Deliverables—Set 1 [QG]

To complete this segment of the project, prepare the following deliverables and export to Excel:

- Chart of Accounts list, saved as: **CH13 Chart of Accounts**

- Products and Services list, saved as: **CH13 Products and Services**

- Customers list, saved as: **CH13 Customers**

- Vendors list, saved as: **CH13 Vendors**

Create Daily Transactions

In this segment of the project, you will create the daily transactions as described for each day, adding customers, vendors, and accounts as necessary. Opportunities to check your figures appear along the way; please be sure your figures match those provided here before moving on. Keep in mind that you will need to add *Riverside, CA 92501* to each taxable sales transaction and you may need to overwrite the calculated sales tax to 8.5%.

Week 1

Wednesday, December 1, 2021

- Sold a Rock Chip Windshield Repair Service to Larry Bloodneck on account using Invoice number 21-101. (Be sure to enable the custom transaction number in Account and Settings→ Sales.)

- Received cash from Dan Greany for Hand Wash with Interior and Electronic Odor Elimination services, using Sales Receipt number 21-102. (Remember to deposit to Undeposited Funds.)

- Received check number 429 from Sean Murphy for Hand Wash and Engine Clean services.

- Used the Visa card to purchase printer ink at PriceCo for $42.99.

- Wrote check number 10010 to Scheideman Property Management for $4,500 for three months' rent (December rent plus prepaid rent for January and February).

- Received check number 461 from Logan Webb for Rock Chip Windshield Repair service.

- Invoice Mike Carson at Carson Car Sales for 4 small-vehicle and 3 large-vehicle Full Interior/ Exterior Detail services; Invoice number 21-105 ($1,395).

- Received cash from Sally Cassen for Paint Protection service for large van.

- Create a purchase order to Patsy's Automotive Supplies for 30 units of Window Cleaner, 25 of Glass Polish, and 25 of Interior Cleaner.

- Create a purchase order to GLJ Car Detail Supplies for 20 Wash Mitts and 20 Dry Towels.

- Create a purchase order to Rosey & Girls Auto Supply, 1511 Seattle Rd., San Diego, CA 92104, for 15 units of Paste Wax, 15 of Vinyl Rubber Dressing, 10 of Leather Conditioner, 10 of Wheel Rim Polish, and 15 of Rubbing Compound.

Thursday, December 2, 2021

- Received cash from Chris McCartney for a Hand Wash with Interior service.

- Received check number 1465 from Dan Thomas for Paint Protection service for a large SUV.

- Received a bill from GLJ Car Detail Supplies for $60 for one case of Mimi's Upholstery and Carpet Cleaner. (Be sure to select Item Details.)

- Received cash from Deborah Michaels for Hand Wash with Interior and Electronic Odor Elimination services.

- Purchased office supplies from Office Superstore for $109.74 with Visa card.

- Sold Engine Clean and Hand Wash to Becky Craig on account.

- Received check number 1642 from Stephen Markley for a Full Interior/Exterior Detail service for a small car.

Friday, December 3, 2021

- Received a bill from Johnson Insurance Co. (Colleen Johnson) for $154.30 for Liability Insurance; due in 15 days.

- Purchased water, soda, and snacks for the waiting room from Thompson's Grocery with Visa card; $36.55 (Office Supplies & Software).

- Received a bill from Patsy's Automotive Supplies for $311.87 for 8 gallons of Jack's Superior Exterior Car Wash at $13.99 a gallon and 5 bundles of Rags at $39.99 a bundle; terms Net 15 days.

- Invoice Ericka Jenson at Jenson Auto Wholesalers for 7 small cars and 2 large cars, Full Interior/Exterior Detail services.

- Receive the products and the bill from GLJ Car Detail Supplies for purchase order number 1002; terms Net 15.

- Received the products and the bill from Patsy's Automotive Supplies for purchase order number 1001; terms Net 15.

- Deposit all the funds in Undeposited Funds into the checking account. (Deposit amount should be $705.)

 CHECK FIGURE *Display your trial balance report from 12/01/2021 through 12/03/2021 and verify that your figures match those shown here.*

Account	Balance
Checking	$9,205
Accounts Receivable	$3,225
Accounts Payable	$985.67
Visa	$189.28

Week 2

Monday, December 6, 2021

- Sold a Paint Touch Up Repair to Mike Carson at Carson Car Sales on account.

- Invoice Ericka Jenson at Jenson Auto Wholesales for 5 small-car Full Interior/Exterior Detailing Services; Invoice number 21-114.

- Sold a Full Interior/Exterior Detailing service for a large SUV to Mike McCollough on account; terms Net 15.

- Received a bill from Patsy's Automotive Supplies for $55.96 for 4 gallons of Jack's Superior Exterior Car Wash at $13.99 a gallon.

- Received check number 622 from Felicity York for a Rock Chip Windshield Repair service.

- Received products and bill from Rosey & Girls Auto Supply for PO number 1003; terms Net 15.

- Received check number 449 from Sean Murphy for Exterior Hand Wash and Engine Clean services as well as one Window Cleaner and a package of Wash Mitts. (Remember to add California Sales Tax.)

- Received payment from Becky Craig, check number 510 for Invoice number 21-110.

- Invoice Annette Helsper for a Hand Wash with Interior service and a package of Wash Mitts, a Dry Towel 3-pack, Window Cleaner, and Interior Cleaner.

Tuesday, December 7, 2021

- Received check number 884 from Skye Simpson for Paint Protective service for a large car and Interior Cleaner and a package of Dry Towels.

- Invoice Mike Carson at Carson Auto Sales for 4 small vehicles and 1 large vehicle, Full Interior/Exterior Detailing services.

- Received payment (check number 2503) from Larry Bloodneck for Invoice number 21-101.

- Received a bill from WebWorks, 1520 So. Main Ave., Corona, CA 92882, for a year (December through November) of web hosting for $600; terms Net 15.

- Received a bill from GLJ Car Detail Supplies for $120 for two cases of Mimi's Upholstery and Carpet Cleaner at $60 a case; terms Net 15.

- Received cash from Cynthia Swan for a Hand Wash with Interior and Electronic Odor Elimination services, as well as a package of Wash Mitts, a pack of Dry Towels, Window Cleaner, and Glass Polish. (Total was $93.64.)

- Received check number 1707 from Mike Carson for Invoice number 21-105.

Wednesday, December 8, 2021

- Purchased carpet for the lobby from Galen Bros. Interiors using the company Visa card for $209.45; (General Operating Expense).

- Invoice Dan Thomas for a Hand Wash with Interior along with Dry Towels, Rubbing Compound, Vinyl/Rubber Dressing, and Leather Conditioner; terms Net 15.

- Sold Paint Protection service for a large vehicle to Lesli Johns for cash.

- Purchased water, soda, and snacks for the waiting room at Thompson's Grocery with Visa card for $41.92.

- Invoice Mike Carson at Carson Auto Sales for 4 small vehicles and 5 large vehicles, Full Interior/Exterior Detail service.

- Sold a Hand Wash with Interior and Vinyl/Rubber Dressing to John McNay on account.

- Received a bill from GLJ Car Detail Supplies for $38.48 for a package of Brushes at $19.99 each and a 3-pack of Buckets at $18.49 each.

Thursday, December 9, 2021

- Received check number 257 from Scott Johnie for Paint Protection and Automotive Paint Sealant Repair for a large car, along with Dry Towels, Paste Wax, Interior Cleaner, and Leather Conditioner; total was $295.57.

- Received check number 1668 for $700 as payment on account from Jenson Auto Wholesalers; apply to Invoice number 21-112.

- Received check number 3355 from Mike Carson for Invoice number 21-113.

- Paid Simpson's Pizzeria $38.44 for a customer appreciation lunch with checking account debit card; (Meals & Entertainment).

- Sold an Interior Detailing package for a large car to Roxy Holden for cash.

- Deposit all funds held in Undeposited Funds into checking account ($3,171.10).

Friday, December 10, 2021

- Received check number 918 from Kimmy Lear for a Paint Protection service for a small car as well as Dry Towels, Glass Polish, Paste Wax, and Leather Conditioner.

- Invoice Chris McCartney for a Full Interior/Exterior Detail service for small car; terms Net 15.

- Received cash from Stacey Byrne for an Interior Detail service for a small car, Leather Conditioner, and Rubbing Compound.

- Received check number 446 from Logan Webb for a Hand Wash with Interior service.

- Paid Wally's, the window washer, $55 with Visa card (Repairs and Maintenance).

- Invoice Ericka Jenson of Jenson Auto Wholesalers for 6 small cars and 5 large cars, Full Interior/Exterior Detailing.

- Pay all the bills due on or before December 18, 2021; starting check number 10011.

- Deposit all funds held in Undeposited Funds into checking account.

 CHECK FIGURE *Display your trial balance report from 12/01/2021 through 12/10/2021 and verify that your figures match those shown here.*

Account	Balance
Checking	$11,641.01
Accounts Receivable	$7,499.64
Accounts Payable	$1,159.59
Visa	$495.65

Week 3

Monday, December 13, 2021

- Wrote check number 10014 to Betty's Cleaning Service for office cleaning for $75; (Repairs and Maintenance).

- Received a bill from City Water Works for $29.88 for water use from December 1 to December 9, 2021.

- Received a bill from District Waste Management for $25 for trash pickup for December 1 to December 9, 2021.

- The local high school had a car wash fundraiser. Raincross donated 5 packs of Dry Towels and 5 packs of Wash Mitts. Create an inventory adjustment to reduce the inventory and then add a new Charitable Contributions expense account.

- Sold a Full Exterior Detailing service package for a large SUV to Dan Thomas; on account.

- Received check number 8811 from Mike McCollough for Invoice number 21-115.

- Purchased general office supplies from Office Superstore with Visa card; $87.40.

- Create a purchase order to GLJ Car Detail Supplies for 10 gallons of Jack's Superior Exterior Car Wash Cleaner at $13.99 a gallon and 5 Water Hoses at $17.99.

- Invoice Pam Swanson for 2 Hand Wash with Interior services and 1 Full Interior/Exterior Detailing for a large car.

Tuesday, December 14, 2021

- Received the products and the bill from GLJ Car Detail Supplies, PO number 1004, ordered on December 13, 2021; terms Net 15.

- Returned a stapler purchased at Office Superstore; record a credit card credit for $18.75.

- Wrote check number 10015 to Dee Motor Company for miscellaneous service supplies and accessories for the display case in the lobby; $258.45 (Service Supplies).

- Invoiced Mike Carson at Carson Auto Sales for 10 small-car Full Interior/Exterior Detailing services, 6 large-car Full Interior/Exterior Detailing services, and 1 Electronic Odor Elimination.

- Received check number 1770 from Ericka Jenson for the balance on Invoice number 21-112 and Invoice number 21-114.

- Received cash from Lesli Johns for Hand Wash.

- Invoice Becky Craig for Glass Polish, Vinyl/Rubber Dressing, and Wheel Rim Polish.

Wednesday, December 15, 2021

- Invoice Ericka Jenson for Jenson Auto Wholesalers for 8 small-car Full Interior/Exterior Detail services and 2 Electronic Odor Eliminations.

- Mike Carson, check number 1414 for Invoice numbers 21-120 and 21-124

- Annette Helsper, check number 1004 for Invoice number 21-118

- Sold Mark Biggs a Full Exterior Detailing for a small car; Mark paid with check number 577.

- Becky Craig returned the Wheel Rim Polish purchased on the 14th for credit; issue a Credit Memo.

- Becky Craig paid her balance due with cash; $13.02.

- Pay the bills from City Water Works and District Waste Management.

- Deposit all the funds held in Undeposited Funds to the checking account ($5,189.91).

Thursday, December 16, 2021

- Transfer $6,000 from the Checking account to the Savings account.

- Invoice Steven Sims for Rock Chip Windshield Repair and Hand Wash services, as well as a package of Wash Mitts, Dry Towels, Window Cleaner, Wheel Rim Polish, and Interior Cleaner.

- Create a purchase order for Patsy's Automotive Supplies for 15 units of Jasper's Window Cleaner 14 oz., 10 of Jasper's Glass Polish 8 oz., and 10 of Jasper's Interior Cleaner 16 oz.

- Received cash from Amber Williams for Hand Wash with Interior service and Leather Conditioner.

- Received cash from Sean Murphy for Hand Wash.

- Received payment from Dan Thomas; check number 448 for Invoice number 21-122.

- Received payment from John McNay; check number 1418 for Invoice number 21-125.

Friday, December 17, 2021

- Received check from Ericka Jenson on account; check number 1801 for $800. Apply to Invoice number 21-132.

- Received products and bill from Patsy's Automotive Supplies on PO number 1005.

- Received cash from Samantha Wilson for a Hand Wash and Exterior Polish and Wax services.

- Sold Hand Wash and Engine Clean services to Pam Swanson on account.

- Write check number 10018 to GLJ Car Detail Supplies for miscellaneous supplies; $87.15.

- Received check number 377 from Larry James for a Hand Wash with Interior and Exterior Wax services, along with a package of Wash Mitts, Interior Cleaner, and Rubbing Compound.

- Pay Patsy's Automotive Services and Rosey & Girls Auto Supply bills; due 12/21/21; starting check number 10019.

- Deposit all funds held in Undeposited Funds into the Checking account.

 CHECK FIGURE *Display your trial balance report from 12/01/2021 through 12/17/2021 and verify that your figures match those shown here.*

Account	Balance
Checking	$11,145.49
Accounts Receivable	$6,911.66
Accounts Payable	$1,079.38
Visa	$564.30
Board of Equalization Payable	$28.85

Week 4

Monday, December 20, 2021

- Chris and Eric both withdrew a $3,000 distribution:

    - Create two new equity accounts: Chris Partner Distribution and Eric Partner Distribution.

    - Create two checks: Chris Christian, first payee; Eric Christian; set to print later.

- Pay all the bills due to GLJ Car Detail Supplies and WebWorks; set to print later.

- Print all the checks in the Print Checks queue; starting check number 10021.

- Invoice Dan Greany for a Full Interior/Exterior Detail service for a large car.

- Received check number 3247 from Seth David for a Full Exterior Detail for a small car, Vinyl/Rubber Dressing, and Leather Conditioner.

- Received check number 488 from Pam Swanson for Invoice number 21-134.

- Write a check to Betty's Cleaning Service for $75; for office cleaning; check number 10025.

- Received cash from Carlos Espinosa for an Interior Detail for a small car, Odor Elimination, and Trunk Shampoo services, as well as Dry Towels and Interior Cleaner.

Tuesday, December 21, 2021

- Invoice Mike Carson at Carson Auto Sales for 7 small-vehicle and 2 large-vehicle Full Interior/Exterior Detail services.

- Received check number 164 from Mary Crofoot for a Paint Protection service for a large car, a package of Wash Mitts, Dry Towels, Window Cleaner, and Glass Polish.

- Received check number 1808 from Ericka Jenson for the balance of Invoice number 21-132 and Invoice number 21-138.

- Received a bill from Galen Bros. Interiors for holiday decorations for the lobby; $218.00; due on receipt (Office Expenses).

- Received a bill from Raincross Power and Gas for service from December 1 through December 17; $205; due on receipt.

- Deposit all the funds held in Undeposited Funds into the checking account.

- Invoice Summit Auto Resellers, 149 So. Armor Rd., Norco, CA 92505, for 8 small-car and 8 large-car Full Interior/Exterior Detailing services, plus Odor Elimination in all cars.

Wednesday, December 22, 2021

- Received a bill from Dee Motor Company for miscellaneous supplies; $189.25; due on receipt.

- Pay all the bills due in December 2021; starting check number 10026.

- Received the telephone and Internet bill from Raincross Telephone and paid online from checking account; $247.85. (Record as a debit card transaction.)

- Ordered two Ceiling Boom Wash Systems from Ultimate Washer; each includes a Ceiling Boom, Wand, and Accessories; wrote check number 10029 for $3,300. Equipment has a three-year expected life; will be installed the week of December 27. (Create a Fixed Asset account: Equipment.)

- Bought 10 $100 gift cards at the bank for vendor and customer holiday gifts; used debit card from checking account (General Operating Expense).

- Bought some paint and wallpaper to spruce up the lobby; Visa card $213.11 (Repairs and Maintenance).

- Bought a used display cabinet, some lobby chairs, a table, and a used flat screen TV for $650 from neighboring business that is remodeling; wrote check to T&M Motors (General Operating Expense).

- Stopped by Patsy's Automotive Supplies and picked up and paid for 10 gallons of Jack's Superior Car Wash Cleaner; paid $139.90 with Visa card; dropped off a holiday greeting with a gift card.

Thursday, December 23, 2021

- Stopped by GLJ Car Detail Supplies and picked up and paid for 5 containers for Mimi's Upholstery and Carper Cleaner at $60 each; paid with Visa card; dropped off a holiday greeting with two gift cards.

- Transferred $5,000 from Savings to Checking.

- Write check number 10031 to Holiday Kitchen for $2,000; donation for toys and food for families.

 CHECK FIGURE *Display your trial balance report from 12/01/2021 through 12/23/2021 and verify that your figures match those shown here.*

Account	Balance
Checking	$4,969.76
Accounts Receivable	$9,296.66
Accounts Payable	$91.05
Visa	$1,217.31
Board of Equalization	$34.55

Prepare Your Deliverables—Set 2 QG

To complete this segment of the project, prepare the following deliverables and export to Excel:

- A report displaying the summary of balances each customer owes at December 23, 2021, saved as: **CH13 AR Aging Summary 12.23.21**

- A report displaying the purchase details for each vendor at December 23, 2021, saved as: **CH13 Purchase Details 12.23.21**

- A trial balance report at December 23, 2021, saved as: **CH13 Trial Balance 12.23.21**

Make Adjustments and Reconcile Accounts

Chris and Eric are closing for the holiday week from December 24 to January 3 to purchase and install new equipment. Although the business is closed for the week, there is lots of activity related to purchasing and installing the new equipment. You will use this opportunity to make any needed adjustments, download the bank and credit card transactions, and reconcile the bank and credit card accounts. Finally, you will prepare the financial reports for Chris and Eric.

Week 5

Monday, December 27, 2021

- Pay Tony Ortiz with Visa card $550 for plumbing services for the new equipment; use the Fixed Asset account: Equipment.

- Write a check to A+ Delivery for $125 for the delivery from Ultimate Washer; use the Fixed Asset account: Equipment; check should be number 10032.

Tuesday, December 28, 2021

- Write a check for $650 to Ernie Molina and Company for installation of the new equipment (Fixed Asset account: Equipment).

Wednesday, December 29, 2021

- There are discrepancies between actual physical inventory and reported inventory. Use this worksheet to make the necessary adjustments; use the Cost of Goods Sold account: Inventory Shrinkage.

Raincross Auto Detailing
Physical Inventory Worksheet

Product	Description	Hand	Count
Dry Towels	Micro Fiber Dry Towels, 3 pack	6	6
Glass Polish	Jasper's 8 oz Glass Polish	31	30
Interior Cleaner	Jasper's 16 oz Interior Cleaner	29	29
Leather Conditioner	Rosey's 6 oz Leather Conditioner	4	1
Paste Wax	Rosey's Exterior Paste Wax	13	10
Rubbing Compound	Rosey's 12 oz Rubbing Compound	12	10
Vinyl Rubber Dressing	Rosey's 8 oz Vinyl/Rubber Dressing	11	11
Wash Mitts	Micro Fiber Wash Mitts, 3 pack	9	9
Wheel Rim Polish	Rosey's 16 oz Wheel-Rim Polish/Cleaner	9	9
Window Cleaner	Jasper's 14 oz Window Cleaner	40	30

- Prepare purchase orders as follows:

  - GLJ Car Detail Supplies: 5 Brushes at $19.99, 5 Buckets at $18.49, 10 Dry Towels at $5.25

  - Patsy's Automotive Supplies: 20 units of Window Cleaner at $1.75

  - Rosey & Girls Auto Supply: 10 units of Leather Conditioner

Monday, January 3, 2022

Eric Christian sent you an email about some debit and credit card transactions made last week during the installation. The email said, "Purchased some gas for delivery at Patel's; you may need to set up a new account for automobile expenses. Bought lunch for everyone at Oscar's; is there an account for Meals and Entertainment? If not, please set one up." Eric included a copy of a receipt for $450 from PriceCo with "GenOpExp" noted on it. Keep all this in mind as you complete these tasks.

- Upload the checking **(CH13 Raincross Business Bank 4673.csv)** and credit card **(CH13 Visa Raincross December 2021.csv)** transactions for December 2021 into the appropriate account via Banking→Upload transactions manually→File Upload. Match or add all transactions.

- Reconcile the bank checking account, savings account, and credit card statements for December 2021. **(CH13 Raincross Business Bank Statement.pdf, CH13 Raincross Business Bank Savings Statement.pdf, CH13 Visa Statement.pdf)**

- Create a trial balance report for December 2021.

- Prepare the following adjusting entry for December 31, 2021: Record the December web hosting expense (use Advertising/Promotion expense) and then make the entry recurring for the following eleven months.

- Print the Recurring Transactions report to PDF.

 CHECK FIGURE *Display your trial balance report for December 31, 2021 and verify that your figures match those shown here.*

Account	Balance
Checking	$3,617.68
Accounts Receivable	$9,296.66
Inventory	$546.13

Prepare Your Deliverables—Set 3 QG

Produce the following end-of-period reports for Chris and Eric Christian, customizing them as necessary. Export each to Excel.

- Trial balance report for December 31, 2021, saved as: **CH13 Trial Balance 12.31.21**

- Balance sheet report for December 31, 2021 (Total Assets equal $27,635.47), saved as: **CH13 Balance Sheet 12.31.21**

- Income statement for the month of December 2021 (rename the profit and loss Statement; Net Income equals $13,688.63.), saved as: **CH13 Income Statement Dec 2021**

- Inventory valuation summary report as of December 31, 2021, saved as: **CH13 Inventory Valuation Summary 12.31.21**

Self-Assessment Answer Key

Chapter 1: Getting Started with QuickBooks Online

Item	Answer	Heading or DYS
1	False	QuickBooks Online Subscriptions
2	True	Introducing QuickBooks Online
3	True	The Gear Menu
4	True	Your Company
5	False	Accrual Basis vs. Cash Basis Accounting
6	True	The Top-Right Navigation Tools
7	True	Updates and the Ever-Evolving User Interface
8	True	The Navigation Bar
9	False	Accrual Basis vs. Cash Basis Accounting
10	False	Account Types and Financial Reports
11	False	Getting Started with QuickBooks Online (chapter opener)
12	False	QuickBooks Online Subscriptions
13	A	Accounting – Behind the Scenes
14	C	QuickBooks Online Subscriptions
15	B	Introducing QuickBooks Online
16	D	The Help Menu
17	D	"User Interface Highlights" video
18	D	Account Types and Financial Reports
19	C	Using the Browser
20	B	Navigating the User Interface *and* The Gear Menu
21	C	"User Interface Highlights" video

Chapter 2: Setting Up a New Company File

Item	Answer	Heading or DYS
1	True	Products and Services
2	False	Products and Services
3	False	Adding and Managing Users
4	True	Adding and Managing Users
5	True	Opening Balances and Historical Transactions
6	False	Opening Balances and Historical Transactions
7	True	Editing the Default Chart of Accounts
8	True	The Chart of Accounts
9	False	Editing the Default Chart of Accounts
10	False	Customizing Your Company File
11	C	Start Date
12	B	Customizing Your Company File
13	D	Customizing Your Company File
14	A	Assigning Account Types
15	B	Assigning Account Types
16	D	Editing the Default Chart of Accounts

Chapter 3: Working with Customers

Item	Answer	Heading or DYS
1	False	Importing Customers from an Excel or CSV file
2	True	Editing, Merging and Making Customers Inactive
3	False	Editing, Merging and Making Customers Inactive
4	True	Recording Sales Transactions
5	False	Creating Sales Receipts and Invoices
6	False	Creating Sales Receipts and Invoices
7	False	Adding Customers and Sub-Customers
8	False	Customizing Sales Form Settings: Appearance *and* DYS 3-4, step #1
9	True	Customizing Sales Form Settings: Appearance
10	False	Receiving Customer Payments
11	B	Importing Customers from an Excel or CSV File
12	C	Adding Customers and Sub-Customers
13	B	Creating Sales Receipts and Invoices
14	C	Creating Sales Receipts and Invoices
15	D	Creating Sales Receipts and Invoices
16	C	Creating Sales Receipts and Invoices
17	B	Creating Customer and Sales Reports
18	B	Creating Customer and Sales Reports

Chapter 4: Working with Vendors

Item	Answer	Heading or DYS
1	False	Editing, Merging, and Making Vendors Inactive
2	False	Adding Vendors
3	False	Working with Vendors (chapter opener)
4	False	Adding Vendors
5	True	Creating Vendor Transactions: Purchases and Expenses
6	False	Accounts Payable Reports
7	False	Customizing Expense Form Settings
8	True	Importing Vendor Data from an Excel or CSV File
9	False	Accounts Payable Reports
10	C	Working with Vendors (chapter opener)
11	C	Creating Check, Expense, and Bill Records
12	B	Creating Check, Expense, and Bill Records
13	B	Tip! under DYS 4-5, step #10

Chapter 5: Banking and Credit Card Transactions

Item	Answer	Heading or DYS
1	False	Managing the Banking Center
2	True	"Banking Center Tour" video
3	True	Undeposited Funds
4	False	Managing the Banking Center
5	True	Setting Up and Using Bank Feeds
6	False	Managing Bank Rules
7	False	Reconciling Accounts
8	False	Other Banking Transactions
9	True	Reconciling Accounts
10	B	Setting Up and Using Bank Feeds
11	B	Managing Bank Rules
12	C	Other Banking Transactions
13	A	Reconciling Accounts
14	C	Preparing Financial Reports
15	C	Reconciling Accounts
16	B	Reconciling Accounts
17	A	Managing Bank Rules
18	D	Setting Up and Using Bank Feeds
19	C	Preparing Financial Reports
20	B	"Tips for Reconciling Accounts in QuickBooks Online" table *and* Reconciling Accounts

Chapter 6: All in a Day's Work

There are no Self-Assessment questions in this chapter.

Chapter 7: Inventory Management

Item	Answer	Heading or DYS
1	False	Purchase Orders
2	False	Inventory Tracking—Behind the Scenes
3	False	First In, First Out
4	False	Non-Inventory Products
5	False	Receiving Inventory Against a Purchase Order—Best Practice
6	False	DYS 7-14
7	C	Enabling Tracking
8	B	First In, First Out
9	C	Customer Returns and Credits
10	A	Cost of Goods Sold Account
11	D	Non-Inventory Products *and* DYS 7-2
12	C	Receiving Inventory Against a Purchase Order
13	C	Adding an Expense to a Purchase Order Payment
14	D	"Inventory Reports" video *and* DYS 7-16
15	B	Inventory Adjustments
16	B	Sales Tax

Chapter 8: Balance Sheet Accounts and Budgets

Item	Answer	Heading or DYS
1	False	DYS 8-5, step #9
2	False	Handling Uncollectible Receivables/Bad Debts
3	B	Recording Other Current Assets
4	D	Recording Other Current Assets
5	B	Journal Entries and Recurring Transactions
6	C	Journal Entries and Recurring Transactions
7	C	Fixed Assets and Long Term Liabilities
8	D	View Recurring Transactions
9	D	Petty Cash
10	D	Creating and Reviewing Budgets
11	B	Note! under DYS 8-7, step #7
12	B	Creating and Reviewing Budgets
13	A	Creating and Reviewing Budgets

Chapter 9: Customizing, Fine-Tuning, and Extending Capabilities

Item	Answer	Heading or DYS
1	False	Customizing Reports
2	False	Customizing Reports
3	False	Keyboard Shortcuts
4	B	Customizing Reports
5	D	Sending Reports
6	B	Adding a Custom Field to Sales Forms
7	B	Enabling Privacy Mode on the Dashboard
8	A	Keyboard Shortcuts
9	C	QuickBooks Labs
10	D	Extending Capabilities with Apps

Chapter 10: Staying on Track: The Accounting Cycle, Classes, and Locations

Item	Answer	Heading or DYS
1	True	Accounting Cycle Steps
2	True	Generally Accepted Accounting Principles and the Accounting Cycle
3	False	Class Tracking
4	False	Delayed Charges and Credits
5	D	Generally Accepted Accounting Principles and the Accounting Cycle
6	B	Accounting Cycle Steps
7	D	DYS 10-1
8	D	DYS 10-1
9	A	Accounting Cycle Steps
10	B	Class Tracking
11	C	Location Tracking
12	B	Class Tracking
13	E	Class Tracking *and* Location Tracking
14	D	Delayed Charges and Credits

Chapter 11: Completing the Accounting Cycle, Closing Books, and Auditing Changes

Item	Answer	Heading or DYS
1	False	Closing the Books
2	False	DYS 11-2
3	True	Creating Financial Statements
4	D	Creating the Trial Balance Report and Making Adjustments
5	B	Adjusting Journal Entries
6	D	Comparing Inventory Quantities and Making Adjustments
7	A	Adjusting Journal Entries
8	B	Creating Financial Statements
9	D	Creating Financial Statements
10	D	Assembling Management Reports
11	D	The Audit Log and Audit History
12	C	The Audit Log and Audit History
13	B	Closing the Books

Chapter 12: Using Payroll in QuickBooks Online

Item	Answer	Heading or DYS
1	C	Run Payroll
2	B	Introducing Payroll
3	B	DYS 12-1
4	B	Run Payroll
5	B	Run Payroll
6	A	Run Payroll
7	C	Run Payroll
8	C	Payroll Taxes
9	B	Payroll Tax Forms
10	D	Payroll Reports

Chapter 13: Bringing It All Together!

There are no Self-Assessment questions in this chapter.

Glossary

accounting cycle Sequence of procedures used for accurately recording business transactions for a period of time; help keep a business's accounting records in line with GAAP and ensure that financial information is accurate

accrual basis Accounting method in which income is recorded when the sales transaction is made and expenses are recorded when the obligation is incurred; used by companies that keep inventory

adjusting journal entries Journal entries used to adjust for depreciation, allocation of prepaid expenses, and corrections to inventory; typically made just prior to the issuance of the period's financial statements (e.g., end of a month, quarter, or year)

apps Third-party application plug-ins that extend QuickBooks Online capabilities

assets In accounting, refers to anything the business owns or is owed

audit history Tracks changes to customer and vendor transactions

audit log Chronological list of activities performed, including who logged in, when, and what each user added, edited, voided, or deleted

balance sheet Statement of the business's assets, liabilities, and equity; reflects the business's financial position on a stated date

bank feeds Feature that allows your bank and credit card providers to automatically share read-only information with QuickBooks Online about money going in and out of your accounts

behind the scenes Accounting that QuickBooks Online performs when a user enters a transaction

cash basis Accounting method in which income is recorded when it is received and expenses are recorded when paid; typically used for businesses that do not carry inventory

center Location in QuickBooks Online that consolidates relevant transaction and contact information; examples include the Sales, Expenses, and Reports centers

Chart of Accounts List of accounts for each transaction in a company's accounting system or general ledger; categorizes expenditures, revenues, assets, and liabilities so you can quickly assess the company's financial health

class tracking Allows companies to keep track of income and expenses by department, project, event, or some other segment; not necessarily tied to one specific customer, vendor, or item; Classes are tracked per line item on a form

cost of goods sold (COGS) account Records the cost of products that are held in inventory and then sold; once an item is sold from inventory, COGS increases by the amount paid for the product when purchased; the difference between the cost and the sales price is income

first in, first out (FIFO) Method of inventory valuation; assumes that the first product purchased is the first product sold and adjusts the inventory and cost of goods sold (COGS) accounts accordingly when a sale is made

fixed assets A company's tangible assets with a useful life of more than one year; examples include buildings, office equipment, vehicles, and machinery

Generally Accepted Accounting Principles (GAAP) Guidelines that businesses use to maintain, prepare, and present financial records to auditors, financial institutions, and other entities; these guidelines help ensure consistency, fairness, and honesty in accounting procedures

location tracking Allows companies to produce financial information reports by location (e.g., for different regions, store locations, properties, departments, or territories); differs from class tracking in that it is limited to one location per transaction form

non-inventory products Purchased products you don't need to track quantities of; for example, a one-of-a-kind mosaic piece for a customer or nuts and bolts used during an installation

other current assets In accounting, refers to what the business plans to use within a one-year period; examples include prepaid insurance, prepaid rent, and security deposits

profit and loss (P&L) statement Reports the income for a period, less all the cost of goods sold and expenses for the period; if income is greater than expenses, the result is a net income, and if expenses exceed income, the result is a net loss

reconciling/reconciliation Process of comparing the transactions entered into QuickBooks Online with the business's bank and credit card statements

recurring journal entry Used for transactions that occur more than once, whether on a fixed schedule or for a set amount (e.g., a loan payment), for a regular bill that has a varying amount (e.g., utility bills), or for other repeated but unscheduled transactions

test drive Free version of QuickBooks Online that is available to anyone as a way to try out the software; no usernames or sign-ins are required

trial balance report Listing of all accounts in the Chart of Accounts and their balances on the date selected; allows companies to analyze their balances and make adjustments to ensure all data is accurate

Undeposited Funds account Account that holds transactions that have not yet been deposited in a financial institution; the amount in this account should always match what is then deposited

Index

Note: Page numbers ending with a "V" indicate that a term is discussed in the video referenced on that page.

NOTES

NOTES

NOTES